the magic of **self-respect**

OSHO

Extemporaneous talks given by Osho
at Rajneeshpuram, Oregon, U.S.A.

the magic of **self-respect**

awakening to your own awareness

DVD: *The Magic of Self-Respect*, Copyright © 2009, OSHO International Foundation, Switzerland

This book is a transcript of a series of original talks by Osho given to a live audience.
The talks in this edition were previously published as *From Ignorance to Innocence* (Chapters 16–30).

All of Osho's talks have been published in full as books, and are also available as original audio and/or video
recordings.

Audio recordings and the complete text archive can be found via the online OSHO Library at www.osho.com
OSHO is a registered trademark of Osho International Foundation, www.osho.com/trademarks

ISBN (paperback)   978-0-9818341-8-4
ISBN (hardback)   978-0-9844444-0-3
Also available as an eBook: ISBN 978-0-88050-766-0

OSHO MEDIA INTERNATIONAL

New York • Zurich • Mumbai
an imprint of
OSHO INTERNATIONAL
www.osho.com/oshointernational

Printed in Singapore

10 9 8 7 6 5 4 3 2

Distributed by Publishers Group Worldwide
www.pgw.com

contents

About the Authentic Living Series

The "Authentic Living" Series is a collection of books based on Osho's responses to questions from his international audience at meditation events.

About this process of asking questions, Osho says:

How do you ask a question which can be meaningful – not simply intellectually but existentially? Not just for verbal knowledge, but for authentic living? There are a few things which have to be remembered:

Whatever you ask, never ask a ready-made question, never ask a stereotyped question. Ask something that is immediately concerned with you, something that is meaningful to you, that carries some transforming message for you. Ask that question upon which your life depends.

Don't ask bookish questions, don't ask borrowed questions. And don't carry any question over from the past because that will be your memory, not you. If you ask a borrowed question, you can never come to an authentic answer. Even if an answer is given, it will not be caught by you and you will not be caught by it. A borrowed question is meaningless. Ask something that you want to ask. When I say "you," I mean the you that you are this very moment, that is here and now, that is immediate. When you ask something that is immediate, that is here and now, it becomes existential. It is not concerned with memory but with your being.

Don't ask anything that once answered will not change you in any way. For example, someone can ask whether there is a God: "Does God exist?" Ask such a question only if the answer will change you – so that if there is a God then you will be one type of person, and if there is no God you will be a different person. But if it will not cause any change in you to know whether God is or is not, then the question is meaningless. It is just curiosity, not inquiry.

So remember, ask whatever you are really concerned about. Only then will the answer be meaningful for you.

Introduction

*"'Respect' is one of the most beautiful words in the English language.
It does not mean what it has come to mean, 'honor.' No, respect simply
means re-spect, to look again. That's the literal meaning of the word; there
is no place for honor. Just look again, look back, look deeply.*
*"Once, you had known your real self. Before you entered and became
part of a society, a culture, a civilization, you knew it. It is not a
coincidence that people go on thinking that their childhood was the most
beautiful part of their life. It is a long-forgotten memory, because there
have been days in your life, the earliest days, which you cannot
remember exactly: only a vague feeling, a kind of fragrance, a kind of
shadow is there.*
*"If you 're-spect,' if you look again and go deep into your existence, you
are going to find the place from where you started losing yourself and
gaining the ego. That moment is a moment of illumination, because once
you have seen what the ego is, the game is finished."*

From *The Magic of Self-Respect*

The quest for the elusive quality of self-respect – or self-esteem – seems
to be central to our greater search to find a way of being in the world
that is authentic and grounded and true. But do we even know what
this "self" is?

In this volume, Osho tackles our notions of who we are, and what the "self"
really is, by examining what it is *not*. The examination begins in an unex-
pected way, with an unflinching look at the most powerful source of all our
notions of what "selfhood" is – our religious teachings. For most of us, these
religious and moral teachings are used from the time we are old enough to
walk, to shape and define our behavior as humans in a world of other human
beings. And as long as we carry the burdens of these imposed beliefs and
superstitions, Osho says, we can't even begin to undertake an honest search
for who we really are. As long as we don't know who we are, any self-

respect that we might enjoy stands on shaky ground, ready to be toppled at any moment if one of our cherished beliefs is challenged.

In his responses to questions from his audience, Osho sheds light on just how much of our experience of everyday life is shaped by religious and social conditioning – and we are not even aware of the fact. In every dimension, he argues, we are constantly being pulled away from the unique nature that each of us is born with. In place of that original and unique self, a false self called the "ego" is constructed, and that false self eventually gains control of our creativity, our ideas about what it means to be successful, our relationships, and our very experience of who we are. At the same time, the collection of egos known as "society" shapes all of our political, educational and religious institutions, which in turn do their part to reinforce the same old patterns onto new generations of innocent human beings.

Discarding the old trinities we all know from the past, Osho introduces the reader to a new trinity – of watchfulness, awareness, alertness. This new trinity is the key to rediscovering our unique nature, the real "self" that lies within us all. And once that discovery is made, whatever falseness we have carried up till now simple falls away of its own accord.

This series of talks takes place in the extraordinary context of a community of meditators, living and working together as part of an experiment to bring meditation to the center of everyday life. As such, it also points the way toward a new way of authentic living that balances the individual need for self expression and creativity, and the need for the whole to function in harmony.

The enclosed DVD is a live recording of one of the talks, and offers a first-hand experience of a contemporary mystic at work.

A note to explain the setting in which this book took place:

As mentioned above, these talks were given by Osho in an extraordinary context. They were held in Rajneeshpuram, the city that was built on land previously known as the Big Muddy Ranch in Oregon, USA. The majority of the population were sannyasins, with Osho staying as a guest. Osho describes the sannyas movement as "simply the movement of seekers of truth." Often Osho uses the phrase "my people" or "my sannyasins" and clarifies that, "the sannyasin cannot be mine, but I can certainly belong to the sannyasins..." During this time in Oregon, the term *Rajneeshee* was coined, referring to the sannyasins.

The backdrop to "life on the ranch" was the often difficult relationship with the people of Oregon. In these talks, Osho takes the opportunity to hammer on the "Oregonians," who become the subject of many of his jokes. The "1000 Friends of Oregon," a group of local citizens, receive particular attention after positioning themselves as the "watchdogs" of land use.

The recording of Chapter 5 was described by his secretary at the time as having been "unavailable" due to technical problems and the original was never given to the editors. A transcription appeared a few days later – with clear omissions and differences from what most of the audience remembers. For example, "That promise you can always remember: I will not leave you under a fascist regime." had become, "That promise you can always remember: I will not leave you in a state of chaos." This manipulation of reality turned out to be a harbinger of things to come. (See subsequent volumes in this series!). We can therefore not completely vouch for every word in this chapter.

innocence is power

Osho,
Is the hypothesis of God not useful in any way? – because the very thought of
dropping the idea of God makes me feel immensely afraid.

It is already too late! The moment one starts calling the idea of God a hypothesis,
the idea of God is already dropped.

The so-called religious people will never use the word *hypothesis* for God. For
them God is not our hypothesis, but on the contrary we are his creation; he is the
very source of existence, he is the most existential being. But when you call God
a hypothesis that means you are putting him in the same category as Euclidian
hypotheses in geometry, or other hypotheses which are only assumptions; they
may prove right, they may not prove right. Only experiment, only experience is
going to decide it, and that too will not be an ultimate decision because future
experiments may cancel it.

A hypothesis is an assumed fact – for the time being accepted as true, but only
for the time being. Nobody can say it will be true tomorrow too. In three hundred
years of scientific growth you can see it: something was true for Newton, it is not
true for Rutherford; it was true for Rutherford, it is not true for Albert Einstein. Better
experiments, better instruments can always change the hypothesis.

So no theologian is going to call God a hypothesis – for the theologian God is
the very truth, and he is not dependent on your experiments. If you cannot find
him it is your failure, not a proof that God does not exist. If you succeed, of course,
he exists. If you fail, *you* fail; God still exists.

Hypothesis is a scientific term, not a theological concept; and science is very honest. Theology is just the opposite, very dishonest. The very word *theology* shows its dishonesty, insincerity. *Theo* means God, *logy* means logic. But nobody has ever offered any logic about God. Every argument goes against God; no argument has been yet produced which proves God. Still they go on calling it theology – "logic of God."

It would have been more honest for the theologians to call God a hypothesis, but you cannot worship a hypothesis, can you? Knowing that this is only a hypothesis, perhaps right, perhaps wrong... But worship is not possible with a "perhaps," with a maybe; worship needs a blind faith that it is so. Even if all the evidence goes against it, then too it is so. That's the meaning of faith. Faith is not logic, it is absolutely illogical. And to call the idea of God a hypothesis means destroying all the churches, all the temples, all the synagogues.

The word *hypothesis* is very significant: it means you are allowed to doubt because you are allowed to experiment and find. It is only a temporary assumption to begin with – one has to begin with something, so for the time being, just to begin with, we accept a hypothesis. But how can you worship it? How can the priest exploit you? It is absolutely against the religious people to use the word *hypothesis*. They will not even agree to call God an idea, because an idea is your mind thing, your projection. To them God is not an idea, God is the only truth.

In India, where religion has taken very subtle forms, they say *you* are an idea in the mind of God, not vice versa. God is not an idea in your mind – because in your mind there is all kinds of rubbish: you have nightmares, you have dreams, you have all kinds of desires. God is also put in the same category? And your ideas change every moment; they are just like clouds, changing their form continuously.

Certainly when you were a child your ideas were different. When you were adolescent your ideas were different, when you became a young man your ideas were different, and when you become old you cannot have the same ideas that you had in your youth. Experience changes everything. It will be simply impossible to retain the same idea your whole life; only a superb idiot can do it. If you have a little bit of intelligence then your idea is going to change with life.

Even to call God an idea will not be acceptable to the religious people – hypothesis is far away. That's why I say it is too late.

You are calling God an idea... And the definition of meditation is to be in a state of mind where no ideas exist, not even the idea of God.

Gautam the Buddha says, "If you meet me on the path cut my head off immediately, because what am I doing there? – disturbing you. The idea of me is a disturbance." It is just like throwing a pebble in a silent lake, and so many ripples, millions of ripples arise. A simple idea thrown in the silent lake of your mind creates millions of waves; it may take you far away from yourself.

Every idea takes you away from yourself; hence the definition of meditation: a state of consciousness without any ideas.

So in meditation there is no way to go away from yourself, you are simply centered in your own being. There is no object that you can see. You are left totally alone. Your consciousness starts turning upon itself.

Consciousness is just like light. The light is here, we are all here; the light is falling on us, on the walls, on the curtains, on everything that is here. These are all objects. Just think for a moment: if all the objects are removed, then there is only light, not falling on anything. But light is unconscious – you are conscious. So when all objects are removed, your consciousness falls upon itself, turns upon itself; it is a turning in, because there is nothing to prevent it. That is the meaning of object: *object* means that which prevents, raises an objection, obstructs, is a hindrance. When there is no object, where can you go? You have to turn upon yourself, consciousness being conscious of itself – there is no idea of God.

In ordinary states of mind, ideas are just rubbish. In that extraordinary space of no-mind, ideas don't exist. So either you have to put God in the category of rubbish, or you have to put him where no objects are allowed.

The word *idea* cannot be used by religious people for God. *Idea* is used by the philosophers, just as *hypothesis* is used by the scientist. For the religious person God is the only reality, but in using the word *idea* you have already gone too far – too far from the so-called reality of God.

But your question is significant from many points. First: you ask, isn't the hypothesis useful in any way? It is useful – not for you but for those who want to exploit you: the priest, the rabbi, the pope, the whole army of all these people around the world. Without the hypothesis of God, what is a pope? What is a *shankaracharya*? Just nobodies! Then who is Jesus? You cannot be a son of a hypothesis, it will look very odd. You cannot be a messiah of a hypothesis. It would be a very strange world if hypotheses started sending messiahs.

God has to be real for all these people to exploit you, and for thousands of years they *have* been exploiting. And they will continue to exploit you for the simple reason that you are afraid to drop this idea.

That shows a tremendously significant point within your being. Why do you feel afraid of dropping the idea of God? Certainly the idea of God is somehow preventing you from being afraid; so the moment you drop it, you start feeling afraid. It is a kind of psychological protection, that's what it is.

The child is bound to be afraid. But in the mother's womb he is not afraid. I have not heard that any child in the mother's womb ever thinks of going to the synagogue or to the church, or reading the Bible or the Koran or the Gita; or even bothers about whether there is a God or not. I cannot conceive that a child in the mother's womb will in any way be interested in God, in the Devil, in heaven, in hell. For what? He is already in paradise. Things cannot be better than they are.

He is completely protected in a warm, cozy womb, floating in chemicals which are nourishing. And you will be surprised – in that nine months the child grows more than he will ever grow in ninety years, proportionately. In nine months he travels such a long journey; from being almost nothing he becomes a being. In nine months he passes through millions of years of evolution, from the very first being up to now. He passes through all the phases.

Life is absolutely secure: no need for any employment, no fear of starvation, hunger; everything is being done by the mother's body. Living nine months in the mother's womb in such absolute security creates a problem, which has produced your so-called religions.

As the child comes out of the mother's womb, the first thing that happens to him is fear. The reason is obvious. His home is lost, his security is lost. His warmth, his surroundings, all that he knew as his world is completely lost, and he is thrown into a strange world, of which he knows nothing. He has to start breathing on his own.

It takes a few seconds for the child to recognize the fact that he has to breathe now on his own – your mother's breathing is not going to help. Just to bring him to his senses the doctor hangs him upside down, and hits him on his bottom, hard. What a beginning! What a welcome! And just out of that hit he starts breathing.

Have you ever observed that whenever you are afraid your breathing changes? If you have not watched it before, you can watch it now. Whenever you are afraid, your breathing will change, immediately. And when you are at ease, at home, unafraid of anything, you will find your breathing falling into a harmony, in a deep accord, becoming more and more silent. In deep meditation it happens sometimes that you feel as if your breathing has stopped. It does not stop, but it almost stops.

The beginning for the child is fear of everything. For nine months he was in darkness, and in a modern hospital, where he is going to be born, there will be just glaring tube lights all around. And on his eyes, his retina, which has never seen light before, not even a candle light, this is too much. This light is a shock to his eyes.

And the doctor does not take even a few seconds – he cuts the connection that is still joining the child with the mother, the last hope of security – and such a tiny being! You know it perfectly well, that nobody is more helpless than a human child, no other child in the whole existence.

That's why horses have not invented the hypothesis of God. Elephants have not thought about the idea of God; there is no need. The child of the elephant immediately starts walking and looking around and exploring the world. He is not as helpless as a human child. In fact, so much depends on the helplessness of a human child that you may be surprised: your family, your society, your culture, your religion, your philosophy – everything arises out of the helplessness of the human child.

In animals, families don't exist for the simple reason that the child does not need the parents. Man had to decide for a certain system. The father and the mother have to be together to look after the child. It is the outcome of their love affair; this is their doing. Now if the human child is left alone, just like so many animals are, you cannot imagine that he is going to survive: impossible! Where is he going to find food? Whom is he going to ask? What is he going to ask?

Perhaps he has come too early? There are a few biologists who think that the human child is born premature – nine months are not enough, because he comes into the world so helpless. But the human body is such that the mother cannot carry the child for more than nine months, otherwise she will die, and her death will mean the death of the child.

It has been calculated that if the child could live in the mother's womb for at least three years, then perhaps there would be no need for a father and mother and the family, and the society and the culture, and God and the priest. But the child cannot live in the mother's womb for three years. This strange biological situation has affected the whole of human behavior, thinking, the structure of family, society; and this has caused the fear.

The first experience of the child is the fear, and the last experience of the man is also fear.

Birth is also a kind of death, you should remember; just look at it from the child's point of view. He was living in a certain world, which was absolutely satisfactory. He was not in any need at all, he was not greedy for anything more. He was simply enjoying being, enjoying growing – and then suddenly he is thrown out. To the child, this experience is an experience of death: death of his whole world, of his security, of his cozy home.

Scientists say that we have not been able yet to create a home as cozy as the womb. We have been trying – all our homes are just efforts to create that cozy home. We have even tried to make water beds, to give you the same feeling. We have bathtubs with hot water; lying down in them you can have a little feeling of the child. Those who know how to take a really good hot bath will also put salt into it, because in the mother's womb it is very salty – the exact amount of salt that is in sea water. But how long can you lie down in a bathtub? We have isolation tanks which are nothing but a search for the same womb that you have lost.

Sigmund Freud is not an enlightened man – in fact he is a little bit cuckoo, but sometimes cuckoos also sing beautiful songs. Sometimes he has significant ideas. For example, he thinks the idea of the man making love to the woman is nothing but an effort to enter the womb again. There may be something in it. This man is crazy, the idea seems to be farfetched; but even if a man like Sigmund Freud is crazy he has to be listened to very carefully.

I feel that there is something of truth in it: the search is for the womb, for the same passage as he had come out from. He cannot reach that womb, it is true. Then he created all kinds of things; he started making caves, houses, airplanes. You see the interior of an airplane – it will not be a wonder if one day you find that in the airplane people are floating in tubs of hot water, salted. The airplane can give you exactly the same situation, but it is not going to be satisfactory.

The child has not known anything else. We try to make it similar – just push a button in the airplane and the air hostess is there. We make it as comfortable as possible, but we cannot make it as comfortable as it was in the womb. There, you had no need even to push a button. Even before you were hungry you were fed. Even before you needed air, it reached you. You had no responsibility at all.

So the child coming out of the mother's womb, if he feels it at all, must feel it as death. He cannot feel it as birth, that is impossible. That is our idea – those who are standing outside – we say that this is birth.

And the second time, again one day, after his whole life's effort... The person has been able to make something – a little house, a family, a small circle of friends, a little warmth, a little corner somewhere in the world where he can relax and be himself, where he is accepted. Difficult – a whole life's struggle, and suddenly, one day, he finds again he is being thrown out.

The doctor has come again – and this is the man who had hit him! But that time it was to start the breathing; this time, as far as we know... Now we are on this side, we don't know the other side. The other side is left to the imagination; that's why heaven and hell, and every kind of imagination has gone wild. We are on this side and this man is dying. To us he is dying; perhaps he is again being reborn. But that only he knows, and he cannot turn back and tell us, "Don't be worried; I am not dead, I am alive." He could not turn in his mother's womb to have a last glimpse and say good-bye to everybody. Neither can he turn back now, open his eyes and say good-bye to you all, and say, "Don't be worried. I am not dying, I am being reborn."

The Hindu idea of rebirth is nothing but a projection of the ordinary birth. For the womb – if the womb thinks – the child is dead. For the child – if he thinks – he is dying. But he is born; it was not death, it is birth. The Hindus have projected the same idea on death. From this side it looks as if he is dying, but from the other side... But the other side is our imagination; we can make it as we want it.

Every religion makes the other side in a different way because every society and every culture depends on a different geography, a different history. For example: the Tibetan cannot think of the other side as cool – even cool is fearful, cold is impossible. The Tibetan thinks that the dead person is warm, in a new world which always remains warm.

The Indian cannot think that it always remains warm. Even four months' heat in India is too much, but for eternity to remain warm – you will be cooked! The Hindu religion had no idea of air conditioning, but the way they describe their paradise, it is almost air conditioned – always cool air, neither hot nor cold, but cool. It is always spring, Indian spring – around the earth there are different kinds of spring, and this is the Indian spring. All the flowers are in blossom, the winds are full of fragrance, the birds are singing, everything is alive – but not warm, *cool* air. That they remind us again and again: cool air continues to flow.

This is your mind that is projecting the idea; otherwise, for the Tibetan or for the Indian or for the Mohammedan, it would not be different. The Mohammedan cannot think that the other world is going to be a desert – he has suffered so much in the Arabian desert. The other world is an oasis – an oasis all over. It is not that after a hundred miles you find a small oasis with a little water and a few trees, no – just oases all over, and desert nowhere.

We project, but to the person who is dying it is again the same process that he has experienced once. It is a well-known fact that at the time of death, if the person has not become unconscious, has not fallen into a coma, he starts remembering his whole life cycle. He goes on back to the first moment of his life when he was born. It seems to be significant that when he is leaving this world he may have a look at all that has happened. Just in a few seconds the whole calendar moves, just as it moves in your movies. That calendar goes on moving, because in a two-hour movie they have to cover many years. If the calendar moves at the usual pace, you will be sitting in the movie hall for two years, and who is going to be able to afford that? No, the calendar just goes on moving, the dates go on changing, fast.

It goes even faster at the time of death. In a single moment the whole life flashes by, and stops at the first moment. It is the same process that is happening again – life has come around full circle.

Why did I want you to remember this? – because your God is nothing but your first day's fear which goes on and on until the last moment, becoming bigger and bigger. That's why when a person is young he may be an atheist, he can afford to be, but as he grows older, to be an atheist becomes a little difficult. If you ask him when he is just coming close to his grave, one foot in the grave, "Are you still an atheist?" he will say, "I am having second thoughts" – because of his fear of what is going to happen. His whole world is disappearing.

My grandfather was not a religious man, not at all. He was closer to Zorba the Greek: eat, drink and be merry, there is no other world, it is all nonsense. My father was a very religious man; perhaps it was because of my grandfather – the reaction, the generation gap. But it was just upside down in my family: my grandfather was an atheist and perhaps because of his atheism my father turned out to be a theist. And whenever my father would go to the temple, my grandfather would laugh and he would say, "Again? Go on, waste your life in front of those stupid statues!"

I love Zorba for many reasons; one of the reasons was that in Zorba I found my grandfather again. He loved food so much that he used to not trust anybody; he would prepare it himself. In my life I have been a guest in thousands of families in India, but I have never tasted anything so delicious as my grandfather's cooking. He loved it so much that every week it was a feast for all his friends – and he would prepare the whole day.

My mother and my aunts and the servants and cooks – everybody was thrown out of the kitchen. When my grandfather was cooking, nobody was to disturb him. But he was very friendly to me; he allowed me to watch and he said, "Learn, don't depend on other people. Only you know your taste. Who else can know it?"

I said, "That is beyond me; I am too lazy, but I can watch. The whole day cooking? I cannot do it." So I have not learned anything, but just watching was a joy – the way he worked, almost like a sculptor or a musician or a painter. Cooking was not just cooking, it was art to him. And if anything went just a little below his standard, he would throw it away immediately. He would cook it again, and I would say, "It is perfectly okay."

He would say, "You know it is not *perfectly* okay, it is just okay; but I am a perfectionist. Until it comes up to my standard, I am not going to offer it to anybody. I love my food."

He used to make many kinds of drinks... And whatsoever he did, the whole family was against him: they said that he was just a nuisance. He wouldn't allow anybody in the kitchen, and in the evening he gathered all the atheists of the town. And just to defy Jainism, he would wait till the sun set. He would not eat before then, because Jainism says to eat before sunset; after sunset eating is not allowed. He used to send me again and again to see whether the sun had set or not.

He annoyed the whole family. And they could not be angry with him – he was the head of the family, the oldest man – but they were angry at me. That was easier. They said, "Why do you go on coming again and again to see whether the sun has set or not? That old man is getting you also lost, utterly lost."

I was very sad because I only came across the book *Zorba the Greek*, when my grandfather was dying. The only thing that I felt at his funeral pyre was that he would have loved it if I had translated it for him and read it to him. I had read many books to him. He was uneducated. He could only write his signature, that was all. He could neither read nor write – but he was very proud of it.

He used to say, "It is good that my father did not force me to go to school, otherwise he would have spoiled me. These books spoil people so much." He would say to me, "Remember, your father is spoiled, your uncles are spoiled; they are continually reading religious books, scriptures, and it is all rubbish. While they are reading, I am living; and it is good to know through living."

He used to tell me, "They will send you to the university – they won't listen to me. And I cannot be much help, because if your father and your mother insist, they will send you to the university. But beware: don't get lost in books."

He enjoyed small things. I asked him, "Everybody believes in God, why don't you believe, *baba*?" I called him *baba*; that is the word for grandfather in India.

He said, "Because I am not afraid."

A very simple answer: "Why should I be afraid? There is no need to be afraid; I have not done any wrong, I have not harmed anybody. I have just lived my life joyously. If there is any God, and I meet him sometime, he cannot be angry at me. I will be angry at him: 'Why have you created this world? – this kind of world?' I am not afraid."

When he was dying I asked him again, because the doctors were saying that it was a question of only a few minutes. His pulse was getting lost, his heart was sinking, but he was fully conscious. I asked him, "Baba, one question..."

He opened his eyes and said, "I know your question: why don't you believe in God? I knew that you were going to ask this question when I was dying. Do you think death will make me afraid? I have lived so joyously and so completely, there is no regret that I am dying.

"What else am I going to do tomorrow? I have done it all, there is nothing left. And if my pulse is slowing down and my heartbeat is slowing down, I think everything is going to be perfectly okay, because I am feeling very peaceful, very calm, very silent. Whether I die completely or live, I cannot say right now. But one thing you should remember: I am not afraid."

You tell me that the moment you think of dropping the idea of God, fear comes up. It is a simple indication that with the rock of the idea of God, you are repressing fear; so the moment you remove the rock, the fear springs up.

I had a teacher in my high school days who was a very learned brahmin of the place. Almost the whole city respected him. He used to live behind my house, and a small path by the side of my house went to his place. Just at the end of my house was a very big neem tree. He taught Sanskrit and was continually teaching about God and prayer and worship. In fact he was indoctrinating everybody's minds.

I asked him, "My grandfather does not believe in God, and whenever I ask him why, he says, 'Because I am not afraid.' Are you very afraid? You seem to be continually hammering this word *God* into our heads, and I see you every morning in your house chanting so loudly for three hours that the whole neighborhood is disturbed. But nobody can say anything because it is religious chanting."

If you do something like modern dancing, or play jazz music, then everybody will be on your neck, complaining that you are disturbing them. He was disturbing everybody, every morning from five to eight – and he had a really loud voice – but it was religious, so nobody could complain.

I said, "Are you so afraid? Three hours every day you have to pray. It must be a great fear if for three hours every day you have to persuade God to protect you."

He said, "I am not afraid. Your grandfather is a rascal." They were almost the same age... "He is a rascal, don't listen to him. He will spoil you."

I said, "It is strange: he thinks you will spoil me, and you think he will spoil me; and as far as I am concerned nobody is going to spoil me. I believe my grandfather when he says that he is not afraid – but about you, I am not certain."

He asked, "Why?"

I said, "Because when you pass the neem tree in the night you start chanting" – because it was known that the neem tree had ghosts in it, so people ordinarily never went near that tree in the night. But he had to go that way because his house was there; otherwise he would have to go almost half a mile round by the main road and then reach his house from the other direction. Going that way round each time was too difficult, so he had found a religious strategy: he would start chanting. As he entered the path, he started chanting. I said, "I have heard you. Although you don't chant as loudly as you chant in the morning, you do chant, I have heard you. And I know there are ghosts so I cannot say you are doing anything wrong."

He said, "How did you come to know?"

I said, "Many times I am there by the side of the neem tree in the darkness; your chanting becomes louder and you start walking faster – that much I know. Why do you chant there if you are not afraid? And if you are afraid of ghosts, then that three-hour morning chanting with God is useless. Can't he save you against ghosts?"

He said, "From today I am not going to chant." Certainly he kept his word. He was not chanting, although he was walking faster than usual. And all that I had to do was to sit in the tree with a kerosene can – empty, so I could beat it like a drum. I simply drummed the can and threw it on top of him. You should have seen the situation! He ran away screaming and shouting, "*Bhoot! Bhoot!*" *Bhoot* is the Hindi word for ghost.

In India the ancient traditional dress is not like western dress. Now it is changing because western dress is more utilitarian; Indian dress is more luxurious but is not utilitarian. If you are working in the field or in the factory, Indian dress is dangerous because the robe is long and loose, it can get caught in any mechanism. Then the dhoti, the lower dress, that too is very loose. It reminds us that once the country must have been in a very comfortable time.

You cannot give the Indian dress to soldiers; otherwise they will not be able to fight, their clothes will be enough to finish them! Even if they had to run away they would not be able to. Can I run in my robe? Impossible. It would be easier to die rather than to run.

This man became so afraid... When the tin can fell on him with a loud noise, his dhoti opened up and he was so afraid that he entered his house without it, naked! His dhoti was left there. I came down the tree, took the dhoti, and with my can I escaped from there.

His whole house was in a chaos. Everybody, all the neighborhood people around were asking what had happened. He said, "That boy disturbed everything. He told me this morning, 'Don't do the mantra. If you are not afraid, don't do the mantra.' He gave me a challenge. Tomorrow I am going to see him about what happened to me. It is because of him that in my old age I have become a laughing-stock. The whole neighborhood has seen me naked!" And in India to be naked, and that too for one of the very respected priests and scholars of the town...

He came the next day and was very serious. I knew that he was coming, so I took the tin with his dhoti inside. When he saw me coming with that tin, he said, "What is that?"

I said, "First, you start. You have threatened, you have told the neighbors that you will come to see me. I have also come to see you – now it is a question of who sees whom. You can impose any punishment you want on me, but remember, I will open this can before the whole school."

He said, "What is in it?"

I said, "*Bhoot!* Ghost! I have caught in it the ghost that made you afraid."

He said, "Ghost? Is this the tin can that fell from the tree?"

I said, "Of course."

He said, "Take it back, it is dangerous."

But I said, "Please look inside and see what is there." I opened the tin can and took out his dhoti and said, "At least take your dhoti back."

He said, "But how did you manage it?"

I said, "Whom do you think was managing it all? You should thank me for taking all the trouble of climbing the tree, drumming the tin can, and then throwing it on top of you; then collecting your dhoti in darkness, and escaping before I was caught. It was just to show you not to lie to me." And since that day, although he knew that I was the person who did the whole thing, he stopped coming by that path, he would go around. I asked him why – "You know perfectly well I was the person."

He said, "I don't want to take a chance. I don't believe you – you may have collected the dhoti and the tin can in the morning, and it may have been really a ghost."

I said, "I am telling you, I was in that tree."

He never came again in the night on that path. My whole family knew that I was the person responsible, because they had seen me going up the tree, but even my family became afraid. They started saying, "Perhaps the ghost took possession of you."

I said, "Strange people! I have said I did it, but now you are projecting new ideas: that the ghost took possession of me, that's why I did the whole thing. You can't take simple facts as simple."

If the fear comes up, that means you have to face it; it is in no way going to help you to cover it with the idea of God.

You cannot have faith again, that is destroyed. Once you have met me you cannot have faith in God, because doubt is a reality, and faith is fiction. And no fiction can stand before a fact. Now God is going to remain a hypothesis to you; your prayer will be useless. You will know it is a hypothesis, you cannot forget that it is a hypothesis.

Once you have heard a truth it is impossible to forget it.

That is one of the qualities of truth, that you don't need to remember it.

The lie has to be remembered continually; you may forget. The person habit-uated to lies needs a better memory than the person who is habituated to truth, because a true person has no need of memory; if you only say the truth there is no need to remember. But if you are saying a lie, then you have to continually remember, because you have said one lie to one person, another lie to another person; something else to somebody else. To whom you have said what, you have to categorize in your mind and keep. And whenever a question arises about a lie you have to lie again, so it is a series. The lie does not believe in birth control.

Truth is celibate, it has no children at all; it is unmarried in fact.

Once you have understood, only once, that God is nothing but a hypothesis created by the priests, the politicians, the power elite, the pedagogues – all those who want to keep you in psychological slavery, who have some vested interest in your slavery... They all want to keep you afraid, always afraid, trembling deep inside, because if you are not afraid, you are dangerous.

You can either be a person who is a coward, afraid, ready to submit, surrender, a person who has himself no dignity, no respect for his own being – or you can be fearless. But then you are going to be a rebel, you cannot avoid that.

Either you can be a man of faith or you are going to be a rebellious spirit. So those people who don't want you to be rebels – because your being rebellious goes against their interests – go on enforcing, conditioning your mind with Christianity, with Judaism, with Mohammedanism, with Hinduism, and they keep you trembling deep inside.

That is their power, so anybody who is interested in power, whose whole life is nothing but a will-to-power, has tremendous use for the hypothesis of God.

If you are afraid of God – and if you believe in God you have to be afraid – you have to follow his orders and commandments, his holy book, his messiah, his incarnation; you have to follow him and his agents. In fact he does not exist, only the agent exists. This is a very strange business.

Religion is the strangest business of all. There is no boss, but there are mediators: the priest, the bishop, the cardinal, the pope, the messiah, the whole hierarchy – and on top there is nobody. But Jesus derives *his* authority and power from God – his only begotten son. The pope derives his authority from Jesus – his only true representative, infallible. And it goes on and on to the lowest priest. But there is no God; it is your fear.

You asked for God to be invented because you could not live alone.

You were incapable of facing life, its beauties, its joys, its sufferings, its anguishes. You were not ready to experience them on your own without anybody protecting you, without somebody being an umbrella to you. You asked for God out of fear. And certainly there are con men everywhere. You ask and they will do it for you. You asked and they said, "We know God is, and you have just to say this prayer…"

Tolstoy has a beautiful story. It became a great trouble for the highest priest in the Russian Orthodox Church, because three men who lived beyond a lake under a tree became very famous; so famous that instead of people coming to the high priest they started going to those three saints.

Now, in Christianity *saint* is a very strange word. In any other language *saint* and the equivalent of *saint* are very respectful words. But not in Christianity – because *saint* means only sanctified by the pope, certified by the pope. Joan of Arc was made a saint after three hundred years. One infallible pope burned her alive. After three hundred years they changed their minds, because people were becoming more and more favorable to Joan of Arc; then the pope thought it was a good time to declare her a saint. She had been declared a witch and was burned alive – and this was done by one infallible pope. Then another infallible pope, after three hundred years, declared Joan of Arc to be a saint. Her grave was dug up again and whatsoever was there – a few bones may have remained – was brought out, worshipped, sanctified. She has become a saint.

"Saint" in the Christian reference is ugly. The Sanskrit word is *sant*, equivalent to saint. If you derive it from *sant*, if you write *sant*, you can read it saint; but *sant* means one who has arrived, one who has known *satya*. *Sat* means the ultimate truth, and one who has realized it is called a *sant* – not somebody certified! It is not a degree or a title that somebody can give to you.

The high priest was very angry because people were talking about those three saints. He said, "But how did they become saints? I have not certified anybody. This is simply outrageous." But people are people… People were still going, so finally he decided, "I have to visit these people. Who are they? They have declared themselves saints! I don't even know who they are. I have not even been informed, and it is in my power only to sanctify a person to be a saint." He was very angry.

He went in his boat – and he had a beautiful boat because he was the high priest and he was higher than the czar as far as religion was concerned. Even the czar and czarina used to come to touch his feet. And he thought, "Who are these fools, unknown, anonymous? – declaring themselves saints!" He went there and found those three very simple people, three old people, sitting under the tree. They immediately stood up, touched the feet of the high priest and they said, "Why did you take all this trouble? You could have sent a message and we would have come." The high priest cooled down a little bit, but he said, "Who declared you saints?"

They said, "We don't know. We didn't even know that we are saints. Who told you?"

The high priest could see that all three were absolutely uneducated and knew nothing about Christianity or religion. And he said, "What is your prayer? Do you know the orthodox prayer? Without it you cannot be even a Christian, what to say about a saint!"

They said, "We are uneducated and nobody ever taught us any prayer. But if you forgive us, we will tell you – we have composed a prayer of our own."

He said, "What! You have composed a prayer of your own! Okay, let me listen to what your prayer is."

One said to the other, "You tell him."

The other said, "You can tell him." They were all feeling very shy and very ashamed.

The high priest said, "You tell it! Anybody tell it."

They said, "We all three will tell it together." Their prayer was simple: "'You are three – God the father, the Holy Ghost and God the son. You are three, we are also three – have mercy on us. This is our prayer. More than that we don't know. We have heard that he is three, and we know that we are three, and what more is needed? 'Have mercy on us – you are three, we are three, have mercy on us!'"

The priest said, "This is unforgivable. You are making a mockery of religion."

They said, "Then you can tell us what the prayer is so we can repeat it."

The high priest told them the prayer, a long prayer of the Russian Orthodox Church. They listened and they said, "Wait, you repeat it again because this is so long and we may forget it. Our prayer is so short, and we never forget it because it is so simple and we always remember that He is three, we are three, have mercy on us. There is no problem about it. Your prayer – if we forget or if we commit some mistake…"

So he repeated it a second time. They said, "One more time." He repeated it thrice, and they said, "We will try."

He was very happy that he had put those fools on the right path. This is prayer, and they have become saints? And he started back, very happy that he had done a good deed. These are the do-gooders.

Just in the middle of the lake he saw all the three old men running, coming, on the lake! He could not believe his eyes. They said, "Wait! We have forgotten the prayer! Just one more time, and we will never bother you again." And they were standing on the water!

The high priest touched their feet and said, "Forgive me. You repeat your prayer, that's perfectly right. And you need not come to ask me; if I have some-thing to ask I will come. I know now whose prayer is right."

Those three persons indicate one simple truth: if you have faith that does not prove that there is a God. But your faith can give you a certain integrity, a certain strength. But the faith has to be very innocent. They were not hiding any fear behind it. They had not gone to any church to learn the prayer, they had not asked anybody, "What is God? Where is God?" – nothing. They were simply innocent people, and out of innocence was their faith.

That faith does not prove that God is; that faith simply proves that innocence is a power.

It is only a story, but innocence is a power. Yes, you can walk on water but out of innocence; and out of innocence, if there is faith. But that very rarely happens, because every parent and every society destroys your innocence before you are even aware that you had it. They go on forcing some belief on you, and that belief you accept because of fear. In darkness the mother says, "Don't be afraid; God is there looking after you. He is present everywhere."

I have heard about a Catholic nun who used to take a shower with her clothes on inside the bathroom. Other nuns became a little worried: "Has she gone Oregonian or something?"

But the poor nun said, "It is because I have heard God is everywhere, so he must be in the bathroom too. And to be naked before God does not look right."

This woman may look foolish but she has a certain innocence. And out of this innocence, if faith arises, then it doesn't matter in what the faith is.

Innocence gives power, but innocence is destroyed, and this is what I am trying to bring back to you, so that you become innocent again. And to become innocent again you will have to pass through these stages.

You will have to drop this idea of God which helps you to remain unafraid. You will have to pass through fear and accept it as a human reality. There is no need to escape from it. What is needed is to go deep into it, and the deeper you go into your fear, the less you will find it is.

When you have touched the rock bottom of fear you will simply laugh, there is nothing to fear. And when fear disappears there is innocence, and that innocence is the *summum bonum*, the very essence of a religious man.

That innocence is power. That innocence is the only miracle there is.

Out of innocence anything can happen, but you will not be a Christian out of that, and you will not be a Mohammedan out of that. Out of innocence you will become simply an ordinary human being, totally accepting your ordinariness, and living it joyously, thankful to the whole existence – not to God, because that is an idea given by others to you.

But existence is not an idea. It is there all around you, within and without. When you are utterly innocent, a deep thankfulness – I will not call it prayer because in prayer you are asking for something, I will call it a deep thankfulness – a gratitude arises. Not that you are asking for something, but you are giving thanks for something that has already been given to you.

So much has been given to you. Do you deserve it? Have you earned it? Existence goes on pouring so much over you that to ask for more is just ugly. That which you have received, you should be grateful for it.

And the most beautiful phenomenon is that when you are grateful, existence starts pouring more and more over you. It becomes a circle: the more you get, the more you become grateful; the more you become grateful, the more you get... And there is no end to it, it is an infinite process.

But remember – the hypothesis of God is gone; the moment you called it a hypothesis the idea of God had been already dropped. Whether you are afraid or not, you cannot take it back; it is finished. Now the only way left is to go into your fear. Silently enter into it, so you can find its depth. And sometimes it happens that it is not very deep.

A Zen story is: a man walking in the night slipped from a rock. Afraid that he would fall down thousands of feet, because he knew that place was a very deep valley, he took hold of a branch that was hanging over the rock. In the night all he could see was a bottomless abyss. He shouted; his own shout was reflected back – there was nobody to hear.

You can think of that man and his whole night of torture. Every moment there was death, his hands were becoming cold, he was losing his grip... And as the sun came out he looked down and he laughed: there was no abyss. Just six inches down there was a rock. He could have rested the whole night, slept well – the rock was big enough – but the whole night was a nightmare.

From my own experience I can say to you: the fear is not more than six inches deep. Now it is up to you whether you want to go on clinging to the branch and turn your life into a nightmare, or whether you would love to leave the branch and stand on your feet.

There is nothing to fear.

jesus, the only forgotten son of god

Osho,
You have said that God is neither a hypothesis nor an idea. Then what is
God? Has anyone ever met God or not?

God certainly is not a hypothesis. A hypothesis can only be part of an objective science. You can experiment upon it, you can dissect it, analyze it.

That's what Karl Marx has argued: "Unless God is proved in a scientific lab, I am not going to accept him." What Karl Marx is saying is that, "I can accept God as a hypothesis, but a hypothesis is not a truth. It has yet to be proved, and the proof has to be scientific."

But if God is put into a scientific lab, in a test tube, and dissected, analyzed, and we know all the constituents that make God, will it be the God who created the world? And if Marx is going to accept God only then, that means God has to be reduced into a thing.

Then what would be the difficulty in manufacturing God? Once you have analyzed all the constituents of God, all the chemicals, then there is no problem. Get your discovery patented, and start manufacturing God. But that manufactured God will not be the God you are asking me about.

God is not a hypothesis, cannot be a hypothesis, because the very word *hypothesis* takes the ground from beneath his feet. God is not to be proved. If science has to prove God then the scientist becomes higher than God. The poor God will be just like a white rat. So you play around and make boxes, and God moves from one box to another, and you find out how much intelligence God has.

Delgado, the psychologist, will be very happy to find God in a mousetrap, because all that psychologists have found about man is not about man, it is about mice. They first find out about the mice, and then they project it onto human beings – because it looks inhuman to dissect a human being, to torture him and to experiment upon him. But it is very strange that the mouse gives clues which help to understand the human mind, human psychology. Certainly man is more developed. You can multiply it, but the basic idea you can get from a mouse.

God, according to the pseudo-religions, is the creator of the whole of existence. According to them, we are his creation. To make God a hypothesis means from now onwards he is going to be our creation. We are trying to reverse the roles, putting the creator as a creature and the creature as the creator. The pseudo-religions will not agree. I also do not agree, but our disagreements are basically different.

They cannot agree because God is above everything; nobody can be above God. The scientist has to be an observer, above, to watch, and then God becomes just a plaything in his hands. He will put electrodes in God's mind. He will have remote control so whenever he wants, God laughs; whenever he wants, God weeps; whenever he wants, God runs; whenever he wants, God stops. The pseudo-religions cannot agree for this reason. They say that God is not a creature, not a thing; he is the creator. He has made you, you cannot be above him, in no way.

My disagreement is that even for something to be a hypothesis a certain probability is needed – not certainty, but at least a probability. God is not even probable. My reasons are totally different. A scientist starts with a hypothesis because he sees some probability in it, some possibility, some potentiality.

God is only a word without any substance in it; a hollow word with no meaning at all.

Perhaps we have to interpret the Bible a little differently. It says, "In the beginning was the Word, the Word was with God, the Word was God." In this reference perhaps it is true, that the beginning of God is nothing but a word. And then the word starts gathering moss around it; as time passes people go on giving more and more meaning to it. What meaning they give to the word is their need. You should remember it.

God is all-knowing, because man has felt in every direction that his knowledge is very limited – just a little light, a candlelight throwing a small circle. Beyond that circle all is darkness; and that darkness creates fear. Who knows what it contains? Somebody is needed who knows. If he is not present, he has to be invented.

God is an invention of man's own psychological need.

He is all-knowing. You cannot be; whatsoever you know, howsoever you know, you can never be all-knowing. Existence is so vast and man is so tiny, so small, that to conceive that your small brain will be able to know all – past, present, future – seems to be a fool's dream. Even a fool will not dream such a thing. But to live in a world surrounded everywhere with darkness is difficult. You cannot be certain even of what you know, because the unknown is so vast, that who can say that if you know a little more, your known will not be found invalid.

In fact that has been the case. The more man knew, the more he became

aware that the knowledge that was knowledge yesterday, today has become ignorance. What about today's knowledge? Perhaps tomorrow this too will become
ignorance.

It became a great psychological need to have someone who knows all.

The priests did a great job, perhaps the greatest job ever done, and did it
perfectly well: they invented God.

It helped in many ways. Man became more certain of himself, more stable,
less afraid, because there is an all-knowing God, all-pervading God, present
everywhere. All that you have to know is the key to turn God in your favor. And
the key was with the priest, who was ready to part with it. Every religion has been
pretending that they have that key which unlocks all the doors, the master key.
And if you attain the master key, you will be just like gods; you will be all-knowing,
you will be present anywhere you want, you will be all-powerful. You just see in
these three words, man's three needs.

Man's knowledge is very limited, very poor. What really do we know? Even
small things can make you aware of your ignorance.

Our power... What power do we have? Perhaps man is the only animal in the
world who has no power. Can you fight with a lion? – with a tiger? Forget about
lions and tigers, can you fight with a dog or a cat? You will be surprised – what to
say about a cat, if even a hundred thousand flies attack you, what are you going
to do? You have never thought about flies attacking, but if they attack, if some fly
turns political, you will be helpless, you cannot survive.

Forget about flies; in fact there are plants in South Africa which catch birds
and animals, suck them completely dry and throw them away. There are science
fiction stories about plants attacking men. In these stories there are plants that
can catch men, they are big enough. If you are in their vicinity their branches can
just catch hold of you like the trunk of an elephant, and crush you completely.
And they have ways to suck your blood. Such perfect surgery – all over your
body their branches will start penetrating you. And how thick is your skin? Just a
little scratch is enough and blood is available. And those trees live on blood; they
are man-eating trees – the man is still alive and they start eating him.

There are science fiction stories about all the trees around you going crazy.
They can go crazy because they have a certain kind of brain, a certain kind
of mind. Now, it is a proved fact that they think, feel; that they have emotions,
sentiments; that they love, they hate. Now there are scientific proofs about all this.

Buddha and Mahavira, twenty-five centuries ago, said not to hurt trees
because they are as alive as you are. People at first laughed: trees – and alive?
But Buddha and Mahavira had no scientific proofs for it. It was only their experience in silence. Sitting under a tree, utterly silent, Buddha suddenly felt that the
tree is not dead, that it is thriving with life. But these were their personal experiences; they could say it, but they could not prove it.

It was left to be proved by another Indian, Jagdish Chandra Bose, who
devoted his whole life to finding scientifically whether Buddha and Mahavira were
right or wrong. And he conclusively proved that trees are alive. He was given a
Nobel Prize for proving trees to be alive. But that was only the beginning. Then

more and more researchers went into it. Just to be alive is not enough.

Soon it was found that they have a different kind of brain system, but they do have one. You should not look for the same brain as you have. This is a stupid human idea, that your brain is the only kind of brain. If there can be so many kinds of bodies, why can't there be so many kinds of brain? And soon it was found that trees have a certain kind of brain system, and the research went on...

Just a few years ago it was found that trees not only have a certain way of knowing which we call a brain, they have a heart too. Certainly it does not beat like yours, because they have their own kind of heart. If their surgeons come to look around you, they will find no heart in you, no brain in you, because they will be looking for their type of brain, their type of heart.

Trees feel emotions, sentiments. For example when a gardener comes to water the tree, the tree feels happy. Now, the happiness can be measured on a graph like the cardiogram. The graph becomes harmonious, as if it is a song, rhythmic. If somebody comes with an ax to cut the tree... He is far away but the graph changes. The man has not even said that he is coming to cut the tree, he has only thought about it, but the tree somehow has become aware of his thought.

If he is not going to cut the tree, and has no thought of it, he can pass by the tree with the ax in his hand and the graph will continue the same. But if he has the thought to cut the tree, then the graph immediately changes, zigzags, all the harmony is lost, there is no rhythm. The tree is shaking with fear. And if he cuts the tree, then the graphs of other trees around start going berserk. They are feeling hurt because one of their fellows, friends, a neighbor, is being cut.

So it is not impossible – if they have sentiments, emotions, a certain kind of thinking... My idea is not outlandish: sometimes they can go crazy, because all these things are needed to go crazy. They have them; and man has done so much harm to them that it is time they should go crazy. And he goes on harming them. There must be a limit, and it is not far away. Man has destroyed the whole environment.

After my graduation I went to the Hindu university in Varanasi to study, because that is the biggest university in India. But I stayed there only twenty-four hours. The man I was staying with was Doctor Rajbali Pandey; he was the head of the department of history. He tried to persuade me not to leave: "Why? – you will not find a better place, at least not in India. It has the best scholars, the best professors, all the best facilities possible. You should think about it."

I said, "I am not going because of this university, I am going because of you."

He said, "What! What have I done to you?"

He had stayed with me once, just accidentally. I was traveling in the same compartment to Jabalpur in which he was traveling. He missed the train that he had to catch from Jabalpur to Gondia – it was on a different line. Our train was late so he was very much worried, "Now, what am I to do?" Only after twenty-four hours – Gondia is a small place – would a very small train, a toy train go to Gondia, and the same train would come back. It takes twelve hours to go and twelve hours to come back, and it is not that far, just the train is such...

So I said, "Don't be worried, come and stay with me." I was staying with one of my uncles. So in this strange way we became known to each other. And in the morning I took him for a walk – Jabalpur is very green, so full of trees that you don't see the houses, you see only the greenery. And he said to me, "I hate these trees, because these trees are the enemies of man. If just for five years you stop cutting them, they will run over the whole city and destroy all the houses."

There is truth in what he was saying, that man has created all these cities by cutting the trees. And if you allow the trees to grow again, they are going to destroy your so-called civilization. He said, "Whenever you come to Benares, you are welcome to be my guest." After two years I had to go, so I stayed with him. And in the morning I was going for a walk, so he said, "I followed you in Jabalpur for a walk, so I will here also."

Benares is barren, no trees at all. The whole university is just buildings and buildings, beautiful buildings because all the Maharajahs of India contributed to make a great Hindu university. The idea was a Hindu university should be parallel to Cambridge, Oxford, or Harvard. So much has been done, and beautifully done; there are marble buildings, great buildings, beautiful hostels, but no trees at all.

I said to him, "Now I understand why you were so much offended by the trees that I love. I cannot survive here. It is true that trees had to be cut to make houses and cities, but that does not mean that trees have to be completely destroyed. Then you will die too. There needs to be a balance because the trees are continuously giving you oxygen. When you breathe in, you take oxygen; the oxygen is absorbed by your blood system and the carbon dioxide is thrown out.

"Trees take the carbon dioxide; that is their food. That's why when you burn a tree you get coal. Coal is nothing but carbon dioxide in solid form, it is carbon. They live on carbon dioxide, you live on oxygen; it is a good friendship. Neither do they have to destroy the civilization, nor do you have to destroy them. You should live in coexistence; that's the only way to live – and here I don't see a single tree.

"And just twenty-four hours here and I am feeling dry. Without seeing greenery your eyes will lose luster. No, I cannot be in this university. It may have great professors, it may have great libraries, it may have great facilities, but I would prefer some huge, big, ancient trees."

And I wandered all over India to find a university where there was something better than Jabalpur. And when I found Sagar I remained there, because Sagar is just unimaginably beautiful. It is a small city, but the city is way beyond a very big lake. The city is on one side of the lake, and on the other side there is a range of hills, and on the hills is the university. And all around, huge trees, and so silent... Benares was so crowded and so buzzing with ten thousand students in the university. Sagar is a small place, and the university was new. I remained there.

Rajbali Pandey once came to Sagar while I was still there to deliver a series of lectures on history, and he saw me and he said, "What happened? I thought you had gone back to Jabalpur."

I said, "First I tried to look all over, perhaps there was something better – and here, you see... The trees in Jabalpur are good but not so huge and not so ancient. And these hills and this lake and those lotuses... It is the right place."

Man has done so much harm to nature, that when I say that one day nature can go crazy, it is not only science fiction, it is possible. If all these trees that we have been cutting and destroying become just a little bit united... I don't think they know anything about trade-unions and things like that. They have not heard Karl Marx' famous slogan: "Proletariat of the world unite, you have nothing to lose but your chains, and you have the whole world to gain." So just change the word *proletariat*: Trees of the world unite, you have nothing to lose, not even chains, and you have the whole world to gain!

If these trees start attacking you, do you think you will be able to survive, even with all your nuclear weapons? – impossible. And it has happened a few times, that's why the science fiction came into existence. In a few places it has happened. Once it happened in Africa, that a certain bird suddenly started attacking people, and it killed many people; before they could kill all those birds, a few people were killed.

It happened once in Indonesia with another bird; the whole community of that species started attacking people. They simply attacked the eyes and they made hundreds of people blind before anything could be done. Because we don't think about these things, we are not prepared.

You have a fire brigade because you know fire can happen. You have the police for the criminals; you have the army if somebody attacks. But if birds start attacking your eyes, by the time you get ready to do something, much harm would have happened. And it was only one kind of bird.

If all birds and all animals and all trees simply decide one day, "It is enough, now get rid of these people," I don't think man can survive, there is no way. All your armies will be useless, all your arms will be useless, all your nuclear weapons will be useless – and then you will understand how weak you are.

You have forgotten your weakness because of all these things. But think of the man in the beginning, when there was nothing, and he felt himself absolutely weak. Just think of before even fire was invented. What was the situation of man? – the weakest animal on the earth.

Fire is perhaps the greatest discovery of man, not nuclear weapons, because it was fire that gave man tremendous courage. Then in the night he could make a bonfire and sleep around it; and the animals were afraid of fire so they would not come. Otherwise sleep was impossible – if you slept you were finished; any animal could take you away.

The whole day you are hunting, and in the night you cannot sleep. In the day you can somehow survive – you can go up a tree, you can hide in a cave – but in the night, when you are asleep, what can you do? And the animals of those days are no longer here – only a few specimens like the elephant, which is not that huge. There were animals ten times larger than the elephant.

For example, the crocodile – there were crocodiles that were many times bigger, which are no longer here. They did not need to chew you if they ate you, they simply swallowed you, they were such big animals. You simply slipped down their throat – and gone! There was no need for chewing or anything.

With these animals, with all the darkness, the people who invented God must have done a service in the beginning. They gave courage. They said, "Don't be afraid. All that you have to do is to be prayerful, faithful." Certainly they took a certain amount of commission, and I don't think that it was bad, because business is business. They were giving you so much, and if you gave a little bit to those people, you should not be grumpy about it.

So a little bit was given to the priest and the priest gave you the confidence and an omnipotent God – omniscient, omnipresent – and you began to start feeling at ease in the world. The priest gave you the idea: "God has created man in his own image, so don't be afraid. You are his special creation. All these animals he has created for you, all these trees he has created for you."

That's the Mohammedan logic still. You cannot talk about vegetarian food because they say, "Why did God create the animals then? The Koran says that God created the animals to eat. When the holy book says that the animals are created to be eaten, how can it be a sin or anything wrong?"

The priest made man, at least in his mind, stronger. Of course they exploited him, and slowly, slowly, there were many more psychological needs. And they had found a great treasure in the word God: it fulfilled all kinds of things, all needs.

The greatest need of man is to be needed.

If you are not needed by anybody in the world you will commit suicide, you will not be able to live. Strange – perhaps you have never thought about it, that you are seeking continuously to be needed. That gives you preciousness, some value, some meaning. Perhaps a woman marries a man simply to fulfill the need that she is needed. And the same may be the reason for the man, that he wants to feel that some woman needs him.

The man has tried to make the woman not earn money, not do any work, not be educated. There are political, economic, and other reasons but the psycho-logical reason is that he wants her to be dependent on him so she is always in need of him, and he can feel good that he is needed. They will produce children and both will feel good that now these children need them: you have some purpose to live for. You have to live for these children, you have to live for your wife, you have to live for your husband: life is no longer meaningless.

And the priest has given you the greatest consolation – that God needs you; so much that he sends his son to save you from going astray. He continually sends prophets, *paigambara*, *tirthankaras*, incarnations, to save you, to keep you on the path. You are not neglected. He is constantly concerned about you.

Krishna in the Gita says, "Whenever there is a need, and whenever people are going astray, I promise you I will come back." Jesus says, "I will be coming back to take my flock." Why have people accepted these things? They wanted some-body to be concerned about them. And if God is concerned, what can be more fulfilling? And when you pray, and by chance if your prayer is fulfilled, then you know perfectly well that in this vast universe you are not just nothing. Your prayer is heard, it reaches to God; not only that, there is a response.

In my neighborhood there was a temple, a temple of Krishna, just a few houses away from my house. The temple was on the other side of the road, my house was on this side of the road. In front of the temple lived the man who had made the temple; he was a great devotee.

The temple was of Krishna in his childhood – because when Krishna becomes a young man he creates many troubles and many questions, so there are many people who worship Krishna as a child – hence the temple was called the temple of Balaji. *Balaji* means… *Bal* means child, and *Balaji* has become the name for Krishna. And then everything is simple because about his childhood you cannot raise all those questions which would be raised later on.

He becomes a politician, a warrior, manages the whole war and collects all those women – anything that you can imagine, he has done it. So in India there are many temples which are of the child Krishna. One of the greatest Krishna devotees, Surdas, a poet, simply sings songs only of the child Krishna; he never goes beyond that. Beyond that he cannot go. Beyond that it is much too difficult, particularly for Surdas.

Surdas was a monk, and he used to go to beg. It is not thought right for a monk to go again and again to the same house, because it may be burdensome to the family. They may not be so rich that every day they can give you food. But the woman who came to give him food was so beautiful that it was irresistible. If she had been only beautiful it would have been possible to resist, but what he saw in her eyes was a tremendous love towards him; that was more difficult – now the temptation became thousandfold. The fire was on both sides.

The next day he went again. The woman placed the food with great love, devotion. And the next day, again he was there; it became a routine. He saw that the woman certainly had fallen in love with him. Of course he was not courageous enough to accept the fact that he had also fallen in love with the woman; he was a monk, he was not supposed to do such things. But what was he doing, going for one month continuously to the same house?

One day is allowed; in certain difficult situations, three days are allowed, but that's all. You may be sick and you cannot go far away, then three days, but not more than that. So the next day when he went, he gathered courage and he asked the woman, "I have been coming here for one month. You have been giving me food every day, better and better more and more. What do you see in me, and why did you never remind me that this is not right for a monk? – one day is allowed, at the most three days. And I see so much love coming from you towards me. I would like to know the exact truth. What is the situation?"

Now, he is throwing all his lust, all his desire on the poor woman; and what the woman said was a great shock. She said, "I simply love your eyes, they are so beautiful and so silent, and I would pray you that you go on coming. We are not poor, but I want to see your eyes at least once a day. I have never seen such eyes." She was not concerned with Surdas at all. She was talking about the eyes as you would talk about a flower, a rose; she wanted to see those beautiful eyes – there was nothing else.

Surdas – that was not his name at that time. In India you don't call a blind man a blind man, because that looks bad, unmannerly; so all blind men in India are called *surdas* – *surdas* means blind man. That was not his name before; but he went home, took both his eyes out, went back with the help of another monk and presented those two eyes to the woman. He said, "You keep these eyes, because soon we will be moving and I will not be able to come every day. You can see these eyes, you can keep them, and for me anyway it is good that I don't have them."

That day he expressed his heart, "I was also feeling a certain desire arising in me. Now I will never see beauty. Now these eyes are closed. The world of beauty is no longer there."

I will not support such a thing because you can be blind but you can still dream of beautiful women, which is more dangerous. Because no real girl is a dream girl, but all dream girls are real when you are dreaming, remember – very real.

You will get frustrated with any beautiful woman. She may be Cleopatra, Amrapali, anyone, but you will get fed up, actually fed up, because this desire for beauty is also a kind of hunger; you are feeding on it. It is a kind of food, a nourishment, but you cannot eat the same food every day. Sooner or later you are going to be fed up. That words *fed up* are very beautiful. The same food can bring nausea if it is given every day to you.

So just by destroying your eyes you cannot go beyond your desire – that is stupid. But Surdas did that. And he was writing poetry only about Krishna's childhood, because how can this man, who has taken his eyes out to avoid desire, think of his god dancing with girls, other people's wives, and living the life of the most materialist person possible? So for him, Krishna never goes beyond seven years of age; he remains just below seven. And in India many temples are called Balaji's temple, which means Krishna in his childhood.

This Balaji's *mandir* was just in front of the house of the man who had made it. Because of the temple and the man's devotion, continuous devotion... He would take a bath – just in front of the temple was a well – he would take a bath there first thing. Then he would do his prayers for hours; and he was thought to be very religious. By and by people started also calling him Balaji. It became so associated that I don't remember his real name myself because by the time I had any idea that he existed, I only heard his name as Balaji. But that cannot be his name; that name must have come because he made the temple.

I used to go to the temple because the temple was very beautiful and very silent – except for this Balaji who was a disturbance there. And for hours – he was a rich man so there was no need for him to be worried about time – three hours in the morning, three hours in the evening, he was constantly torturing the god of the temple. Nobody used to go there, although the temple was so beautiful that many people would have gone there; they would go to a temple further away because this Balaji was too much. And his noise – it can only be called noise, it was not music – his singing was such that it would make you an enemy of singing for your whole life.

But I used to go there and we became friendly. He was an old man. I said, "Balaji, three hours in the morning, three hours in the evening – what are you asking for? And everyday? – and he has not given it to you?"

He said, "I am not asking for any material things. I ask for spiritual things.

And it is not a matter of one day; you have to continue your whole life and they will be given after death. But it is certain they will be given: I have made the temple, I serve the lord, I pray; you can see even in winter, with wet clothes..." It is thought to be a special quality of devotion, to be shivering with wet clothes. My own idea is that with shivering, singing comes easier. You start shouting to forget the shivering.

I said, "My idea about it is different but I will not tell you. Just one thing I want because my grandfather goes on saying, 'These are only cowards; this Balaji is a coward. Six hours a day he is wasting, and it is such a small life; and he is a coward.'"

He said, "Your grandfather said that I am a coward?"

I said, "I can bring him."

He said, "No, don't bring him to the temple because it will be an unnecessary trouble – but I am not a coward."

I said, "Okay, we will see whether you are a coward or not."

Behind his temple there was what in India is called an *akhara*, where people learn to wrestle, do exercises, and the Indian type of wrestling. I used to go there – it was just behind the temple, by the side of the temple – so I had all the wrestlers there as my friends. I asked three of them, "Tonight you have to help me."

They said, "What has to be done?"

I said, "We have to take Balaji's cot – he sleeps outside his house – we have just to take his cot and put it over the well."

They said, "If he jumps or something happens he may fall into the well."

I said, "Don't worry, the well is not that deep. I have jumped into it many times – it is not that deep nor is it that dangerous. And as far as I know Balaji is not going to jump. He will shout from the cot; sitting in the cot, he will call to his Balaji, 'Save me!'"

With difficulty I could convince three persons: "You have nothing really to do with it. Just alone I cannot carry his cot, and I am asking you because you are all strong people. If he wakes up in the middle it will be difficult to reach the well. I will wait for you. He goes to sleep at nine o'clock, by ten the street is empty and eleven is the right time not to take any chances. At eleven we can move him."

Only two persons turned up; one didn't turn up, so we were only three. I said, "This is difficult. One side of the cot... And if Balaji wakes up..."

I said, "Just wait, I will have to call my grandfather."

And I told my grandfather, "This is what we are going to do. You have to give us a little help."

He said, "This is a little too much. You have some guts to ask your own grandfather to do this to that poor man who does no harm to anybody except that he shouts six hours a day, but we have become accustomed to it..."

I said, "I have not come to argue about it. You just come, and anything that you want, anytime, I will owe it to you; you just say, and I will do it. But you have to come for this thing, and it is not much – just a twelve-foot road has to be crossed without waking up Balaji."

So he came. That's why I say he was a very rare man – he was seventy-five!

He came. He said, "Okay, let us have this experience also and see what happens."

The two wrestlers started escaping, seeing my grandfather. I said, "Wait, where are you going?"

They said, "Your grandfather is coming."

I said, "I am bringing him. He is the fourth person. If you escape then I will be at a loss. My grandfather and I will not be able to manage. We can carry him, but he will wake up. You need not be worried."

They said, "Are you sure of your grandfather? – because they are almost of the same age; they may be friends and some trouble may arise. He may tell on us."

I said, "I am there, he cannot get me into any trouble. So don't you be afraid, you will not be in any trouble, and he does not know your names or anything."

We carried Balaji and put his cot over his small well. Only he used to take a bath there, and once in a while I used to jump into it, which he was very much against – but what can you do? Once I had jumped in, he had to arrange to take me out. I said, "What can you do now? The only thing is to take me out. And if you harass me, I will jump in every day. And if you talk about it to my family, then you know I will start bringing my friends to jump into it. So right now, keep it a secret between us. You take your bath outside, I take my bath inside; there is no harm."

It was a very small well, so the cot could completely fit over it. Then I told my grandfather, "Go away because if you are caught then the whole city will think that this is going too far."

And then, from far away we started throwing stones to wake him up, because if he did not wake up the whole night, he might turn and fall into the well, and something would go wrong. The moment he woke up he gave such a scream! We had heard his voice, but this…! The whole neighborhood gathered. He was sitting in his cot and he said, "Who has done it?" He was trembling and shaking and afraid.

People said, "Please at least get out of the cot. Then we will find out what has happened."

I was there in the crowd, and I said, "What is the matter? You could have called your Balaji. But you didn't call him, you gave a scream and you forgot all about Balaji. Six hours training every day for your whole life…"

He looked at me and he said, "Is that too a secret?"

I said, "Now there are two secrets you have to keep. One you have already kept for many years. This is now the second."

But from that day he stopped that three hours shouting in the temple. I was puzzled. Everybody was puzzled. He stopped taking a bath in that well, and those three hours evening and morning he just forgot. He arranged a servant priest to come every morning to do a little worship and that was all.

I asked him, "Balaji, what has happened?"

He said, "I had told you a lie that I am not afraid. But that night, waking up over the well – that shriek was not mine." You can call it the primal scream. It was not his, that is certainly true. It must have come from his deepest unconscious. He said, "That scream made me aware that I am really an afraid man, and all my prayers are nothing but trying to persuade God to save me, to help me, to protect me.

"But you have destroyed all that, and what you have done was good for me. I am finished with all that nonsense. I tortured the whole neighborhood my whole life, and if you had not done that, I may have continued. I am aware now that I am afraid. And I feel that it is better to accept my fear because my whole life has been meaningless and my fear is the same."

Just in 1970 I went for the last time to my city. I had a promise with my mother's mother that when she dies – she had taken it as a promise – that I would come. So I had gone. I just went around the town to meet people and I saw Balaji. He was looking a totally different man. I asked him, "What has happened?"

He said, "That scream changed me completely. I started to live the fear. Okay, if I am a coward, then I am a coward; I am not responsible for it. If there is fear, there is fear; I was born with it. But slowly, slowly as my acceptance grew deeper, that fear has disappeared, that cowardliness has disappeared.

"In fact I have disposed of the servant from the temple, because if my prayers have not been heard, then how is a servant's prayer going to be heard, a servant who goes to thirty temples the whole day?" – because he gets two rupees from each temple. "He is praying for two rupees. So I have disposed of him. And I am perfectly at ease, and I don't bother a bit whether God exists or not. That is his problem, why should I be bothered?

"But I am feeling very fresh and very young in my old age. I wanted to see you, but I could not come, I am too old. I wanted to thank you that you did that mischief; otherwise, I would have continually prayed and died, and it was all just meaningless, useless. Now I will be dying more like a man freed, completely freed." He took me into his house. I had been there before; all the religious books were removed. He said, "I am no longer interested in all that."

You ask me: "If God is not a hypothesis, if God is not an idea, then what is God?" It is not a hypothesis because there is no way for science to discover God. Science does not move inwards, it moves outwards, and there you will find the world of things.

If you want to know consciousness, that center is within.

So God is not a hypothesis. God is not an idea because an idea is a philosophical concept, and philosophers only go on weaving thoughts, ideas, rationalizations – and they create great systems of thought...

If you look into their systems of thought you will be immensely impressed. For example, Hegel or Kant... If you are not alert, you will be surprised at what a palatial system they have made – but there is no base. And it is not a palatial building either; if you come closer you will find it is made of playing cards. A little breeze and the whole palace will fall down, because there is no base to it.

Philosophy is baseless. It makes castles in the air. Ideas are just ideas: you can project any idea you like, nobody can prevent you; and once you project the idea you can find all kinds of rationalizations to support it. There is no difficulty.

One man came to me, he was an American. He was a professor in a Christian theological college. Jabalpur has one of the greatest theological colleges in the whole of Asia, where they train ministers and priests and missionaries, and they go on sending them all over Asia to convert people to Christianity. There they teach everything – if you just go and see, you will laugh. I used to be invited there to speak on some subject.

This professor became interested in me. He took me around the whole college. In one class they were teaching how you have to stand up when you preach in church, in public; on what sentences you should put the emphasis, what words should be pronounced loudly, what gestures should be made with your hands.

I was simply amazed and said, "What are you doing? Are you making these people actors or ministers?" And these people go on doing that acting – every priest will do the same. It is a training, a kind of exercise; there is no heart in it.

If there is heart in your words, the emphasis will come on its own. If there is something that has to be expressed by your hands, the hands will take care of it, you need not do anything. If something comes to your eyes, it will come. You are not to bring it, otherwise the whole thing becomes hypocrisy.

He became friendly. One day he brought me a book which said that in America – I don't know how far it is true – number thirteen is thought to be something bad. He showed me that somebody had done this research in his theological college under him: that thirteen is really bad. So he had collected all the information about how many people die every month on the thirteenth. People die every day, but he had taken only the figures for the thirteenth: how many wars have broken out on the thirteenth, how many disasters, calamities, earthquakes. From the whole of history he had collected thousands of facts – that all this had happened on the thirteenth.

So the professor was saying to me, "This man has done a great job. He has really proved it." That professor told me – I don't know, because I have never stayed in any hotel, but the professor told me, "In America the thirteenth floor is simply missing because nobody wants to stay on the thirteenth floor." So after the twelfth, comes the fourteenth! Great idea! Even deceiving God just by changing the number.

I told him, "Do one thing... I would like to meet your student too. So tomorrow when I go to my university, I will be coming here at this time. Keep your student in your room."

I asked the student, "Have you thought about number twelve or number eleven before you submitted this thesis? And this professor who is your guide for a PhD thesis should have been intelligent enough to tell you that you should look for each date, and only then can you prove that the thirteenth is bad.

"If on the first there were only five wars and on the thirteenth there were five hundred, then it proves something. If on the second only five people died, and on the thirteenth, fifty thousand people died, it proves something. You count the whole month; you have to present thirty-one days and compare them. There is no comparison here.

"You have simply collected anything that is bad, that happened on the thirteenth. I can tell anybody to collect for the twelfth, or eleventh, or tenth, and the same kind of facts will be collected and the same number of facts. This is not a thesis, this is simply stupidity. You wasted your time, and your professor has been wasting his time."

He had been working on this thesis for three years and he was getting a scholarship for it.

Once you get an idea – it may be the date thirteen, it doesn't matter – you can make a great philosophy out of it.

God is not an idea, although philosophers have tried...because philosophers are trespassers; they simply don't believe that any territory is not their territory. They will enter into every direction, into every dimension, and they have some idea for everything. A philosopher never says, "I don't know." He knows! And not only does he know, but he will give you all the arguments and proofs that his knowledge is valid. So how can they leave out such an important area like God?

They have discovered four arguments for God. Christians have accepted those four arguments, but none of those four arguments has any validity. They are all bogus.

The first argument I have talked to you about is that everything needs a creator; hence God is needed. Now it is clear that this is not an argument. Immediately the question is shifted back – who created God? And then there is no end to it. But this is thought to be the most important argument brought in by philosophers in support of God.

It has been so easy for the atheists to laugh at these philosophers and these theologians: "What kind of arguments are these people giving?" But atheists have not been very different either.

One very famous atheist, Diderot, was speaking and he stood up and told the audience, "If God exists and you say he is all-powerful then let him stop the clock, this very moment. I will wait one minute." He waited one minute. The clock did not stop. He said, "Now you see he is not powerful. He cannot even stop the clock. He is not even courageous enough to accept my challenge."

But are these arguments? Some cunning person can manage to fix the clock so that at nine it will stop. And when it reaches nine, he stands up and says, "God, prove yourself: if you are real let the clock stop within one minute; otherwise it will prove that you don't exist." And the clock stops; God is proved. These are arguments? Neither stopping the clock nor not stopping the clock can make any substantial contribution to the proof of God.

Hence I say God is not an idea. You ask me: Then what is God? It is simply a word, a meaningless word, hollow inside, with no substance in it.

Samuel Beckett has written his masterpiece, *Waiting for Godot*, a very small piece of tremendous importance. Two persons are sitting under a tree. Both are hobos. One hobo says, "It is getting late and he has not come yet."

The other says, "I also think that he must be coming." They are waiting for Godot who has never said to them, "I will be coming." Nobody knows who this Godot is. They have never met him, but just to pass time they have invented this idea of Godot, because those two hobos, what are they going to do the whole time? So they sit and they wait, and they argue, "I don't think he is a man of his word."

The other says, "No, I know perfectly well that if he has promised he will come. He may be a little late but he will come, don't be worried." This conversation continues, and then one becomes fed up and says, "I am going. It is enough. Now I cannot wait."

The other says, "Then I am also coming with you; we will wait there together, wherever you go. Anyway what is the point? Do you think you will meet him there? We don't know where he is."

When I first came across this small play, I thought perhaps Godot was German for God – these Germans are just such crackpots that they can make anything out of anything, so they must have made God a Godot. But I inquired of Haridas. Haridas said, "No. In Germany we don't call God Godot, we call him Gott."

So I said, "I was not very far off: G-o-t-t, Gott." I said, "You have come very close to Godot. It is perfectly okay. My guess was not absolutely wrong, I was on the right lines that it must be some German idea of turning God into Godot."

But whether you call him God or Gott or Godot, it doesn't matter because the word means nothing – so you can call him anything. It is simply a word without any meaning at all, so you can play with it. And in fact that's what Samuel Beckett was doing. He means God. He doesn't say so, but it is a clear-cut indication – waiting for God; but then it would have lost some beauty. When he makes it waiting for Godot, you know who Godot is yet you cannot say that you are speaking against God.

Nobody has seen him. Nobody has met him. Nobody has heard him. Still everybody is waiting for him: now he must be coming, it is time, he should be here.

What are the Jews doing? Waiting, waiting. And they were angry when Jesus said, "I have come." He was disturbing their waiting. Just think if you had gone to those two hobos and you had said, "Okay, I have come." They would have both killed you – "You think you are Godot? Do you know who Godot is? Are you trying to deceive us?" Even if Godot himself had come, they would not have believed that he was Godot – because how he can prove that he is Godot? They don't have any photograph. They don't have any address, a phone number. How can they recognize him? They have not seen him before.

That's one thing which should be clearly understood. When Moses sees God, nobody asks him, "How did you recognize him? – because you have not seen him before." Recognition needs you to have seen him before; otherwise some charlatan or somebody may be deceiving you. "How, on what grounds...?"

When Jesus hears voices of God, or Mohammed hears them, how do they recognize that those voices are God's? Have they heard him before? Their recognition is not valid. They may have heard some voices, many mad people hear them. They may have seen somebody, many mad people see somebody. You can go into any madhouse and you will see a madman alone talking to another who is not there, and not only talking, but answering also from his side.

There is a game of cards that one man can play. In trains, once in a while, I came across a person...because I would not speak in the trains. That was my only time to be silent, otherwise in the cities with five meetings a day... So only between two cities, on the train, was the time when I would be silent and rest. But

I saw people playing cards, alone. I was puzzled: this was a great religious game! They had a partner, and for that partner's side they also played; they knew both sides and they knew both hands of cards.

Those two hobos were not doing anything new. All these religions for centuries have been doing just that, waiting for Godot, because waiting at least keeps you hoping that tomorrow… If not today, then tomorrow – but it is going to happen. And when so many people are waiting, somebody must know, somebody must have heard, somebody must have seen – he must have spoken to *somebody*! And then there are people who say, "He has spoken to me."

I used to receive so many letters. Even now I receive them, but I don't see the letters because I stopped looking at all this rubbish. I used to receive letters – and still they come but my secretary simply reports to me: "Fifteen or twenty letters of this type have come, saying that they have seen God and they want to meet you so that you can see whether their realization is true or not."

"*They* have seen God," I said, "they should have asked him. Why should they bother me? I am absolutely unconcerned with you and your God; why should you bother me? If you have seen God then what is the suspicion? Why should you need a certificate from me?"

Just pure hallucinations, imagination, continual listening to idiotic sermons… Millions of people waiting with great expectation – the imagination fires up: just a little effort and you will see God.

But remember, whatever you see is not you. Whatever you see is some object. And religion's basic concern is not objective. Its basic concern is your subjectivity. When all seeing disappears, all hearing disappears, and all thinking disappears… When all your senses are silent, in that silence it transpires.

priests are the devil's agents

Osho,
What is the difference between a religion and a cult? – because the Christians
go on calling the people around you a cult. It seems difficult for them to
accept us as a religion. What could be the reason behind it?

It is a complex question. You will have to understand many things before the
question can be answered.

Religion is an individual experience. Only an individual can be religious. The
cult is an establishment, it is an organization, it has nothing to do with religion at all.
It exploits in the name of religion. It pretends to be religious and lives on the past.

For example, Christians will say that they have a two thousand year history.
But the past is dead, it is a corpse. This is a very strange world in which we live.
When Jesus was there, Jews could not accept him as religious: he and his followers
were a "cult."

Jesus is a religious man so there was the fragrance of religion around him,
and those who were sensitive, available, receptive, came close to Jesus. This
coming to Jesus was not a question of any intellectual conviction; it was more
like a love affair. They simply fell in love with the man. The religious man never
converts anybody, but his presence inspires many people to be with him. A
religious person has no followers, only fellow travelers – it is impossible for
a religious person to insult somebody by calling him a follower.

When Jesus was crucified, a strange thing happened, something that has
happened to almost all the religions. The same type of people who had crucified
Jesus – the rabbis, the priesthood – the same type of people gathered around the

dead religious phenomenon, which had gone, which was not there anymore.

It is just like the fragrance of a flower. The flower is gone, the fragrance lingers on a little – and then it is lost. Religion cannot have a continuity. It will always be individual, here and there. One individual becomes enlightened and suddenly people start becoming attracted towards him as if by a magnetic force.

Jesus is not an intellectual; he is not even educated. He is not a theologian; he cannot argue for God or for religion. In all his teachings there is no argument, they are statements. A philosopher argues, a religious person states. The philosopher argues because he does not know; it is through argument that he wants to come to a conclusion. But the religious person knows it. He states it, it is a declaration – and he also knows that there is no way to prove it. No argument is going to be supportive of it.

But once that magnet disappears... The priest is the most cunning part of humanity – and clever. He is a businessman, he sees the opportunity of a great business. While Jesus is alive, it is dangerous to be with him. No businessman will come close to him – only gamblers may risk it and be with him. It is dangerous to be with him: he can be crucified, you can be crucified.

But once he is dead it is a great opportunity for business. Then a new kind of people start gathering around: they are the priests, the popes, the imams, the rabbis – learned, scholarly, argumentative, dogmatic. They create the dogma, the creed. They create the cult.

On the dead body of a religious person, a cult is created. Christianity is a cult.

Friedrich Nietzsche used to say... And I feel that he has the tremendous quality of seeing certain things which others go on missing. The man was mad, but sometimes mad people have a very sharp intelligence. Perhaps that is the reason that they go mad. Friedrich Nietzsche says, "The first and the last Christian died on the cross two thousand years ago. Since then there has been no Christian at all." And he is absolutely right.

Jesus was the only Christian, although he never knew the word *Christian*. He knew only Aramaic, the language which he spoke, and a little bit of Hebrew, the language which the rabbis spoke. But he had no idea of Greek. The word *Christ* is a Greek word, and the word *Christian* comes out of *Christ*. Jesus never in his life heard the words *Christ* or *Christian*. The Hebrew word for Christ is *messiah*, so Jesus knew *messiah*.

But once he died... And it was very strange that when he was alive, overflowingly alive, and was ready to give, to share, to pour his being into their being, the people were avoiding him. But once he was dead, the priests were not going to miss the opportunity.

The priests immediately gather around the dead body of a Buddha, of a Jesus, of a Lao Tzu, and they immediately make the catechism. They start making a church on the dead body.

If Jesus comes back, the pope will be the first person to ask for his crucifixion again, because Jesus will disturb the whole business. That's what he was doing the last time he was here.

Why were the rabbis angry? The business was going so well, everything was settled, everybody was satisfied and suddenly this man Jesus comes and starts disturbing people's minds. He starts people thinking, inquiring, seeking. The establishment cannot tolerate such a person, because if you start seeking and searching, soon you will find that the establishment is standing on a dead body.

I have heard that one day the bishop of New York phoned the pope, a long distance call, and he was really in a very shaky condition. He said to the pope, "A hippie-like man has entered the church and when I asked him, 'Who are you?' he said, 'Can't you recognize me? I am your Lord Jesus Christ, exactly.' What am I supposed to do in such a situation?"

The pope said, "You idiot! Just call the police. If he is just a hippie, there is no problem. If he is really Lord Jesus Christ then let him be imprisoned before he creates any disturbance – and get moving. If he is the Lord, just get busy and phone the police – and be quick to get him imprisoned."

The same trouble will be there. Jesus has promised in the Bible, "I will be coming back," but I can tell you authoritatively that he is not going to come – one experience was enough. Who wants to be crucified again? And that time at least there was a consolation: these were Jews, orthodox, traditional; they could not understand the revolution that he had brought. This time, even that consolation will not be there. It will be the Christians, his own people, who will crucify him.

Last time, Jesus had prayed to God, "Forgive these people because they don't know what they are doing." What is he going to do this time? He will have to pray, "Forgive these people – they know perfectly well what they are doing." But they will do exactly the same thing.

A cult is a business, a religious kind of business. It has a religious jargon; it has no experience. Yes, once somewhere in the past there may have been a flower, but it is gone. Centuries have passed, and since then the priest goes on pretending that he is the representative of that fragrance. Nobody can represent fragrance: it comes with the flower and goes with the flower. But the priest can create a plastic flower, can even put French perfume on it... And that's what he has been doing in all the religions.

Religion is rebellious, is bound to be so, because religion starts saying things that the tradition will oppose. Only one of these two can exist: either the mass, unintelligent crowd mind which creates the tradition, or a man like Jesus or Buddha or Mahavira. They are alone. And what they are saying can be understood only by the chosen few. What they bring to the world is something so otherworldly, that unless you can have a heart to heart contact with them, there is no way of understanding them – you will misunderstand.

Jesus is misunderstood. Socrates is misunderstood. Al-Hillaj Mansoor is misunderstood. Whenever you find a religious man, it will be simple to ascertain that all around him there will be misunderstanding. But once he dies, things settle down. Once he dies the priesthood makes a new business. Now, Jews have been suffering almost a heart attack for nearly two thousand years, for the simple reason that they missed the business. Christianity is now the biggest business in the world, and they missed. And Jews are not the people to miss when there is a business; they have the eye to see it.

I have heard a story...

It has been happening for centuries that every year on a particular day in the Vatican, the chief rabbi of the city comes with roll in his hand to Saint Peter's Square where the pope waits for him. Jews and Christians gather in thousands to see this meeting of the pope and the chief rabbi, but what transpires between them, nobody knows. The rabbi bows down, gives the roll to the pope. The pope bows down – that's all.

The next morning, the roll is sent back to the rabbi to keep for the next year. For two thousand years no pope bothered to look into it, but this Polack pope became curious: what is this? What kind of convention is this that has been going on and on? And every time the rabbi gives it to the pope and the next morning it has to be sent back, ceremoniously – the same roll goes back. What exactly is in it? He opened the roll. It was very ancient – two thousand years old. And do you know what he found? It was the bill for the Last Supper!

The Jews were still asking, "Pay for it at least." And of course Jesus died without paying, so...

Religion is basically rebellion against dead traditions, meaningless conventions. It is a revolution to bring the birth of a new man, of a new consciousness.

The cult is not concerned with the new man. The cult does not want the new man *ever* to be born, because with the old, things are so at ease, why create trouble? Who knows what the new man will be?

And they are right. The new man is going to be trouble. He is not just going to accept any idiotic concept; he will ask questions. He is not going to be faithful. He will be basically a man of inquiry. He will doubt – he will not believe.

A religious man doubts, but never believes. He inquires, because doubt leads into inquiry; and he questions till he finds the answer on his own. Then there is no question of belief or faith – he *knows*.

If you ask him, "Do you believe in God?" he will say no. You will be surprised – a religious man saying no! And if you ask him, "You are a religious man and you say that you don't believe?" he will say, "Yes, I repeat it again: I don't believe because I know; belief is for those who are blind. A blind man believes in light, a man with eyes knows. Do you believe in light?"

But the believers are docile, ready to submit, to surrender to any idiotic concept. Ask the Christian, "What do you mean by the virgin birth?" – and each Christian believes in it; if you don't believe in it you are not much of a Christian.

Just a few days ago a bishop in London was thrown out of his bishophood because he said, "I don't believe in the virgin birth."

If you don't believe in the virgin birth, then you are not a Christian, so what right have you to be a bishop? And you are spreading dangerous ideas in people's minds. Tomorrow you will say, "I don't believe in the Holy Ghost." It is bound to come, that "Who is this fellow, the Holy Ghost? Doing unholy things, making a poor virgin Mary pregnant, still he remains the Holy Ghost!"

And if you suspect the virgin birth and the Holy Ghost, how long can you believe in a God? – because out of the trinity you have already doubted two. The third you have not seen, and you cannot meet a person who has seen him. They will quote scriptures, but scriptures cannot satisfy a religious man. He wants to taste truth himself. But that creates difficulty for the cult. The cult may be any: Hindu, Mohammedan, Christian, Jewish; it doesn't matter – these are all cults. Perhaps there has been a religious man in the beginning. I say "perhaps" because priests are so cunning they can make a whole church even without a real religious man's dead body; that is not such a necessity.

I am reminded of a small story.

A young devil comes running to the chief devil and says, "Do something quickly; just now one man has found truth. I am coming directly from there. Something has to be done. His truth has to be stopped, otherwise he will destroy our business."

It is obvious, if people become truthful and people start discovering truth, what business has the devil left? But the old devil laughed and he said, "You are too young, too new to the business. Our people are already there."

He said, "But I didn't see anybody."

The old devil said, "You will take a little time to understand. Did you see the priests around the man?"

He said, "Yes."

The devil said, "They are our people. They won't let the truth go anywhere. They will make a dogma out of it and they will not leave the man who has found the truth. Let him find it. They will surround him – they will become the mediators between him and the masses, and they are our agents."

All priests are the devil's agents. They have no interest in truth, no interest in inquiring about the ultimate reality. Their interest is how to exploit man's fear, man's greed.

They exploit your fear by creating hell. They exploit your greed by creating heaven. They exploit your helpless state by creating God. They give you certain scriptures, mantras, prayers, and they say, "These will save you; you are protected. You need not be worried, you are not helpless. And we are always there between you and God – you can depend on us." They don't know of God at all. They have nothing to do with God. But God is a beautiful concept to exploit people who are feeling psychologically sick, afraid, fearful – and the whole of humanity is in the same situation.

Whenever a religious man comes, he starts transforming you, not consoling you, because by consolation, your sickness is not going to disappear. Only by transformation can you be absolutely on your own, can you be absolutely contented with yourself and with existence.

But the priest does not want you to be contented. He wants you to be discontented; otherwise why will you go to the priest? For what? He does not want you to become courageous. He wants you to be cowards forever, because only cowards will come crawling to his feet. Why would the courageous come to him? There is no need.

The religious man destroys the need for the cult; hence, whenever there is a religious man and around him the climate of religion, all the cults will be against him.

So this is a strange situation – Christians calling us a cult! *They* are a cult. Hindus are calling us a cult; they are a cult because their religious people died two thousand, three thousand, five thousand years ago. And nobody actually knows whether there has been any religious person in the beginning at all or whether it was a fiction from the very beginning.

George Gurdjieff, one of the most penetrating intellects of this century, used to say, "There has never been a Jesus Christ. It was only a drama that used to be played; and slowly, slowly, the priests became aware that this drama can be utilized: 'Make it history.'" One thing is certain, that except for the Christian New Testament, there is no reference to Jesus Christ anywhere, in any scripture.

If a man of the caliber of Jesus was there, it is impossible that somewhere in the Jewish scriptures his name would not have been entered – and particularly when he was crucified. Crucifixion makes his name the most historical name. In fact, now we know history only according to Jesus: before Christ, after Christ... That's how we know history. That man becomes the central point of our whole history. Such an important person is not even mentioned anywhere: neither in Jewish scriptures, nor in Roman scriptures – Judea was under the Roman Empire.

Certainly in the Roman files Jesus must have been referred to. If you crucify a man, at least he deserves a place somewhere in your bureaucratic files. But nowhere, except those four gospels which are written by his four disciples... He is simply non-existent. If you just lose those four disciples' gospels, Jesus becomes only gossip. Gurdjieff was very insistent that he was just gossip, and that cunning people had used the drama and made history out of it – and a great business of course!

It is bound to be the case, that while I am here nobody is going to accept you as a religion. And you are a religion only while I am here. The moment I am gone, the best way is to disperse just like a fragrance. The worst way is to become a cult. Then these people – Christians and Jews and Hindus and Mohammedans – will accept you also as a religion. They will accept you as a religion only when you have become a cult. Do you see the strange logic of the world? When you have lost contact with a living experience, then of course you are as dead as they are, and of course dead people don't argue. And one dead person pays respect to another dead person – it is just courtesy, simple manners.

But how can the dead people be respectful to a living person? They are dead; that hurts. They don't know; that hurts. They have only beliefs – and who knows whether those beliefs are true or not. There are three hundred religions on the earth, three hundred different dogmas, creeds. Do you think all three hundred dogmas and creeds can be true?

Truth can only be one.

You may verbalize it differently, but you cannot make two creeds out of it. Your languages may be different. Your concepts about it may be different, but anybody can see that it is about the same truth.

You must have heard the story of the five blind men who went to see an elephant. In the first place, blind people should not go to see something; that is an absurdity. But they were curious, and the whole village was agog because for the first time an elephant had come to the village. So they also decided, "Let us go."

They could not see but they said, "We can at least touch and feel, and we will see what this elephant is." And they all five touched the elephant, of course from different angles. Somebody touched the leg of the elephant; he said, "I have found it. The elephant is just like a pillar, the pillars that we have in the temple, exactly like a marble pillar."

Another man said, "You idiot, you must be touching some pillar, because what I see is totally different." He was touching the ear of the elephant, and he said, "It looks like a fan."

In India, in the hot summer, before electricity came into being, there used to be fans hanging from the ceiling. And one person, a poor person, would go on pulling the fan with a rope the whole day, and the fan would give you, at least for the few rich people, cool air the whole day. Or people would be standing on both sides with two big fans the shape of an elephant's ear, and they would both be fanning you.

So the second man said, "This is impossible what you are saying."

A third one contradicted them both, and the fourth one contradicted all three. Then the fifth one said, "You are idiots; I should not have come with you, because it is nothing but a brush" – he was holding the tail. "And so much ado about nothing; just a brush hanging with something... I don't know what it is hanging with because I can't see." They were all quarreling the whole way back home.

But how can you decide when you are blind? You should accept one thing, that you cannot see. If you don't accept that then there is going to be trouble.

These cults have no eyes. I have asked bishops, rabbis, *shankaracharya*s, Jaina monks, Buddhist *bhikkhus*, "Have you experienced it? And at least, for once, be sincere and be truthful."

And they have all told me, "In private we can say we have not experienced it, but in public, if you ask us, we will absolutely deny that we have ever said it – because in public we have to pretend. We have studied..."

When I spoke for the first time in Mumbai, in 1960, a Jaina monk also spoke with me. We were the two to address the meeting. He spoke before me because he was a well-known person; I was absolutely unknown. And when he finished and I stood up, people from the hall started leaving because nobody knew me. I had to tell those people, "Just for five minutes, stand still wherever you are. After five minutes you are free to leave or to sit down." Of course they stopped because I was asking for just five minutes and it wouldn't have looked good to go out just like that.

I said, "Just for five minutes – look at the clock and after five minutes just empty the hall; there is no need to be here. But I have just a few things to say in five minutes. First: this man who spoke before me knows nothing; he is just a dodo!" Many who were standing sat down. I said, "For five minutes, stand up! For five minutes keep standing then you can either sit or go out."

This man had been talking about Mahavira, the founder of Jainism. Mahavira's original name was Vardhaman. Mahavira is a given name. *Mahavira* means very courageous, a great warrior – because in Jainism, truth has to be conquered. That is the exact meaning of *Jaina*; *Jaina* means the conqueror. *Jainism* means: the religion which teaches you how to conquer the truth – and Mahavira conquered it, so his name was changed from Vardhaman to Mahavira. Now, Vardhaman is almost forgotten.

That monk was saying, "Vardhaman was born as a son to a king," and "Vardhaman renounced the palace, the kingdom," and "Vardhaman became realized." And he was using both names – Vardhaman and Mahavira – without any trouble, and all the people who were present there were Jainas so they understood it.

But I said, "This man does not understand that he is talking about two persons, and he is very confused." The people looked at me. I said, "Vardhaman is one person; Mahavira is totally another. When Vardhaman died, then Mahavira was born; they never met. This man has been talking as if they were one person and was saying that Mahavira was born to redeem you all from suffering, from misery."

I said, "That's a lie, because Mahavira himself has said, 'Nobody can make you miserable, and nobody can make you happy, except you.' So how can he redeem the whole world? He cannot redeem a single person. He himself is saying the truth: 'It is you who cause your misery. If you understand the cause of your misery, you stop causing it.' And ecstasy is your nature. Misery is your effort, your great endeavor, your success.

"To be miserable, you have to stand on your head, upside down. You have to be as unnatural as possible, you have to swim upstream. To be ecstatic, blissful, you just go down with the river. You are in a let-go. You simply allow your nature to be what it is. Mahavira says, 'Nobody can make you miserable. Nobody can make you happy' – and this poor fellow was saying that Mahavira was born to redeem the whole world."

I said, "Five minutes are over, now you can decide: either you sit down or get lost." They all sat down, but the monk was very much puzzled. It was an air-conditioned hall but he started perspiring. But he was a sincere man, and when I finished, he whispered in my ear, "Can you come to my temple just for ten minutes? I cannot come to your place – otherwise I would have come – because my followers will not allow me to go anywhere." Such a great monk with so many followers, and going to meet some unknown person; and someone who has made a mockery of him, who has criticized him on every point.

I said, "There is no problem; I will come."

I went there. Nearly one thousand people had gathered because people came to know that I was coming, and they had seen what had happened in the morning.

But the monk said, "I want to talk to him in private, so please sit outside; we will be going into the small room."

We went in. He closed the door and started weeping, crying, tears...and he must have been seventy years old. I said, "But why are you crying?"

He said, "I am crying because for the first time I felt that I really don't know anything. For fifty years – because I was twenty when I became a monk – for fifty years I have been teaching people *as if* I know. I have called you just to confess that I don't know anything. I cannot say it in front of people – I am not that coura- geous – because if I say that in front of people, I will be thrown out.

"No, for fifty years I have not worked. I have been worshipped for fifty years. I have been looked after; thousands of people think of me as their master, and if I say that I don't know anything, they will kill me. They will say, 'Then why have you been deceiving us for fifty years?' I cannot say it to them, but I wanted to unburden my heart to you – I don't know. First I was shocked, angry, by what you said in the morning, but as I started thinking about it, everything seemed to be right.

"First I was thinking to stand up and argue against you, but I saw clearly that no argument was going to help – because I am not arguing; what I am saying is simply stating." He said, "I would love to know myself. Enough of belief – fifty years I have wasted; and I am just standing where I started."

This happened to many religious leaders with me. When they were alone they accepted what I was saying, but in public they have a different face, a different mask. Now, these people – they may be Christians, they may be Jews, they may be Hindus – they don't know. Knowing is not a function of a crowd. I can see, you can see, but there is no way that we can both see from the same place.

You cannot see through my eyes. I cannot see through your eyes. I can nei- ther stand in your space, where you are standing, nor can you stand in my space, where I am standing.

Exactly like that, religion is absolutely individual. And whenever you organize it, the priesthood immediately takes over. If the man who has experienced is alive, he may try to make sure that the religion does not become a cult.

That's what my whole effort is.

So as long as I am here with you, it is not going to become a cult. But once I am gone then it will be very difficult to avoid, because up to now, there are so many religions in the world and nobody has succeeded.

Krishnamurti tried his best. Nobody has done so much against becoming a cult, but it seems not to be succeeding. He dissolved the organization in 1925. An organization had been made for him, The Star of the East, to spread his truth and experience to the whole world. He dissolved the organization. He returned the castles and the money and the land, and everything that had been donated to the organization, to their original owners. And he said, "I don't want any followers."

He has been continually saying from that time, "Nobody is my follower," but there are people who say, "We are Krishnamurtiites." Now, what can you do? He is still alive, and every day he is saying, "Nobody is my follower, and I am not your leader, teacher, master, anything." But people just repeat these words and say, "We are Krishnamurtiites."

When Krishnamurti dies they will again join together, because the master is dead now and something has to be done in his memory – make a temple, make a church, make a memorial, make an organization – so his truth goes on living.

Truth is not some thing. It is not a thing that you can preserve. It disappears with the person who has experienced it.

Can you preserve love? There may be two great lovers and you see the phenomenon of love happening; can you preserve this phenomenon? Those two lovers die; can you preserve that climate? – that transfiguration that was happening between those two persons? How can you? It is not a thing; you cannot hold it in your hands, and you cannot put it in a safe deposit. You cannot make a temple out of it or a church out of it or a creed out of it.

Love happens between two persons – truth is even more difficult: it happens within a single individual being. At least in love there were two, and there was something visible outside also. Any observer could have seen something intangible but yet comprehensible transpiring between two persons. You can see it in their eyes, in their faces.

Once I was traveling in a train, and a couple was with me, a very old couple, a Spanish couple. They had come to India to travel. The man must have been eighty, the woman must have been seventy-five; it was time they should have been in their graves. But I was surprised to see their love – because we had to be together for twenty-four hours – in each and everything that they did, just small things. It is not in big things that you have to show your love, just small thing. But I could almost touch their love. It was so visible you could see it. I asked the old man, "This is a rare phenomenon; how long have you been together?"

He said, "If you count the years, we must have been together for at least sixty years – she was fifteen when I first met her – but those sixty years don't seem to me as sixty years; they have all become a small moment, condensed, herenow. I never think of all those moments that have passed because this moment contains all of them."

But once these people are gone, you will not find that aroma, that aura, that feel. It will be gone too; it is too subtle.

With truth it is even more difficult, because it is a single individual who has experienced his own being and is so full of ecstasy that if you allow, he may overflow; if you are available, he may enter in you.

If you are reluctant and resistant... This phenomenon is so delicate that a little resistance on your part and you miss it. So anybody who comes here with a certain prejudice, a certain mind, a certain idea, is going to miss me. If he comes here open, vulnerable, then he will taste something of religion, he may smell something of religion. And that is the only way to know religion: to be in close proximity to a religious man. It is infectious.

But you cannot get it even if you hug pope the Polack. There is nothing... A

Polack is just a Polack. He may also hug you and may crush your bones, because a Polack hug is a little difficult on the ribs. But you will not find anything.

I have met thousands of people who are known as great religious masters and teachers. India is so full of sages and saints you can meet them anywhere. There is no need to seek and search. They are seeking and searching for you, and fighting: "You belong to me, not to yourself" – whosoever catches hold of you first. But they are all parts of a certain cult, repeating parrot-like – exactly parrot-like or you can say computer-like – scriptures, great words. But words only mean that which the person *has*.

When Jesus says "truth" or Buddha says "truth," the word has meaning in it. When the Buddhist monk says "truth," there is no meaning in it; it is an empty word, there is no content in it.

You ask why they can't accept you as a religion. It is obvious: they are in the marketplace; everybody is shopping and peddling his own goods. Now you come as a competitor, and you start selling new things which are more attractive because they are alive. They become afraid that their young people, their young boys, their young daughters, may get attracted to you – and they *are* getting attracted, they are not wrong. And that's what makes them freak out: these people should be going to church or to the synagogue – what are they doing here, in this place? They should listen to the rabbi, to the minister – what are they doing here?

And certainly when they see you, they cannot figure it out. They have a certain idea: you should fit with that idea, then you are religious. And certainly I am trying my best so that you cannot fit in with anybody's idea – including mine! – so that you can be just yourself.

My whole religious approach is to give you back to you.

You have been stolen. You have been covered, conditioned in every possible way. They have closed all the doors of approach to yourself.

My whole work is just to make doors and windows in you. And if I can withdraw all the walls and leave you just an open sky, you will know what religion is. But you will not fit with anybody else's idea of religion. They are going to call you all kinds of names. For them, cult is a condemnation, so they call you a cult.

Just the other day I was looking at a panel on the TV with one rabbi and two Christian priests – one must have been Catholic, one Protestant or something, different denominations – discussing me and what is happening here. And the rabbi said, "It is a cult."

The coordinator asked, "What is a cult? – and what is the difference between a cult and a religion?" And what the rabbi said, I agree with, but for a totally different reason.

The rabbi said, "A cult is when there is a charismatic person and people are hypnotized, magnetized by him, surround him; and when the man dies the people disperse – no tradition is created. That is a cult."

What he is saying, I am also saying – exactly the same but for different reasons. He says, "If the cult survives the death of the founder, then it becomes a religion." When Jesus is alive it is a cult, because it is his charismatic personality… When Jesus is dead then it becomes a religion. A very strange idea: religion being born out of a cult. The cult should not be a condemnatory thing; it is the mother of religion, it is the womb from where the religion comes. It is a potential religion.

But he was saying, "The cult is bound to disappear because it was only the charismatic person, it was his charisma, his magic that kept people together. Once he is gone, then there is nothing to hold onto. Then people disperse and the cult dies." I say this is actually the definition of religion.

In a more intelligent world there will be no tradition. Religious people will be born, and with a religious person a religion will happen. Many more people will come, become close to him and will drink out of his well. Jesus says, "Eat me, drink me." Yes, they will eat, they will drink and they will be transformed in the whole process. And when the religious person is gone, certainly there is no need to make a tradition, because tradition will be dead.

Yes, you loved your father but when he died you took him to the grave. You didn't say, "He was my father, how can I take him to the grave or to the funeral pyre? I am going to keep him in my house. I loved him, he loved me..." No, when your father is dead it is sad but a natural phenomenon. Everybody who is born is going to die. You say good-bye to him with all your gratitude. The same should be the case with every religious teacher.

Jesus is perfectly good, but Christianity is a disease. Moses is perfectly good, but Judaism is a curse. And the same is true about all of the religions. The people at the very source were really beautiful, but every beautiful flower dies. Even beautiful stars die and disappear, and don't leave even a single trace behind. So what is the need for any religious person to leave a tradition behind him?

I am not going to leave a tradition behind me.

While I am here, enjoy the moment. Celebrate the moment. Why be bothered for the future? And remember one thing: anybody who tries, after me, to make a tradition is my enemy, is not my friend and is not your friend either. He belongs to the devil. He is now creating a church – and then the popes will come and everything. Then the businesses start and businessmen come in and religion disappears completely.

It is better it disperses in the universe, rather than becomes a part of the religious marketplace.

So whenever people ask me, "What is going to happen to your religion when you are not?" I say, "Why should you be worried? While I am here, it is enough." And there will be people... Somebody will blossom and there will be religions. People will go on blossoming, but don't make traditions because those traditions prevent other people from blossoming. Leave the space. If you had not been told to be a Jew or a Hindu or a Mohammedan or a Christian, and space had been left for you, perhaps you may have blossomed by now. But from the very beginning they started clipping you, cutting you, cropping you...

Mukta was my gardener in Pune. She was always moving around with scissors, and whenever she would see me she would hide her scissors. I said, "Don't do this. Why are you unnecessarily cutting these trees?" One tree particularly she used to call a monster, because she wanted to cut it. So first you have to call it a monster and then it becomes easy to cut.

First you give it a bad name – it is a cult – and then it is good to destroy it. It was a monster. And it was such a beautiful tree, it was growing huge, but whenever I was not watching, she was cutting it. If it is a monster, then let it be a monster; it is that tree's nature. Who are we to destroy it or to give it the shape of our ideas? Mukta has been in difficulty with me because she is Greek and follows the tradition of Aristotle – logical, mathematical. She wanted to create a European garden around my house.

I said, "It is not possible." And a European garden, particularly the English garden, is so much against nature, because where in nature do you find symmetry? But in an English garden you will find symmetry. They will cut two trees symmetrically, will make lawns symmetrical, will put plants symmetrically... Symmetry is unnatural, nature is asymmetrical.

So in a Zen garden in Japan you will not find any symmetry. Even if there is, the Zen people won't allow it; they will disturb the symmetry – something has gone wrong.

Nature is wild, and when it is wild it has freedom.

A religious person is also wild. In his wildness is his freedom and in his freedom he finds truth. In his freedom he finds himself. In his freedom he finds everything that there is to be found in existence.

But a cultist remains full of rubbish and crap, borrowed empty words; maybe great words – *God, soul, truth* – but all empty because he has not lived any of them. And unless you live it, it has no meaning.

Only life gives meaning.

So it is true that they will not accept you as a religion – but why bother about them? Who cares? I am not interested that they should accept us as religion. We don't need anybody's acceptance, recognition, certificate. Who are they?

Those three people in the panel finally decided, "It is time now that we should have a dialogue. We should go to these people and we should have a dialogue." I simply laughed at the idea – the Jew sitting there, and on each side the two Christians sitting there.

The Jews did not have the courage to have a dialogue with Jesus – or do you think the crucifixion was a dialogue? What dialogue can they have with me? If they know, there is no need for them to come here. If they do not know, then it is going to be a monologue. I will speak and they will have to listen. A dialogue is not possible.

If you also know, and I also know, there is no need for a dialogue – silence is enough.

If you don't know, and I don't know, then too there is no point in a dialogue, because it will not be a dialogue, it will become a wrestling match.

I say I know. So with me there is only one possibility – a monologue.

CHAPTER 4

religion is rebellion

Osho,
Is it not possible in any way to preserve your living religion and not let it be
reduced to a cult like Christianity? The very idea of your religion being
reduced with time to a cult is unbearable.

It is almost impossible to preserve a religion as a religion. Up to now nobody
has succeeded in doing it.

But I said it is *almost* impossible, not absolutely, because we are fortunate in
seeing all the failures of the past: all that helps a religion to become a cult can be
dropped from the very beginning. We know that many people have tried before.
Their efforts are also helpful.

There is not an intrinsic impossibility of a religion remaining a religion. The
reasons that reduce it to a cult are not very fundamental.

The first thing: it is not "my religion." I have nothing to do with it. In fact,
when I ceased to be it came into being. This is the first thing to remember – it will
help the religion to remain a living current. Do not make it a certain kind of
religion – Christianity, Hinduism, Buddhism – no, just let it be pure religion. Let it
be just religiousness.

Nobody can reduce religiousness to a cult. That is absolutely impossible. And
what I am doing continually is withdrawing all possibilities, all potentialities, which
can reduce it to a cult. For example, I have removed God. Without God it is very
difficult to reduce a religion to a cult. That's why Christianity is more of a cult
than Buddhism.

This is our blessing, because we can look back upon the whole of history.

And only fools say that history does not repeat itself; it continuously repeats, unless you prevent it from repeating itself. If you have accepted the idea that history never repeats itself you are not going to prevent it from repeating itself, there is no need. I say to you that it always repeats itself, unless somebody intelligently prevents it.

Judaism, Christianity, Mohammedanism, Hinduism, are all God-oriented. Jainism, Buddhism, Taoism, Confucianism, are not God-oriented. And the difference can be seen immediately. The God-oriented religions become cults immediately.

God is a very dangerous concept because in the name of God comes the priesthood. If there is no God it is very difficult to create a priesthood. In Jainism there is no priesthood. They have to borrow priests from the Hindus for their worldly rituals; for example, marriage. They don't have any priests, their religion is against Brahminism. But Hindus have the greatest and the longest-standing priesthood; the most sophisticated, cultured, very solidly based establishment.

When my first uncle was getting married... At that time I became aware of a strange thing, that a brahmin had been called. I asked my father, "Jainism is against Brahminism, it was a revolt against the brahmin ritualistic, magical religion. And the marriage is being performed by a brahmin? From the very beginning the marriage is invalid. Can't you manage to have a Jaina perform the marriage?"

He said, "You raise inconvenient questions, but I must accept that your questions are never wrong. We may not be able to answer them, we may have practical difficulties in answering them, but that is really our problem – and we get angry at you! Now, the ritual is going to be performed; everybody is ready – the bride and the bridegroom, all the guests and the brahmin have come – it is just about to begin and you are starting to ask a troublesome question."

I said, "It is my uncle's marriage. I have every right to be concerned that it is done rightly."

My father wanted me to be quiet. He said, "You can have a few rupees but get lost, go away."

I said, "This is not the time – no bribery is going to help. I am going to create trouble; I am not going to allow this brahmin to do the marriage ceremony. Just the very idea... He is your enemy; the brahmins are continually condemning Jainism, all their scriptures are full of condemnation. Jainas are continually condemning brahmins, their whole philosophy is against brahmins. I will not allow it. Either the marriage has to be performed by a Jaina, or I am going to create trouble."

And I created trouble. I stood up and I asked all the Jainas – all the elders of the society were there – I asked them, "What is the meaning of all this? Can anybody answer me?"

One old man said, "This question has been arising in me my whole life – because I must have seen thousands of marriages. Each time the question was there, but I was not courageous enough to inquire. This boy is right. And one has to begin someday."

I told my grandfather, "Now, you come to my help. What this brahmin is doing, anybody can do. If you allow me, I can do it."

They said, "That will be too much. Let some elderly person do it."

I said, "That's okay."

The same old man performed the ritual. That was the first marriage in India amongst Jainas performed by a Jaina. I said, "Don't be worried. Whatsoever the brahmin is saying in Sanskrit, you say in Hindi. In fact it is better to say it in Hindi, because both the bride and the bridegroom will understand what you are saying. What the brahmin says is all nonsense – all Greek and Latin! He may be simply talking gibberish, and you think he is saying great things. All that is wanted is a commitment, a promise, a word given before the society that you will take care of each other. All else is non-essential."

And that old man performed it in Hindi. The brahmin was so angry because he lost his fee... And that was the beginning. After that marriage in my city no Jaina marriage was performed by a brahmin.

Jainas have no priesthood because without God what is the function of the priest? Things are interrelated. God is absolutely needed to create the hierarchy – then the messiah, then the pope, then the cardinals, then the bishops, then the priest... And it goes on and on; from the bottom to the peak, so many steps. But they are all possible only if you accept the peak, and the peak is fictitious. God is fictitious.

If I had met Jesus I would have told him, "God is fictitious. I am not denying you anything; I am simply saying that unless you prove God as a fact, your messiah-ship is out of the question – so there is no need to deny it, as the Jews are denying it, saying that you are not the messiah, not the true messiah."

Just a few days ago I saw a film, a beautiful film on a Jewish family, a very orthodox Hasid family. The Jews don't accept Hasids as really equal to them, they are outcasts. The Hasids even today don't accept the nation of Israel, because they say, "Israel will be established when the messiah comes – but where is he?"

Their logic is perfect. This Israel is created by the politicians, not by the messiah. They don't accept this nation – and I agree with them that this is just a creation, a forced creation. It is not a nation that grew naturally; hence the Jews in Israel are going to be in trouble forever.

The Jews think that the Americans have done them a great favor by creating Israel; it is not so. They have done something worse than Adolf Hitler did, because this is going to be a constant problem. Israel had not existed for centuries; it was a Mohammedan country, Palestine, surrounded by Mohammedan countries.

Now just because you won the Second World War and you happened to be in control of the land of Palestine, you forced the creation of a nation. It is arbitrary. The people are Mohammedans, it is their country. Israel may have been, thousands of years before, the country of the Jews. But for thousands of years it has been a country of the Mohammedans, and suddenly you simply change the map. And surrounded by the whole Mohammedan world... In the Middle East all the countries are Mohammedan.

This small country, Israel, is going to continuously suffer; and how long can America help it? And how long are American Jews going to pour their money into Israel? Sooner or later the truth of history will have to be accepted. If America had been really compassionate towards Jews, they should have given them an Israel in America. Oregon would have been perfectly good! I propose it: let Oregon be Israel. But what kind of compassion is this? – putting Jews there. They will never be able to live at ease, never.

So when I saw in this film the rejection of Israel by the Hasids... Of course their reason is different. I have always been against the creation of Israel. I was a child when it was created but even then my first reaction was that this was absolutely idiotic.

The country is populated by Mohammedans – all around there are Mohammedan countries, they are all together – and you put the poor Jews amongst this vast ocean of enemies. Previously they had somehow escaped from that Israel – history was more compassionate to them. And there was no need for a nation; they were living all over the world. The whole world had become their nation. When you lose your nation, the whole world becomes your nation – why bother about a nation?

My reasons were different: that this was a political strategy to keep a military base – because Israel will always need the help of America, so America will always keep its military base in Israel, which is close to Russia. And the Jews are not going in any way to be against America because they are protected by America; they are almost slaves of America.

Without America Israel would be immediately finished, they would be slaughtered; so they depend on America, and their dependence is a guarantee that America has a base in the Middle East. Other Mohammedan countries will not give you a base – you are Christians, and Mohammedans and Christians have been fighting for fifteen hundred years, crusades upon crusades.

My reason is different, but the Hasidic reason is worth consideration. They say the scriptures are clear that the messiah will come and reestablish the kingdom of Israel. Where is the messiah? Franklin Roosevelt? Winston Churchill? Who is the messiah? Then this Israel is bogus!

I like the idea. But for me it is bogus for different reasons, but it is bogus; on that I agree with the Hasids. Without God you cannot have a messiah. I would not have argued with Jesus that "You are not the messiah," because that is a secondary question. The primary question is that "You have to prove God exists."

But because Jews accepted God, they never argued on the basic point. And on the secondary point you cannot argue because Jesus says, "God has sent me." And the Jews had been accepting other prophets sent by God, so what was wrong with poor Jesus? – why should he not be accepted? But if God had been denied, then... "There is nobody to send you. First you prove the existence of God – then only the secondary question arises; then we will discuss it." And Jesus would have been at a loss to answer and the crucifixion would have been easily avoided.

But Judaism is God-oriented, Mohammedanism is God-oriented, hence Mohammed becomes his messenger. And somebody has to be the messenger, otherwise how is there going to be any kind of communication between God and his creation? – a mediator is absolutely needed. It appears logical.

The people in the Arabian countries believed in God, so they could not raise the basic question. They only argued that, "You are not the right messenger." But how can you prove who is the right messenger and who is the wrong messenger? You are fighting on very secondary issues. The real fight has to be on the primary issue.

In Jainism there is no possibility of a messiah. Nobody can declare that "I am a messiah"; people will simply laugh and say that you have gone mad. Nobody can declare that "I am a messenger of God"; he will be just a laughingstock, people will just joke around. He cannot say, "I am an incarnation of God," because God does not exist. From where are you getting this incarnation – an incarnation of nobody?

So in Buddhism, Jainism, Taoism, Confucianism, no problem arises about the messiahs, messengers. And then how can you have popes and bishops and priests? This is the whole ladder. If you accept the highest rung on the ladder you will have to accept the ladder. But if the ladder is going nowhere, if it is just standing on the ground and leading nowhere, reaching nowhere, all the rungs on the ladder will become meaningless.

I have denied the idea of God.

And with God disappears all messiahhood. You cannot declare me a messiah even when I am dead. You cannot declare me an incarnation, even when I am dead. You cannot declare me a messenger.

Do you see the simple fact? – that even when I am dead you cannot go against me. How can you create a cult? – because I am denying all the necessary ingredients for a cult. I am saying there is no messenger. I am saying there is no *avatara*.

But although Mahavira saved Jainism from the priesthood, he could not save it from becoming a cult, because he brought in a new concept – the *tirthankara*.

You have to understand: that concept is totally different from a messiah. A messiah is one who comes from God; that's the exact meaning of *avatara*. Literally it means descendance – coming down from above. *Tirthankara* means growing up from below. It is man who has blossomed to his fullness, who has achieved the ultimate. It is not a descendance of anybody; it is a growth. It is from the roots, it grows like a tree.

The *avatara* is upside down, the messiah is upside down, hanging from above, coming downwards; they are a kind of fall. A *tirthankara* is man risen up to his full potential.

Mahavira thought...and that was the concept of Buddha, the same – they were contemporaries, and they both thought, "This way we avoid the priesthood, God, because we have made man the central point."

One Baul poet of Bengal... *Baul* means mad, and they are really mad people – madly in love with existence. One of the most important of the Bauls is Chandidas. His famous statement is, "*Sabar upar manush jati, tahar upar nahin*: Above all is the truth of man, and above that there is nothing." Now man becomes the ultimate truth.

It was a great revolution – to throw God from his throne and put man on his throne.

But a cult still came into being. They forgot something, but we can remember it. They were experimenting; they were the first people, and they have done a great deal. They have cut out almost half the possibilities, but the other half of the possibilities are enough to create a cult: they made the *tirthankara* an extraordinary man, a superman. They had to, because the question was of continuous comparison – Hindus have *avataras*; they are all supermen with divine power.

The ordinary people would like to follow a man who has divine power, rather than only a man. Naturally, when you are going to shop, you shop for the best and the cheapest. Now, Mahavira was neither. He was the costliest because his discipline was very difficult; that was the price you had to pay if you were to follow him. If you were to go on that path of austerity, that was the price you had to pay to become a superman – and still you would be a man.

So much trouble, so much fasting, living naked... The Jaina monk cannot even use fire. In the night when it is cold, winter, he cannot use a blanket, he cannot even use fire. There are naked Hindu monks also but they are not troubled: they do two things which are very inventive of them. First, they always sit with a bonfire in front of them, so they are warm. And second, they go on rubbing, all over their body, ashes from the fire. So all the pores in the body which breathe are closed – not completely, otherwise they would be dead, but closed enough so that their body heat does not go out. Then there is also the heat from the outside which prevents them from being cold.

The Jaina monk is also naked, but with no heat, with no ashes rubbed on his body. He shivers. Shivering is the only method, the natural method to create a certain heat. Shivering is a natural protection against cold. You shiver, the body starts shaking; that creates a certain movement, exercise in the body, and creates heat. That's all they can do the whole night. In the summer they are naked under the sun. They are completely burned up, with little food to eat and a small quantity of water to drink.

So the path is arduous, and what do you gain? You are just following a man who is not even a descendant of God, who is not even a relative of God, who is not even a messenger of God. Who knows whether he is mad, sane, insane? He is just a man, just like you. While, in comparison, there are messengers of God, messiahs of God, *avataras* of God, God himself coming down...

So in the market it was a difficult thing to sell. Hence they had to raise the *tirthankara* to the same status as the *avatara*, the messiah, even higher. This is simply the market economics. The *tirthankara* is omniscient, omnipotent, omnipresent; he has the qualities of God. The messiah is only the messiah, the messenger is only a messenger, but the *tirthankara* has all the qualities of God himself. This created the base, the loophole for turning the religion into a cult.

Hence I am insisting that I am an ordinary man. You cannot put me up for sale – who is going to buy me? When Jesus is available, Mohammed is available, Krishna is available, Mahavira is available, Buddha is available, do you think anybody is going to go for me? – a simple man, an ordinary man, himself insisting continually on his ordinariness.

I have been denying miracles, saying that they have never happened, they never happen, and they will never happen. Mahavira and Buddha both faltered on that point – but they were pioneers. I have twenty-five centuries of experience behind me. I am standing on their shoulders; I can see far away. They could not think that these things would become their very weaknesses. They all – because Krishna was doing so many miracles, Rama was doing so many miracles... What to say of Rama – even his devotees, just in his name can do miracles.

For example, between India and Sri Lanka there is an ocean, and it was a problem for Rama to cross the ocean to attack Sri Lanka and get his wife back. But his disciple, the monkey god, Hanumana, said, "Don't be worried. Your name is enough." And in his name he started throwing stones in the ocean – and because of Rama's name the stones were floating, not drowning.

The whole army of monkeys and of donkeys, and perhaps Yankees, all were there; so he started throwing stones, rocks, in the name of Rama, and the rocks started floating – soon there was a bridge. They passed over the bridge just by the using the name. Hanumana said, "You need not be worried, your name is enough. You don't need to do anything."

Now, where such stories are going around what chance you have got to compete? Buddha's disciples had to invent stories, Mahavira's disciples had to invent stories. They are all invented stories; and invented in such a way that they made Mahavira and Buddha superior to Rama, to Krishna, to the Hindu trinity, the Trimurti – Brahma, Vishnu, Mahesh.

When Buddha became enlightened, the story is that all the gods – Brahma, Vishnu, Mahesh – all three came down to touch his feet, because an enlightened person is far higher than any gods. You should note that in Judaism, Christianity, Mohammedanism, God is always singular; in Hinduism God is always plural – it is "gods," thirty-three million gods.

The chiefs of all these thirty-three million gods are these three, Brahma, Vishnu, Mahesh. The moment Buddha became enlightened, all three ran down from paradise to touch his feet. For seven days Buddha remained silent. It was Brahma, Vishnu, Mahesh, these three gods, who persuaded him to speak because even gods don't know the supreme truth. Even gods are eager to hear from you: What have you attained? What's your realization? What has it done to you? Buddha argued in many ways, but finally he was persuaded by the three gods.

His argument was very good. He said, "If I speak, in the first place what I have experienced will not be conveyed through the words. Secondly, even if a little fragrance of it goes with the words, where are the people who will be able to receive it? Where are the people who are available? And who wants truth in the first place? People want consolation."

But the three gods said, "You may be right about ninety-nine point nine percent of people, but still there is point one percent of people left who are available, who are receptive, who are willing to go to the further shore. Will you disappoint them?"

Now this whole story is just to prove that even gods are not enlightened. And in

Buddhism and in Jainism both, gods are people who have earned much virtue, and because of their great virtue they are rewarded with paradise. But there is a time limit to it. Sooner or later the reward for their virtues will be finished; they will have to come back again to the earth and again move into the wheel of life and death.

That's why there are thirty-three million gods, because with one god how can you manage this idea? So many people, in millions of years, have been virtuous, religious, truthful, honest – they all have to be rewarded; paradise is a reward.

In Christianity, Mohammedanism, Judaism, you don't have anything above heaven. In Jainism and Buddhism, you have something above heaven. Heaven is only a pleasure place, a holiday, a pleasure resort – a holiday from this continuous wheel of misery, anxiety, anguish. One needs a little holiday, a long weekend.

Heaven to the Jainas and the Buddhists is only a long weekend. But don't forget! – it comes to an end and you fall back again into the same rut. And now it is even more unbearable because you have lived in such tremendous pleasure and splendor and now again you are living this boredom called life. It becomes more of a hell than it was before because you have something to compare it with.

The *tirthankara* does not go to heaven, the buddha does not go to heaven – remember. The enlightened person goes to *moksha*, which is beyond heaven. From there, there is no coming back. One has got out of the wheel of life and death completely. It is not a holiday resort.

Do you see my point? The Jainas and Buddhists had to create something above heaven. They had to give qualities to their *tirthankaras*, better, higher, superior to even those your god has, because it was a question of simple competition in the marketplace. But they forgot that this competition is going to be their very failure.

They succeeded in attracting people: almost the whole country's intelligentsia was influenced by them. Only unintelligent people, the masses, remained with Hindu gods. The intelligent people could not bow down to a monkey god – it looked so idiotic; they could not worship a tree. Just any kind of a stone, you paint it red, put two flowers on it, and wait. Soon, somebody else will come and put flowers, somebody else will come and put a coconut – and a god is born, you have given birth to a god. And this happens every day.

The corporations in India, the municipal committees in India are in continual trouble. In the middle of the road a god appears! Now you cannot remove it; that is interfering with the feelings of religious people – and soon a temple will arise there. First any stone colored red, any shape will do – because with thirty-three million gods, who knows how many shapes they have? Just all that you need are worshippers, and worshippers are available. Then neither the government can remove it, nor can anybody else remove it.

And when the god is there, a shelter is needed for it. A temple is going to be raised there, just in the middle of the road. To remove it means immediate riots; people will be killed and slaughtered, and that fire will spread all over the country; so it is better to allow the god to remain there. It destroys the beauty of the road, it disturbs the traffic, it is dangerous, it can cause accidents, but there is nothing you can do.

In India only Jaipur has straight and plain roads – the only town, the only city – and it is perhaps the most beautiful city in India. But it happened because the man who made it, Jai Singh – he was the king of Jaipur state – was an atheist. And he called from south India, from the Nizam of Hyderabad... The Nizam of Hyderabad had a very intelligent chief minister, Mirza Ibrahim. Jai Singh was born a Hindu but he asked Nizam to give Mirza Ibrahim to him for at least a few years while he was making Jaipur. He wanted it to be India's Paris.

And he almost succeeded; he made something tremendously beautiful. And why did he ask a Mohammedan? He told Mirza, "I don't want any nuisance – because it is going to happen: everywhere temples and mosques and things will start happening, and our whole plan will be disturbed.

"So if a temple appears – you are not a Hindu, simply remove it in the night. No hustle, no bustle about it; the way it appears, the same way it disappears. In the morning it is not there at all. Nobody should even be suspicious that it is disappearing; everything should go quietly, but in the night the whole temple is to completely disappear. And if any mosque appears, I am not a Mohammedan... Perhaps you will feel it is difficult...?"

Mirza said, "That's true: A mosque I cannot remove."

Jai Singh said, "That, I will do."

They removed many temples, many mosques that were appearing, and Jai Singh proved right: they were bound to appear because Jaipur has the biggest roads. Now, on any crossroad where he wanted a garden to be, Hindus would love to have their temple. Where you can find such a beautiful place? And you need not buy it, you need not ask anybody for it, because for God there is no question.

And all that you have to do, simple things... You just go in the night, you put a round stone – dig a little hole in the earth, put in the round stone – and the next morning you declare that in the night a God appeared to you, and he said that at such and such place he had been waiting for many, many centuries, and now it was time that he should be brought to people's notice and a temple should be raised.

Soon crowds will rush to check whether the dream is true or not. And it is going to be true: a god is found! – and it is god's own indication, you cannot interfere. But Jai Singh managed very well. The god would appear; they would start working, and in the night the god would disappear. And Jai Singh would say, "What can I do? The way he appears, the same way he disappears. We cannot prevent him from disappearing; we cannot prevent him from appearing, what can we do?" That's how he managed to have beautiful streets in Jaipur.

While he was alive, Jaipur had only one color, red. All the houses, on the main streets were made exactly the same; so for miles you could see the same houses. It looked so beautiful. And they were all made with red stone, nothing else was allowed. The whole city was red stone. And with the greenery, the red stone is so beautiful because green and red are the basic colors of nature. Nature knows only two colors, red and green.

Since Independence everything has been disturbed. Every year I would go there, and I would see gods appearing, temples being raised in the middle of the street, on the corner of the street, anywhere. Now, the secular government cannot do anything. The man had made it so beautiful... And now people are painting different colors on their houses because how can you prevent them, it is their house.

Jai Singh was a crazy king. There was no question of anybody raising the idea that a house could be of any other color. In Jaipur only one color was allowed: "If you don't want that color, get out of Jaipur" – and he was whole and soul!

Even in his time, efforts to change it were made in the Supreme Court of India. But the Supreme Court said, "As far as internal affairs are concerned we cannot do anything; that is our agreement with the king – only on foreign affairs, but this is not a foreign affair. He is absolutely sovereign. If he wants the red color, we cannot do anything. If he wants only one kind of model for all the houses, we cannot do anything."

But now... When I visited the last time, I almost felt like crying, because they have destroyed the whole thing. All those beautiful lanes with similar houses had something poetic; and all those red stones with green trees... The whole place was a vast garden. Now all kinds of colors have appeared. Old houses are being demolished, skyscrapers are being made. People are changing their houses because people don't want a similar model, the same model, and nobody can prevent them. On the streets – temples, mosques, *gurudwaras*; in the name of religion you can do anything.

Buddha and Mahavira tried, but were not aware of all the implications. I am aware of all the implications. You may not be able to see what I am trying to do: I am destroying all the bases, so that when I am gone you will not find a single base to make a cult out of my religion.

Hence I said, it is *almost* impossible, because people are so stupid that out of their stupidity they can start inventing things for which I am not even leaving a single seed. For example: just the other day a letter was brought to me. Professor Vijay Chauhan, a professor in Washington University, gave an interview about me saying that we were great friends, and we used to have long discussions.

I have never seen this man, what to say about long discussions! – and friendship? Yes, I have heard his name, so I know who he is, but I have not seen him. His mother was a great poetess, Subhadra Kumari Chauhan, and because of her I used to go, once in a while, to her house, and she used to recite her poems to me. She just had mentioned to me, "I have two sons, one is Ajay Chauhan, the other is Vijay Chauhan – but it is strange that whenever you come they are not at home. I would like you someday to meet them." But she died and that day never came. I was never introduced by her to her two sons.

Ajay Chauhan I have seen, just on the road, but we were not acquainted with each other. But this man, Vijay Chauhan, I have not even seen – and he is saying that he was a great friend and for hours we used to discuss philosophy, religion, and great problems.

Now, many letters of this type come. Sheela asks me, "Do you know this man?" – she brings the photograph. "This man says that he knows you from your very childhood, and you have stayed with him many times in his home." I see the picture...and my memory is not bad, not *so* bad. I have never seen this man in my whole life, not even heard his name.

One letter was from New York; I had never heard the name. The man was from India; he says that he is a great poet and I have been quoting his poetry in my lectures. I have never known his name, I have never known any poetry connected with him, any book written by him. But he says that we are great friends. Now what to do with these people? Once I have gone, all kinds of stories will start.

It will be for you to stop all these kinds of stories. Remember, whatsoever is meaningful I have told you, and whatsoever I have not told you is meaningless: that should be the criterion.

If somebody comes and says, "I have seen a miracle..." And there will be people; it gives them importance – that I performed a miracle. Yes, a few times I have performed a miracle.

One man, Doctor Bhagwandas – he is a professor now; we studied together in the same university, although he was in a different department. But we were friendly; he used to come, and he used to go for a walk with me. He invited me once to go to his home. His home was not very far away from the university, just fifty miles.

So I said, "Next Saturday we can go. It is not far away." We went there; we were both sleeping in the same room, on two beds. Between our two beds was a small table with a clock, because I wanted to get up at three. At that time I used to get up at three, but in case I went on sleeping, I told him to put on the alarm – but he had no alarm clock.

He said, "I don't have an alarm clock here."

So I said, "Then forget about it." I went to sleep.

But he felt uneasy, so he went to the neighbor, borrowed an alarm clock and put it in the middle on the table. I was asleep. Because of my habit of getting up at three, I woke up at three, and I heard the tick tock of the clock by my side, so I looked. It was a luminous clock, so I could see that there were still five minutes to go before three o'clock. So I covered myself, and from inside the blankets I said, "Bhagwan" – his name was Bhagwandas, and I used to call him Bhagwan – "It is five to three."

He opened his blanket, and looked at me covered in blankets. He looked at the clock... Five to three! He said, "What?"

I said, "It is five minutes to three. After five minutes wake me up."

He said, "You are already awake."

I said, "Just in case I fail asleep, because there is no clock and..."

He said, "No clock!"

And the next day the whole town was talking about it: a miracle! Exactly five minutes! The next day I told him, "There was no miracle, nothing; I was just joking. I just looked at that clock and I thought, this is good... You think that I didn't know about the clock because you must have brought it in later on after I had fallen asleep."

But he wouldn't believe me. He said, "You are trying to just drop the idea of miracles, but it was a miracle."

I said, "I am saying that it was nothing."

I explained the whole thing to him, but he said, "This is all mere explanation."

Now what to do with these people? Once I am not there, they will all be there... And I have been in hundreds of homes, and many miracles I have performed – but none of them was a miracle. I was just joking, and when I found there was a possibility, I never missed it.

So remember it, that I have never performed a miracle, because miracles as such are impossible. Nobody has performed them.

But the gullible mind...

A man came to me almost in the middle of the night; it was twelve, I had been asleep for three hours. He knocked on the door, and made so much noise that I had to wake up and open the door, and I asked, "What is the matter? What do you want at this time of the night?"

He said, "I have a terrible pain in my stomach, and this pain has been coming on and going away, coming on and going away, for at least three months. I go to a certain doctor, he gives me medicine, but no permanent cure has happened. And just nearabout ten, this pain came; it was so terrible that I went to the doctor and he said that this pain was something spiritual – he suggested your name."

I asked him, "Who is this doctor? Is his name Doctor Barat?"

He said, "Yes."

Barat was my friend. He was an old man, but he loved me very much. So I said, "If Barat has sent you then I will have to do something. But you have to give me a promise that you will never say anything about this to anybody, because I don't want to be disturbed every night, and I don't want patients to be here the whole day. I have other things to do."

He said, "I promise, but just help me. Barat has told me that if you give me just a glass of water, with your hand, I will be cured."

I said, "First give me the promise." And he hesitated, because if he has found such a source of miracles, to give such a promise...

He said, "You don't see my pain; you are talking about your promise. Just give me a glass of water – I am not asking much."

I said, "First you give me a promise. Take an oath in the name of God" – and I could see that he was a brahmin and he had... Brahmins of different faith believing in one god or another god have different marks on their forehead; those are trademarks, so you can judge, and know who the man is worshipping. So I knew that he was a devotee of Shiva, and I said, "You will have to take the oath in the name of Shiva."

He said, "This is very difficult; I am a loudmouth, I cannot keep anything to myself. Such a great thing, and you are asking me to make a promise. I may not be able to keep it because if I keep it then it will be more painful than my pain.

I won't sleep, I won't go anywhere, I won't talk to anybody because it will be just there waiting to come out."

I said, "You decide. I have to go to sleep, so be quick."

He said, "You have created a dilemma for me. Whatsoever I do I will be in trouble. This pain is not going to go away because to keep your promise... And you don't know me – I love gossiping. I am a liar; I go on lying – and this is the truth."

But I said, "Then you decide. Keep your pain."

Finally he said, "Okay, in the name of Shiva I give you the promise. But you are too hard, too cruel."

I gave him a glass of water. He drank the water and he said, "My God! The pain is gone!"

Now, there was no miracle, but because I haggled so much about the promise he became more and more certain that the miracle was going to happen: "Otherwise this man would not insist so much." The more I delayed, the more I insisted, the more he became certain that there was something in it. That certainty worked.

It was simple hypnosis, he got autohypnotized; he became ready. If I had given him the water directly, the pain would not have disappeared. This much of a gap of haggling was needed. And I reminded him when he was leaving, "Remember, if you break the oath, the pain will be back."

He said, "You have destroyed me. I was thinking that when Shiva meets me I will be able to fall at his feet and ask his forgiveness; and I have heard that he is very forgiving. Now you have destroyed that too – and the pain will come back."

I said, "Certainly the pain will come back, once you utter a word."

And the next day he was there. He said, "I could not manage it. At least I had to go to Doctor Barat and tell him, 'All your medicine and medical knowledge is nonsense. Just a glass of water did what you could not do in three months. And you have been taking fees each time I was coming – give my fee back. If you knew it beforehand then for three months you have been cheating me.' But the pain came back."

He came running to me, "I am a fool, but what to do? I just could not resist putting this Doctor Barat right in his place. For three months I have been suffering and he knew the cure, and he went on giving me this tablet and that, and then he started the injections. Finally he started saying, 'You may need surgery' – and just a glass of water! And he did not suggest that at all."

I said, "I cannot help you. Now the water won't work; you have broken the promise – the miracle will not happen again. Now go to Doctor Barat and take his medicine, or do whatsoever you want."

But he went around, even though still in pain, saying, "I have seen a miracle."

These people are there – sometimes very educated people, but deep down they are as gullible as any uneducated person. Once I am not there, you have to remember it, that all my miracles were simply jokes and nothing else; that I have been enjoying every opportunity. If there was an opportunity to manage a miracle, I have not missed it. But there was no miracle at all. If you know just a little bit of human psychology you can do great things which are not prescribed in the psychology literature and textbooks – because they are not concerned with that.

But if you know a little bit of human psychology, just a little bit – not much is needed... And man is ready, he wants the miracle to happen. He wants to see the miracle happen; he is ready for the messiah. He is hankering, desiring deep down to find someone who is higher than him, more powerful than him; then he can follow him.

But I have been cutting all the roots. You ask me, "Is there any possibility of your religion not being reduced to a cult?" Yes, there is a possibility, only one possibility – and that is that sannyasins go on becoming enlightened, so there is always a chain of enlightened people around.

Buddha's religion was not reduced to a cult for five hundred years. For five hundred years the chain continued; there was always somebody who was enlightened, so in some way the Buddha consciousness was present. It remained alive. But after five hundred years the gap came, and then for six hundred years Buddhism was just a cult.

Then came Bodhidharma. Bodhidharma created a new dimension, Zen, which is still alive fourteen hundred years later. This is the longest time any religion has been alive. Bodhidharma has got the trophy, because in Zen, continuously in these fourteen hundred years, there has not been a single day when there was not somebody alive and enlightened – no break, no gap. Hence it is possible – difficult, but possible.

All that you have to remember is: no God, no priesthood, no holy scripture, no miracles, no superman. For the first time in the whole of history I am saying that an ordinary man can be enlightened. In fact only an ordinary man can be enlightened. Ordinariness for the first time is given this much respect. So don't try to make me someone extraordinary.

I am trying in every way so that you cannot make me in any way special. I go on doing everything that will prove that this was not a superman or a messiah or a *tirthankara*. I will not fit with any image. You cannot manage to make me extraordinary. Beware of the human tendency: one wants one's master to be extraordinary. But this is what leads ultimately to the death of religion.

You should not desire your master to be extraordinary. You should rather rejoice that an ordinary man has become enlightened. That means he has opened the doors to enlightenment for everybody. You need not be the only begotten son of God, you need not be a *tirthankara* earning virtue for millions of lives, you need not be born with special qualities, talents.

Have you seen the statue of Mahavira? In India you may have visited a Jaina temple – otherwise you can look in a book. On all twenty-four *tirthankaras* you will see a few very strange things. One is that all twenty-four statues look exactly alike. You cannot say which is which, who is who. Even Jainas cannot say, so they have made small symbols under every statue: under one statue a lion, under another statue something else, under another statue the swastika. You may not be aware of it but just underneath the statue there is the symbol which indicates whose statue it is – Mahavira's? – otherwise there is no difference.

Now, this is not possible. These twenty-four people were born over ten thousand years; there is no possibility of them all being similar – the same face, the same nose, the same body, the same proportions. You will see one thing more strange: all their ears, their ear lobes, will be touching their shoulders – such long ear lobes. That is especially needed if you are a *tirthankara*.

I have seen foolish Jaina monks massage their ear lobes, pull them to make them longer, because the longer they are, the more respectable you start becoming. It is possible that perhaps Mahavira had long ear lobes – I don't think *that* long; he was a man, not a donkey. Otherwise all donkeys have at least one quality to help them become a *tirthankara*. I have seen one man with ear lobes that long, so it is possible that Mahavira had them – but twenty-four people!

It is all imagination. Once Mahavira becomes established, then whatsoever he has becomes a necessary characteristic for anybody else to become a *tirthankara*. All *tirthankaras* have also to be molded again into the same pattern.

Remember, I don't have any talents – because religion is not a talent. Music is, poetry is, painting is.

Religion is not a talent. Religion is simply seeing yourself.

You may be a painter, you may be a poet, you may be a musician, you may not be anybody, but you *are*! This is not a talent, this is your existence. And to experience it is everybody's birthright.

You can save this living religion only so long as you go on meditating and you go on creating new flowers, new blossomings – so that you never become a desert; there is always some oasis. Just a single person amongst you is enough to keep the religion alive and prevent anybody from reducing it to a cult.

But please don't call it *my* religion. It has nothing to do with me. It is simply religion. You have to understand, as totally as possible, that just a pure religion has more possibility of surviving, because then you don't put any boundaries on it.

I have not put any boundaries on it. And I don't want to put any boundaries on you of discipline, of morality, of virtue. I have given you freedom, and I have given you individuality, and I have given you just a little taste of something that is always yours.

You just have to claim it.

enlightened organization
is organic harmony

Osho,
Isn't organization a necessity for a religion to survive?

Unfortunately, it is. Religion needs some kind of organization, but a problem arises. Organization in itself is a political entity; organization does not need religion at all. To survive, religion needs organization. To survive, organization needs no religion at all. There is the crux of the whole problem.

There have been in the past efforts to create religion without any organization, seeing that all the organizations somehow end up in being anti-religious. For example, the Catholic Church – it is a very solid organization but only an organization; there is no religion left. Religion is a disturbance as far as the hierarchy of the organization is concerned. Religion is a continuous trouble; religious people will be trouble.

The Catholic Church has been throwing out all the people who are really religious from the church because those people will not support this criminal act of destroying religion. They will oppose it, they will rebel against it. But the church has so much authority. The head of the church, the pope, is a religious head and also a temporal head; the Vatican is his kingdom, a political nation. Once it was big, vast; now it is only eight square miles, but still he is the temporal head and the spiritual head.

There are religions where the temporal head is separate and the religious head is separate, but then there were problems of conflict. The temporal head has all the power of the army, the law, the state; and the spiritual head has no temporal power. For example in Hinduism, the Shankaracharya is only a spiritual head. But that creates this other problem: a continuous conflict between the state and the religion – and of course the state is powerful.

You have to remember that the higher a thing, the more fragile it is. The lower a thing, the more strong it is. Roots are strong, flowers are not; although roots are meaningless if the flowers disappear – the roots have meaning only because of the flowers. But the tree is not as stupid as man; so there is a harmony between the flowers and the roots, there is no conflict.

Flowers represent the spiritual fragrance, and the roots represent the state, the army and all its power.

The roots can deny food to the flowers and the flowers will die and disappear within no time. But no tree is so stupid: there is a harmony; the roots go on supporting the flowers, the leaves, the branches. And it is not only one-sided. The flowers, the leaves, the branches go on taking rays from the sun and carbon dioxide from the air, and they go on continuously sending them to the roots.

It is a communion, there is no question of conflict. But in religion it has been a problem. If you keep them apart then soon the state starts trying to control the religion. For example, in England the church is separate but the queen is really the head of both: of the church and of the state. The church has its own head but there is a crowned head who is over him. What can the archbishop of Canterbury do against the queen?

In Russia the situation was the same. The church was separate, the czar was separate, but the whole power was in the hands of the czar. So it was just for show that the head of the church crowned the czar as if he was above the czar. But he knew and everybody knew that this was only ceremonial. In reality he had to follow the czar and the state, support the czar and the state, because without the czar, the church would die: it wouldn't have any support, financial or other-wise. That's why Catholics tried to make church and state, one: to give both powers into the hands of one man so there was no conflict.

But the trouble is when a man becomes politically powerful, that political power tends to corrupt him. He may misuse it; it is almost certain that he will misuse it.

In the first place, if the head has both temporal and spiritual power, then the people who are spiritual will not make any effort to become the head, because the spiritual person does not want to get involved in power politics. Then, only the people who are politically minded become involved in the organization. They may be in a religious robe, they may be bishops and cardinals and ministers and they may have studied theology, but they are not spiritual people. If they had been in the world they would have tried to become the president or the prime minister; it is just accidental that they are in the religious robe. Their ambition can be fulfilled here only by becoming the pope. So they will make every effort to become the pope.

When they have the power they are bound to misuse it. They were never spiritual in the first place.

Hinduism tried another thing also. If you make one person a spiritual head there is a possibility that the person is not really spiritual. You may have erred, because there is no criterion by which to judge, and it cannot be decided by election because people have no idea what spirituality is. How are they going to decide who is spiritual? They can only nominate. It cannot be chosen in an election – if you have an election you bring politics in.

The Catholic pope is elected, so naturally the politically minded cardinals make every effort to approach all those people – perhaps there are two hundred cardinals who choose the pope – so there is an undercurrent of campaign, an election campaign, continuously. Even when there is a pope the campaign continues because popes don't live long, for the simple reason that by the time the person becomes a pope he's nearabout seventy. So you can hope that within two, three, four or five years he will be gone.

A Polack is going to be tough – you cannot hope that he will be gone so easily, he may stay longer. His predecessor was only in office for nine months – that is more gentlemanly, but who expects a Polack to be a gentleman? That was more gentlemanly: in nine months the previous pope disappeared to give an opportunity for another person to become a pope. But very few people are so generous.

Hinduism tried to ensure that their religion would have many heads; all would be nominated. But then there is another problem: great confusion. Hinduism is a great confusion – you can't even call it one religion. It is a thousand and one religions together, because there is no central control. Anybody can gather disciples and can become a head and nobody can prevent it.

The idea was to give freedom but it turned out to be confusion. Any idiot can find a few other idiots who are always available everywhere. There are so many sects in Hinduism; each sect has many sub-sects and each sub-sect has its own head. They don't even have a talking relationship with the other heads of the same religion! They are continually fighting in the courts because sometimes it happens that two persons claim that they are the head and if they can give some kind of proof...

One of the most important temples in India for Hindus is in the Himalayas, Badrinathdham. For almost ten years it has been locked under police control because the court is unable to decide who the head is, because the Shankaracharya who died ten years ago wrote two wills. He wrote one will perhaps twenty, thirty years earlier when he found somebody who was potentially very capable, and he forgot about the will because he lived so long. For thirty years he must have kept it somewhere. That man stole the will.

And when the Shankaracharya was dying he was asked – by that time that man had left him – so he chose another person and made another will; the first will could not be found in his papers. Now before the Allahabad High Court there are two wills from the same man and both persons are claiming that they are the head. And the temple is one of the richest temples in India so it is not only a question of being head: it has money, it has power, it has lands – and it has millions of followers.

But both wills are from the same man. Now, how to decide? The signature experts have decided that both signatures are from the same man. There are eyewitnesses for both. But neither Shankaracharya is able to function because the court goes on postponing, simply for the reason that they don't see any way of deciding it. They are simply hoping that one of these two dies, so *that* will decide the case. Otherwise it won't be decided.

Hinduism has so many sects because each person in Hinduism... The caste system is very strict but as far as thinking is concerned you are absolutely free. If you are born in the house of a shoemaker you cannot change it, you will have to remain a shoemaker. No other profession will allow you in. You cannot move from one caste to another caste; that movement is absolutely closed.

So for centuries your forefathers and their forefathers and their forefathers and their forefathers were all making shoes – so you will make shoes. If they were weaving clothes, you will weave clothes; you will be a weaver. If they were carpenters, you will be a carpenter. There is no movement as far as your business, trade, lifestyle is concerned, but as far as thinking is concerned there is no bondage. You could move from being a follower of Shankaracharya and you could become a follower of Vallabhacharya, another spiritual head, a contemporary of Shankaracharya's and against Shankaracharya.

Sanskrit is such a language that with just a little logic everything can be interpreted in many ways. Each word has many meanings; that gives beauty to it. It gives it poetry because you can play with the word in so many ways, it does not have a fixed meaning. But it is also dangerous: you cannot write signs in Sanskrit because then there will be so many interpretations, and that is what has happened. On the Gita there are one thousand famous commentaries, to say nothing about non-famous commentaries! – there will be many thousands more. But there are one thousand very famous commentaries.

It is thought that anyone who writes a commentary on three of the scriptures – the Vedas, Badarayana's *Brahmasutras* and Krishna's Shrimad Bhagavadgita – becomes an *acharya*, a head: he can create a following. Now it is not very difficult to write commentaries on these three scriptures.

Many commentaries are available. Shankara wrote one in his own time. Vallabhacharya wrote differently, a totally different interpretation. Ramanujacharya wrote one, different again from both. Nimbarkacharya wrote one different from them all – not only different but quite the opposite. But the Gita is capable of being looked at from any angle. It gives tremendous freedom to think, to comment, but it also creates great confusion.

So Hinduism is not a religion like Christianity, Judaism or Mohammedanism. In Mohammedanism there is one prophet, one god, one book – that's all. In Hinduism there are thousands of scriptures, all of tremendous value; and on each scripture there are thousands of commentaries, and every commentary has some value, some insight. Then there are commentaries upon commentaries... Shankara writes a commentary on the Gita; then among Shankara's followers one follower writes one commentary on Shankara's commentary, and another follower writes another commentary on Shankara's commentary – because the commentary is also as vulnerable to interpretation as the original. Then *their* disciples go on writing more commentaries.

If you just look, Hinduism is like a tree: each branch brings new branches, then small branches, then more small branches. And they are all creating a great noise, great controversies – one cannot say what exactly Hinduism *is*. Organization has been avoided in a way, but the religion has not been saved – it has fallen into a confusion. It has not become a cult and a creed; it has become a confusion.

Seeing this situation, Mahavira's orthodox followers... They are called Digambaras because they live naked, their monks live naked. *Digambara* means one whose only clothing is the sky – nothing is between him and the sky. To avoid confusion, to avoid commentaries, to avoid organization, they simply destroyed all Mahavira's scriptures.

So Digambaras don't have any scriptures of Mahavira – a strange act, just to preserve his teaching. It is given by word of mouth to the disciple but is not in a book. You cannot sell it in the market; nobody can write a commentary on it. The teaching goes on silently, transferred from one generation of monks to another generation of monks. It was a great effort of tremendous courage to destroy all the scriptures, so you could not print them. But what happened was that even by transferring it from individual to individual, there were different versions, because naturally...

You are all listening to me, but if you all go back home and write down what I have said, do you think you will be reporting the same? Tomorrow morning you can look at all the notebooks and be surprised that everybody has got something else, has laid emphasis on something which you have completely ignored. You have not heard it at all, but somebody else has heard only that. What you have heard, she has not bothered about.

So even though they tried to avoid written scriptures and remain consistent, there are different versions. There are only twenty-two naked monks now; I have met all twenty-two. I was puzzled that they all have different versions from their teachers, and they are giving a different version to their disciple who someday will become a naked monk. They are training the disciple, and they think in this way the purity of the message is preserved.

But I asked them, "Have you ever compared notes with the other twenty-one?"

They said, "No, that is never done. What my teacher has given to me, I will give to my chief disciple, and he will give it to his chief disciple."

But I said, "I have met all twenty-two and you are all saying different things." If it was in a book at least there would have been some possibility to come to some agreement. Now there is no way to come to any agreement. There are twenty-two religions arising from one source – which they have destroyed. So now there is nothing to fall back on and check; and you cannot prove anybody is wrong or anybody is right.

The other sect of Jainas is the Shvetambaras. The name, *shvetambara*, means white-robed; they are not naked, they use white robes. They have scriptures but they have many sects themselves. And on such small points there is so much difference that one cannot imagine what will be happening about spiritual, philosophical things.

They have strange disagreements – about whether Mahavira was married or not, there is a difference. One sect believes he was not only married, he had a daughter. The daughter was married – he had a son-in-law, and the daughter and the son-in-law were both initiated by Mahavira. Not only that, they believe that the son-in-law slowly became more political, thinking, "I am the son-in-law of Mahavira…" He must have been hoping that he would succeed him. But Mahavira simply did not encourage him. It came to such a point that he rebelled against Mahavira with five hundred other monks and made a totally different religion.

Now this is so much that it cannot be just invented – and for what? But the other sect says that he was never married because *tirthankaras* are not married. That is part of the definition of a *tirthankara*, that he remains unmarried; so how could Mahavira have been married? He was not married.

And to say that he had a child means he had a sexual relationship – that is an absolutely ugly thing to think of a *tirthankara*. Then you are doing more and more harm: the *tirthankara's* daughter is married! Now the daughter of a *tirthankara* – his blood – thinking of marrying? Impossible! And worse, you say that the son-in-law rebelled against him. How could anybody have rebelled against a man like Mahavira – what to say about the son-in-law! – it is impossible. This whole story is bogus, according to the other sect. Their scriptures say that he was never married, there was no question of a daughter, no son-in-law, no rebel.

If on such points, which are factual, there is so much difference, then what to say about the teaching! On every point there is a difference. To avoid the differences the orthodox Digambaras destroyed the scriptures – but just destroying the scriptures won't help. You have to create a certain mythology around it. And the mythology is that Mahavira never spoke. So there is no question of there being any scriptures – he never spoke.

Now the Shvetambaras have the scriptures, sermons of Mahavira on each subject, detailed instructions for the monks about each special thing: how he has to sit, how he has to stand up, how he has to walk, how far he can see. He should look only four feet ahead so he never sees a woman, because looking four feet ahead, at the most you can see the feet of a woman, that's all.

He should walk very slowly, very carefully, so he does not kill any ants or anything. He should carry a woolen brush with him so that before he sits he brushes the place. It has to be woolen so that no ant or anything is killed by it, it is so soft. Such details! – that he has to have three pieces of clothing, one begging bowl, one brush, one small mattress which he keeps rolled under his arm. He should not sit on anybody else's clothes because you can't be certain about the vibrations of other people… And Digambaras say Mahavira never spoke!

What did he do instead of speaking? He had chosen twelve chief disciples with whom he had a mind-to-mind communication. He didn't need to speak to them; it was a silent communication to twelve teachers. Those twelve teachers were to tell all the other monks what they had heard in Mahavira's silence. Now a very complicated affair… And all those twelve didn't agree, so from the very beginning there have been twelve versions of Mahavira's teachings.

To avoid organization Mahavira said, "Now, there will be no successor to me." But that did not make any difference. Yes, there is no one successor to him, but there are thousands of heads of small sects. They don't claim to be successors of

Mahavira, they don't say they are *tirthankaras*; they are teachers of Mahavira's teaching. But all those teachers are continually in conflict about everything.

The same happened to Buddha. While he was alive he did not allow what he was saying to be written down – you were simply to understand him, to experience him. And your experience and your understanding you shared with people. Otherwise there was every possibility that people would start worshipping those books – like Mohammedans worship the Koran, Christians worship the Bible.

"So it is better not to have my words," Buddha said to his disciples, "in a book form." When he was saying it, of course it was going to be so. But when he died the disciples were in difficulty because there were so many people saying different things, something had to be decided – already there was chaos.

Then three hundred disciples together compiled what Buddha had said. The compilation was done in a closed place because there was so much conflict and they did not want people to know that the chief disciples were in conflict and fighting: "This was not said by Buddha..." So in a closed place somehow they came to some agreement, through negotiations, following the middle path: "If two persons are saying two things then come to the middle and keep that." But that was a hodgepodge.

Buddha would not be able to recognize that those were his words – those were three hundred people's agreement. Now, three hundred people in disagreement, coming to an agreement – you can imagine what the outcome will be. Yes, to the world they could then show that they had a scripture, but those who understand – how can they deceive them? Buddha avoided making any head of his religion. That created thirty-two sects immediately after his death.

There were other teachers in Buddha and Mahavira's time too. One was Sanjay Vilethiputta. He avoided even initiation, he said, "Simply listen to me. If you feel like doing what I am saying, you do it, but I will not initiate you. If I initiate you, soon you will create an organization. You will need an organization to keep all the people who are my disciples together. There are so many reasons for them to be together – for their security, for their safety, because they will be persecuted by the other religions. And if they are left alone in the vast ocean of enemies, they will be destroyed."

And in India they have a very simple method of destroying anybody. India is a country of small villages, very small villages, millions of small villages. In a small village there are only twenty houses; twenty families are living there. They can destroy anybody by a simple method, a very nonviolent method. They decide that a man is not to be accepted as part of them, so he cannot be invited to any marriage, to any ceremony.

Nobody will talk with him. He's not allowed to take water from the village well. If the river is five miles away, he has to carry his water from there. When crops are to be cut, nobody is to support him. Otherwise, in a village, that's the way: when one person's crops are ripe, the whole village helps him to cut the crop. Then somebody else's are ready and the whole village helps him. Single-handedly, he will be in immense trouble.

Nobody will talk to him. People should not recognize him on the street, should not say hello. You will kill the man – and he cannot go anywhere else because in India people are tethered to their land. Nobody is going to purchase his land, his house. If he wants to leave he can leave, but where is he going to go and what he is going to do?

It's a very easy, very nonviolent, but really cruel method; far more cruel than killing the man. His children will not be playing with other children, his wife will not be meeting with any other woman. He's boycotted.

So Sanjay Vilethiputta said, "If I initiate you an organization will be necessary. I will not give you initiation, then it cannot be known to others that you are my followers. You just go on living, experiencing, doing what I have told to you. And if you feel to convey it to somebody, you can convey it, but there is no question of initiation. So nobody knows that you belong to Sanjay Vilethiputta."

But what happened? We don't have Sanjay Vilethiputta's scriptures. The man must have been of immense intelligence because Buddha criticizes him, Mahavira criticizes him. Otherwise, Mahavira and Buddha would not criticize a man who had no status. He must have had a status exactly the same as Buddha and Mahavira. Mahavira does not criticize Buddha, he was too young. Mahavira was too old; it was below him to criticize Buddha.

It happened to me... It was Gandhi's one-hundred-year celebration year, a century was complete; if he had been alive he would have been one hundred years old. So one year, a whole year of celebrations was made in India. And I made it a point that for the whole year I would criticize him because that was the right time. So I spoke all over India, criticizing him everywhere.

The oldest Gandhian was Kaka Kalelkar. He was one of the very early disciples and by then was the most authoritative person. When he was asked in New Delhi what he thought about me, he said, "He's too young, and youth is bound to be rebellious. When he is my age he will not criticize Gandhi." I was in Ahmedabad when I received the message. Someone from Delhi brought me a newspaper and showed me that this is what he had said.

I said, "My comment is that Kaka Kalelkar has gone senile. If youth is rebellious and if it is to be decided by age... He has not said anything against my arguments. He's indicating my age, that I am saying these things because I'm too young; he's not saying anything against what I have said. Then naturally the simple answer is that he is senile. He's too old to understand; he's lost his brains and he should be in his grave.

"As far as I am concerned, one thing is certain: even in my grave I will criticize Gandhi because my arguments have nothing to do with my age, no relevance to my age. Gandhi was against everything that has been invented after the spinning wheel. I cannot conceive that even if I am three hundred years old I will support this idea that the spinning wheel should be the last invention of man, and after that everything is evil!"

Now almost twenty years have passed and I am still of the same opinion. Gandhi, about certain things, was absolutely fanatic. He wanted the world to remain at least three thousand years back, stuck there, not to move from there. And the reason he was giving was absolutely meaningless. The reason was that at that time people were happy, people were moral, people were religious, people were spiritual. Now, all these things are wrong.

In Mesopotamia they have found a stone – the whole civilization of Mesopotamia has disappeared – it is a six thousand year-old stone with writing on it. If you read it you will think it is from somewhere in today's newspaper's editorial. It says, "Young people are getting lost" – the generation gap, six thousand years ago – "the young people are disobedient and don't listen to their fathers and mothers and elders. This is the age of degradation" – six thousand years ago!

And it was the age of degradation. Mahavira, Buddha, Krishna, were all teaching people continually – Mahavira for forty years, Buddha for forty-two years – and what were they teaching? "Don't steal, don't lie, don't lust after other people's women." Now if people were not doing these things then Mahavira and Buddha were both insane, completely insane. When people are not stealing, what is the point of teaching for forty years continually, "Don't steal"?

I was in Bhopal sitting in my host's bedroom, and I saw on the wall a small notice: "Please don't spit on the floor." Strange... I said, "People do?"

He said, "Yes, in Bhopal this is the trouble. Only in Bhopal is this the trouble: people chew betel leaves and spit them out wherever." He said, "You are surprised? You will find this kind of notice in every nice house." But this notice is enough proof that people are spitting. Otherwise I have never seen that notice anywhere in India.

In my university, one day I saw one of the professors spitting betel leaf on the floor – the pan that Indians go on chewing. Taru is here, she is an expert in it! I saw him spitting there, just in front of me. I was sitting alone and he was sitting in another corner and he just spat by the side of the chair. I went over and asked him, "Are you from Bhopal?"

He said, "Yes, I have just been transferred from Bhopal."

I said, "That explains it." He said, "What?"

I said, "We will now have to keep a small notice here that says, 'Please don't spit on the floor.'"

He said, "Strange, but it is true that only in Bhopal people spit, and this is general. And nobody cares about those notices. Notices are there – in fact they remind you to spit. You may be chewing your pan joyfully and suddenly you see that board, and the desire to spit arises. They don't prevent anybody."

If Gandhi says everything was moral three thousand years ago, then to whom was morality being taught? If everything was spiritual, then what was the need of so many spiritual leaders? If everything was good then why do you go on remembering only a few good names? – Buddha, Mahavira, Krishna – that can be counted on your fingers.

If everybody was good, Buddha and Mahavira would have been lost in the crowd because the whole crowd was good. Just because you remember these few names shows that they rose above the masses; so high, that even three thousand years, five thousand years afterwards, you can still see them. The masses have completely disappeared; there is no description of the masses at all.

But Gandhi was adamant about technology: the telegraph, the telephone...

I don't see that the telegraph or the telephone are in any way violent. In fact these are very nonviolent things; they should be supported by nonviolent people. If you don't have a telephone then you will have to walk down to the place, and walking may kill a few insects. Or if you drive the car there then you are going to kill a few small insects on the road – or you may have an accident, kill somebody or get killed yourself. The telephone is saving you from all this violence.

I don't see that I can change my argument anytime, because it is a simple argument. It has nothing to do with my age.

Mahavira did not criticize Buddha. To me that is a criticism of Mahavira. It was an egoistic attitude to think, "He is too young and I am too established; he is just starting from scratch – who cares about him?"

But he could not ignore Sanjay Vilethiputta. Neither could Buddha ignore him, so it seems the man must have been of great influence. We find his name in the books of his enemies, and we find a few things that he must have been teaching – that too in the books of his enemies. His books are not available because there was no disciple to preserve them, no organization to preserve them.

And we cannot trust what his enemies were saying against him because this is an old logical strategy: to describe, to destroy, to criticize your enemy, first you impose a certain doctrine on him which is not really representative of the person. It may be similar but first you impose a similar doctrine on the person's name – knowing perfectly the loopholes because you are imposing the doctrine – and then criticize it. Then whosoever reads your book will find your criticism is perfectly right. This has happened to me, that's why I know.

One of the great Hindu monks, Karpatri, has written a whole book against me; and when I saw it I wondered how he managed. Statements that I have never made, he makes in my name, and then criticizes them. Now, anybody reading his book will think that he has finished me completely. He has not even touched me.

His secretary has written the introduction to the book, and seems to be an intelligent man because in that introduction he says, "We are obliged to Osho because he created this opportunity and the challenge for all those who think to reconsider everything and not just to accept anything without reconsidering it."

The secretary is a follower of Karpatri, so he thanks Karpatri for doing a great job in accepting the challenge of Osho and criticizing him. He came personally to give me the book. I looked in it here and there and I asked him, "You are the secretary to Karpatri" – he was a Hindu sannyasin himself – "Have you not noticed that these statements are not mine? Most probably the book was dictated to you."

He said, "I was afraid that you were going to say that."

I just looked here and there in the book and I told him, "This statement is not mine. Not only is it not mine, it is contrary to me, absolutely against my statements. You are an educated person: how did you allow it to happen? You should have prevented it, because this book is absolutely false and whosoever reads it will have a totally wrong concept of me."

So you cannot trust these people – because I have compared what Buddha said about Sanjay Vilethiputta, and what Mahavira says about him is something else. Buddha quotes Sanjay Vilethiputta's philosophy differently, Mahavira differently. That shows certainly that nobody is representing the other person accurately. That is dishonesty. The honest person should first state the other person's argument in its totality, in its full strength, and then he should criticize it.

But without an organization Sanjay Vilethiputta is completely lost – we don't have anything of his to compare. And we don't have any disciple's notes because he never initiated anyone. So perhaps within one or two generations the thing must have disappeared – and the man's contribution must have been of immense value.

Krishnamurti is doing exactly what Sanjay Vilethiputta did. He abandoned the organization and for almost sixty years he has been trying to help people individually to understand – but nothing has happened; he's the most frustrated master ever. And now at the age of eighty-five he creates the Krishnamurti Foundation in England. This is the experience of sixty years – that he understands that the moment he dies there will be nobody even to preserve his words. What to say about his experience – even his words will not be there.

What is happening around me is totally different from what has been done up to now, because nothing has been successful; in one way or another every effort has failed.

Now the effort around me is not to create an organization like the Catholics because then the whole power becomes concentrated in one person – and that is dangerous. That creates ambition in others to reach to the highest post. They forget about spirituality, growth. Then their whole effort is how to become the pope. Deep down that desire... So it becomes another world, an other-worldly politics. And all the power in one person's hand is always dangerous.

Around me the effort from the very beginning has been to decentralize power. So around me many parallel organizations are slowly being created, and each organization is autonomous, functioning in one direction.

For example, Rajneesh Foundation International will be looking after my words and other religious affairs. The Academy, another organization, will be purely esoteric. For the Academy I have created three circles of people. They will be the Academy; they will have the spiritual power in my physical absence. It will have all the best, the most intelligent sannyasins in there. Their combined intelligence will be enough – a power unto itself.

Then the commune will have a separate body of its own. Now there are almost one dozen communes around the earth, and all the communes are patterned exactly alike. They are coming up to the standards here; Europe is almost there – in Europe there are ten communes now.

Small centers have dissolved into bigger communes because small centers can be crushed very easily; only communes can live. So now the Zurich commune has hundreds of people; Medina, in London, has hundreds of people; Berlin has hundreds of people. So now these people can stand up for themselves and will not be easily persecuted.

Each commune is autonomous. Still they are all alike, exactly patterned like the commune here. Their clothes are of the same quality; their food is of the same quality – because I was shocked when I heard that a few communes were so poor that they were only eating bread and soup.

So I am now sending Sheela for three days every month to each commune, to see that the religious work is carried out according to my vision, and so that no sannyasin living in any commune feels that he's deprived of any facility. All the facilities should be absolutely similar, and each commune is autonomous.

Our sannyasins in many ways are very innocent people. They may be very educated but they are innocent people – and after becoming sannyasins they have become more innocent. Therefore there is no problem; it needs a simple common sense.

Organization cannot be avoided. We just have to be a little more sophisticated and more scientific and more mathematical about it. We have to use it rather than being used by it. So I am not against organization, but we can learn from the past. Whatsoever has happened in the past we can avoid, and we can do something totally new which has never been done.

If you can see all the possibilities which destroy religion... Before they get hold of my religion I am going to finish all the possibilities. Sannyasins can have a totally different organization. That promise you can always remember: I will not leave you under a fascist regime.

In the past what has happened? These people created their organizations at the very last moment when they were dying; or mostly the organizations were created after the founders were dead, because when the founder was alive, there things were going perfectly well, so who bothered about it. But when the founder was dead, immediately the need...his absence was there. And it was such a big emptiness that it was impossible for people to connect. They had connected with the founder, but they had no interconnection amongst themselves.

And that's really what organization is. The word is very meaningful; it comes from *organ*. Your hand is your organ, your leg is your organ; your nose, your eyes – these are your organs. And your whole body is the organization. And they're all functioning in immense harmony.

How many parts you have – and they're all functioning in harmony; you are not even aware of it. Everything is going on so silently that scientists say that if we were to make such a mechanism that works so silently and does all the work that the body does, we would need at least a one square mile area to make it in the factory.

Even today it is not possible to turn bread into blood – how your body does it is an everyday miracle. Millions of living cells are within you; you are almost a city. There are seven million living cells, perhaps having a certain small brain of their own, because their work is so intelligent you cannot say they don't have any brain.

Everything is being shifted, is being supplied to the place where it is needed. Care is even being taken by those small cells inside you so that the nourishment should reach first to the parts which are most essential. Your brain gets the nourishment first, the legs can wait a little.

But if just for few minutes – I think six minutes – your brain does not get oxygen, it starts disintegrating. So the first thing is – and how these small cells are doing and deciding it is a mystery – oxygen should reach to the brain. When the brain's need is fulfilled, then second-grade organs, third-grade organs, fourth-grade organs... That way it should move.

You are a city of seven million living beings. This is an organization, and this is what it should be. All our separate organs should be connected, helping each other, remembering where help is needed more, and first; and remembering that your whole function is to be enlightened, so the torch of enlightenment remains burning. There is no gap. And I'm taking every care that there will be no gap.

Bodhidharma will feel jealous of me.

personality: the carbon cop-out

Osho,
Why were you so mischievous in your childhood?

D o you think I am different? Not a bit. I am still the same. I did not allow my childhood to be spoiled by anybody. And what you think of as mischievous, I have never thought about it in that way. Even today I don't think that anything I have ever done was a mischief. I had my reasons, and very valid reasons.

For example: the first day I entered high school from my middle school... In high school they used to have a prayer at the beginning of the day. It was a very famous song of Mirza Iqbal, who was one of the greatest Urdu poets of this age. As far as the language is concerned, it is certainly a great piece of art, but the philosophy behind it is ugly. The song says: "My country, my nation, is the best of all the nations. My country is a beautiful garden and we are nightingales in this garden..." And that's the way it goes on.

I said to the principal who was standing in front of the two thousand students and fifty teachers, "I will not participate in this prayer because to me this is absolute rubbish. Every country thinks of itself in the same way and every country has its ego in it.

"You ask the Chinese, you ask the Japanese, you ask the Germans, you ask the English, you ask anybody – they all think the same. So what Iqbal has written is simply rubbish as far as the philosophical background is concerned. And I am against the very concept of "nation." The world is one; I cannot say that my country is the best of all the countries.

"And I don't even see the reason for singing the song. It is not only that

I am against nationalism, the song is untrue too, because what do you have? – poverty, slavery, starvation, sicknesses, increasing population and increasing problems. And you call this our garden and we are its nightingales! I don't see a single nightingale anywhere! These fifty teachers are here; can anybody raise his hand and say, 'I am a nightingale'? Let him sing, and let us see! These two thousand students are here; can anyone say it? Look at these poor students."

And they used to come from faraway villages, miles every day, from at least a twenty mile radius around the city, because there was no other high school except this. "They walk, they come utterly tired, they are hungry. And I have seen what they bring with them: just dry bread, not even buttered, and a little piece of salt. That's all that they bring every day and every day they eat it.

"These are your trees, this is your garden? So factually also it is not right. And I don't care whether Iqbal is a Nobel prize-winning poet or not. I don't care. It does not make me feel like singing this song; in every way uttering a lie."

The principal was so annoyed and so irritated that he could not speak for anger; he became almost red. Trembling, he went into his office and brought out his cane which was very famous – but he rarely used it. He told me to put both my hands in front of him, and he said, "This is my answer, and remember it."

I said, "These are my hands. You can beat my hands or my whole body if you want, but before you start, remember that from here I am going directly to the police station, because this is legally prohibited. Both you and your cane will be behind bars."

It was illegal to beat any student, but nobody cared. Still today, in India, students are beaten. And the law that students should not be physically beaten has existed for at least fifty years. So I said, "You decide. Here are my hands, this is your cane; you are here. And remember, these two thousand students are eye-witnesses, fifty teachers are eyewitnesses, and you will leave your signature on my hands. Leave it there! If you have any guts, beat me."

I can remember even today that he remained almost like a statue. The cane fell from his hand. He just turned back and went into his office. I told all the students, "Now you need not be worried; we are finished with this song. Unless they find something reasonable, we will simply be standing here for ten minutes in silence."

Now, do you call that mischief? It *can* be called mischief, and it was mischief in the eyes of my principal. He reported to my father that I had misbehaved.

I told my father, "You have to come with me. *He* has misbehaved. He should have answered me, told me that I was wrong. He should have convinced me that the song is right. Instead of that, he brought his cane to beat me. Is that an argument? Is that right behavior? Who has done the mischief, he or I? And then he had no guts even to beat me. I gave him the challenge; my hands were before him. I was ready to take as many beatings as he wanted, but I told him that I would go directly to the police station which is not far away from the high school, and that soon he would be behind bars because beating is illegal. Now who has misbehaved?"

My father said, "Forget about it."

I said, "I cannot forget about it. You have to come with me. It has to be decided – because the man has some nerve to tell you that I was mischievous, that I was misbehaving, that I insulted him before the whole school, all the teachers and all the students. You have to come with me."

Now, my father said, "Forgive me – perhaps you are right."

I said, "No perhaps – if you don't come with me, I will drag that principal here."

So I had to take my father, and he had to follow, persuading me all the way: "Leave it. It is not such a big thing; he simply mentioned by the way that you misbehaved."

I said, "That is not the question. He has to say it in front of me. This is back-biting. *He* is mischievous."

And when the principal saw that I was coming with my father, he again became afraid that there was, it seemed, some more trouble. And I said to him, "Now you tell my father what I have done, and what you have done: saying behind my back to my father that I have been misbehaving, doing mischief, insulting you before the whole school. Repeat it! – because I don't agree with any of it.

"You have insulted me by not answering my argument. Not only that, you wanted to beat me. Not only that, you are a coward: you could not even beat me. Now, this is very slimy, that you go around and tell my father. You prove it – that it was mischief.

"In fact, all the nations that have been proclaiming themselves the best nation in the world are mischievous. Their mischief has accounted for millions of lives; the whole of history is full of it, and still we go on doing the same thing.

"Small children are being told to repeat every day something which is absolute nonsense, and unrealistic too. There is no fact supporting it. A country which has been a slave for two thousand years cannot say, 'In the whole world we are the best' – the best slaves, or what? A country which is ninety percent poor, where one meal is difficult...

"There are days when millions of people in India sleep only by drinking water, just to keep the feeling that the stomach is full. This is the best country in the world! – whom are you trying to befool? These children will become conditioned to the idea. This is a strategy of the politicians: that tomorrow these children will become soldiers, and they will die for the 'best country of the world,' not even knowing that this is not true.

"And even if it is factual, then too it is egoistic, and it should not be a prayer. Accepting, just for the sake of argument, that it is true – that one country is the best in the world, the richest, the most well-educated, well-cultured, has every-thing that is needed so all the facts support it – still I say such a prayer is wrong, because a prayer should not be ego-fulfilling, a prayer should be ego-destroying."

The principal said to me, "Forgive me, and please forget it, and I hope that we will never come into any conflict again."

I said, "That depends on you. If you behave, and you promise to behave, perhaps the situation may not arise. Was it not possible for you to accept my argument humbly? – because it was true. Do you think that would have been an insult to you? It would have raised your status before the whole school, that you are a man of some dignity, that you do not hesitate even to respect the right argument from a child, that you respect intelligence.

"You missed that opportunity; you brought your cane. And then again you created trouble for yourself; you gave me another chance to prove you are a coward. You are unintelligent, you have no respect for intelligence or for a child – and you are a coward: you should have beaten me! What would it matter if you were behind bars? – it was a question of your principles. If you were right, then it would have been good to be behind bars. But be right, and fight for it!"

For three years he avoided me like anything. But I will not say it was mischief although it will appear so. I don't see a single point supporting the idea that it was mischief.

For three years, while I was in the high school, we continued the silence. The ten minutes' silence continued instead of prayer, because they could not come up with something better. Whatsoever they brought up I was capable of finding faults with. And without my approval, I was not going to allow it. So finally they decided, "Let this boy be gone from here, then…" And the day I left the school and went to the university…

I came back in some holiday and I went there to see what was happening: and the children were repeating the same song again. I went to the principal and I said, "I have just come to check. It has not reached your mind at all – again you started the same thing."

But he said, "Now please leave us alone. I was afraid that if you failed, then you would be here for one more year. I was praying for you to pass. I had told all the teachers to support you, to help you so that you pass. Any way you should not fail, otherwise one more year… But now, leave us alone."

I said, "I will not be coming again and again. I have just come to check and to see whether you have any mind or not, and you seem to be absolutely unintelligent. You are a postgraduate in science, and that too in mathematics – which is just an extension of logic – but you can't understand a simple thing. I will not be coming here because now I am occupied in the university. There are so many problems there, I cannot take care of your school."

One of my high school teachers was a certain Mr. Nigam; he used to teach chemistry. I knew him, the whole city knew about him, but he was such an angry, violent and idiotic man that nobody raised a voice against him. He killed his wife, but I was the only witness.

I was a witness because I was sitting in a mango tree. The mangoes were getting ripe, and it was nobody's tree so I was not stealing. In India, mango trees are planted along the roads. They give shade and they give the most delicious fruit also; so, many people out of charity plant mango trees. Municipal committees, corporations, plant mango trees. So it was a public tree and nobody could say to me, "You are stealing" – or anything.

But this mango tree was just by the side of this Mr. Nigam's compound, outside his compound, and he was not aware that somebody was sitting in the tree. It was getting a little dark, the sun was almost gone, and I saw him dragging his wife along. He pushed the wife into the well – there was a well in his garden – and then he started shouting, "My wife has fallen into the well!"

Neighbors gathered. I also came down, but I thought it better first to inquire of my father, "Do I have to get involved in this or not? – because I am the only witness that this man pushed his wife."

My father said, "In the first place, what were you doing there?"

I said, "I was just picking a few mangoes. Even if it is a crime, it is not such a crime that a man can throw his wife down a well and I should remain silent. If there is some punishment for it, I am ready. Just two mangoes I have taken. If somebody wants the price, you give the price, but just suggest to me what I am supposed to do. Should I speak? – because that man is trying to prove that his wife fell."

And his wife died – the well was very deep. My city is such that half the city is on top of a hill, and the other half is in the valley. Cycling is very difficult in my city. You can come down very easily, but going up you have to walk with your bicycle, you cannot go on the cycle. Cycle rickshaws are not yet possible because of this situation. So half is on top of the hill, and it is a very plain hill – then suddenly the slope.

The middle city is on the slope, and the other half, the main city, is in the valley – the main market and everything. So in the valley wells are very easy to make. You can dig a well alone, there is not much of a problem: six, eight feet, that's enough, and you reach the water because the river is just by the side. But on the top, you have to go down at least sixty feet.

This Mr. Nigam used to live on the top, so the well was very deep, sixty feet deep, and then the water was very deep.

By the time people gathered, his wife had died. Perhaps she died before she reached the water. Sixty feet falling in the well... She must have hit something. The well was not very big, so she must have hit the sides, because when her body was brought up, it was bleeding from many places. Her head and body were bruised and bloody, so she must have died on the way down – or perhaps the little bit of life that remained was finished when she reached the water.

Now this man, when on the first day he came to teach... The first thing is the attendance; so everybody who is present says, "Yes, sir," or "Present, sir," and for whoever is not present, nobody speaks, so he is marked not present. I said, "Yes, mister."

He looked at me and he said, "Don't you hear everybody saying 'Yes, sir'? – and you say 'Yes, mister.' Don't you have any respect for a teacher?"

I said, "I have respect for people who are respectable. I know you perfectly well. The day your wife was pushed into the well, I was sitting in the mango tree in front of your house. I can still open up the case. And you want me to call you sir?

"There is a student in the class who lives by the house of the prostitute. You visit that prostitute almost every day. Do you want me to call out the name of the boy, and ask him to stand up and say that he sees you every day in the prostitute's house? There is a boy here whose father sells wine and all kinds of drugs. He can stand up for me and tell you what kind of things you go on purchasing from his father. And still you want me to call you 'sir'?"

Now certainly it looks like mischief, but not to me. He was very angry and annoyed. He took me to the principal, and the principal said, "It is better you settle it yourself."

But he said, "No. This boy is going to spoil the whole class. He was saying to the class, 'From tomorrow nobody calls him "sir."' "

I said to the principal, "These are the reasons; now you tell me whether we have to call this man 'sir.' As far as I am concerned, even calling him 'mister' is too much. If he does not agree to 'mister,' then I am going to find something worse."

The principal took him aside and said, "You had better settle for 'mister.' It is not a bad word, it is perfectly respectable. There is no harm, because what he is saying... And he has proofs. And what he is saying is that he is an eyewitness that you pushed your wife. He is dangerous, he can go to the police and you may be in trouble. And he is not afraid of your violence or anything which your neighborhood is afraid of."

That man settled for "mister." The whole class called him that. And then I started spreading it into his other classes, "You have to call this man 'mister.'" Finally he resigned. Seeing that the whole school knew about everything that I had been saying, he resigned; not only resigned, he left the city and moved to another town.

It can be thought of as mischief, but I don't think it is mischief. I had valid reasons and still I will stand by what I did; it was perfectly right. In fact this man should have been thrown out of the school long before, thrown out of the city long before. And it was a good nonviolent strategy that I applied.

He left on his own. I was the only person at the station to say good-bye to him. And I can still remember the way he looked at me as if he wanted to kill me, then and there. But the train moved, and I went on waving to him; I went on running up to the end of the platform. And I said, "Don't be worried. I will be coming to visit sometime, wherever you are."

This world, from a child's standpoint, looks very different. You will have to understand it from a child's standpoint because his standpoint is nonpolitical, fearless, innocent. He sees things as they are. And if every child is allowed to behave according to his understanding, you will see that every child proves to be mischievous. It is your attitude that interprets it as a mischievous act because you are not thinking from an innocent vision.

It continued in the university. One of my vice-chancellors was Doctor Tripathi, a very famous historian. He was a professor of history at Oxford, and then he became vice-chancellor at Sagar University; an old man, a world-famous authority on history. And the first address that he gave to the whole university was on the birthday of Buddha.

He said with great feeling, "I always think that if I had been born in Buddha's time, I would have gone and sat at his feet and tried to understand the wisdom, the light, the vision that this man has brought into the world."

I was there. I stood up and said, "Wait a minute, please."

He said, "Have I said anything wrong?"

I said, "Certainly. Have you been to Krishnamurti? You have lived in England; Krishnamurti is often in England – have you been to this man's feet to learn the great wisdom, the vision?"

He said, "No, I haven't."

"Then," I said, "you would not have gone to Buddha either. Did you go to Raman Maharishi?" – who had just died a few years before. "He was alive your whole life, and he was known all over the world as one of the most enlightened masters ever. And he was here in India, just living in one place, Arunachal. He never moved from one small hill in the south, he always remained there, his whole life.

"He went there when he was seventeen, and he died there; he must have been eighty-five. He never left, all these seventy years. He was just living on that small hill. From all the world over people were coming to him. Did you go there?"

He said, "No."

I said, "Then can you repeat that you would have gone to Buddha? I can say with certainty that this is mere oratory. You are befooling others, you are befooling yourself. You have to accept the fact that you would not have gone. Why have you not gone to Raman, to Krishnamurti, to Meher Baba? These people were available your whole life.

"But you think yourself a far higher authority, more and better educated than these three people. You have wisdom, you have vision, you have light – what can these people give you? I say to you with absolute certainty, you would not have gone to Buddha. Do you agree with me or not?"

There was silence for a moment, such silence as rarely happens in a university convocation hall, pin-drop silence. And the man said, "Perhaps the boy is right. In fact I have no right to speak on Buddha because I have never been interested in enlightenment, nirvana, meditation. And he is right that I would not have gone to Buddha. For what? – because my interest is not in these things. And he has pointed out clearly that I know three persons – these three persons are well-known as enlightened masters – but I have not gone. And they have been very close to me.

"Krishnamurti has been very close; just an hour's drive and I could have seen him many times. I have been speaking in Chennai University, from where Arunachal is only a few hours' drive. I have been speaking in Pune University, and Meher Baba lives there in Pune – but I have not bothered." He apologized to me before the whole university and asked me to come sometime to his home; he would like to talk with me. I will say this man was at least intelligent; he was not annoyed.

My professors told me, "This is not right, particularly for you, because your scholarship depends on him. He can cancel your scholarship, and he has every opportunity in many ways to harm you, because he will appoint those who are going to be your examiners. He will appoint the one who is going to take your verbal examination. And your future... After your MA, he is the person who will decide whether to give you a research scholarship or not."

I said, "Don't be worried about anything. I have taken care of everything today."

They said, "By doing this mischief?"

I said, "The man has offered an apology and still you are calling it a mischief?"

They said, "Yes, a disturbance in a public place making him look stupid."

I said, "I was not trying to make him look stupid, and he proved that he is not stupid. And I have asked many students: they all said that their respect for him in their eyes has increased because he was ready to accept that what he had said was just oratory. You can go on sometimes carried away by words; one word takes you to another word.

"People who have been speaking their whole life – professors, teachers – go on saying things which they don't mean. You have to pull them back: 'Where are you going?' Just one word leads to another word, that word leads to another word... You have to pull them back. Of course pulling on anybody's leg looks like mischief, but it was not. And he has not accepted it as mischief."

I went to him, and he said, "You have done something great to me. In my whole life nobody has ever disturbed me while I was speaking. And you disturbed me on such a point that I had no way to deny you; and I loved you for the simple reason that you had the courage. Whatever you need and whenever you need it, always remember I am here. Just let me be informed about it and every facility, everything that is in my power will be available to you."

And I didn't have to say anything to him. He, without my asking, made arrangements that from the university cafeteria I should receive a free pass for two years, and that my scholarship should be granted. And you will be surprised that before deciding on my examiners, he inquired of me, "Do you have any preference for whom you would like?"

I said, "No, when you are deciding I know that you will decide on the best people. I would like the best, the topmost people. So don't think whether they will pass me or fail me, give me better marks or lower marks; that is absolutely irrelevant to me. Choose the best in the whole country."

He chose the best. And strangely, it turned out to be very favorable. One of the professors that he chose for Indian philosophy, the best authority, was Doctor Ranade of Allahabad University. On Indian philosophy, he was the best authority. But nobody used to choose him as an examiner because he had rarely passed anybody. He would find so many faults, and he could not be challenged; he was the last person to be challenged. And almost all the professors of Indian philosophy in India were his disciples. He was the oldest man, retired. But Doctor Tripathi chose him, and asked him as a special favor, because he was old and retired by then, "You have to."

A strange thing happened – and if you trust life, strange things go on happening. He gave me ninety-nine percent out of a hundred. He wrote a special note on the paper that he was not giving a hundred percent because that would look a little too much; that's why he had cut the one percent, "But the paper deserves one hundred percent. I am a miser," he wrote on his note.

I read the note; Tripathi showed it to me saying, "Just look at this note: 'I am a miser, I have never gone above fifty in my whole life; the best I have given is fifty percent.'"

But what appealed to him were my strange answers, that he had never received before. And that was his whole life's effort – that a student of philosophy should not be like a parrot, just repeating what is written in the textbook. The moment he would see that it was just a textbook thing, he was no longer interested in it.

He was a thinker and he wanted you to say something new. And with me the problem was I had no idea of the textbooks, so anything that I was writing could not be from the textbooks – that much was certain. And he loved it for the simple reason that I am not bookish. I answered on my own.

He appointed, for my viva voce, a Mohammedan professor of Allahabad University. He was thought to be a very strict man. And even Doctor Tripathi told me, "He is a very strict man, so be careful."

I said to him, "I am always careful whether the man is strict or not. I don't care about the man, I simply am careful. The man is not the point: even if there is nobody in the room, I am still careful."

He said, "I would love to be present and see it because I have heard about this man that he is really hard." So he came. That was very rare. The head of my department was there, the vice-chancellor was there, and Doctor Tripathi. He asked special permission from the Mohammedan professor, Sir Saiyad, "Can I be present? I just want to see this, because you are known as the hardest examiner, and I know this boy – he is also, in his way, as hard as you are. So I want to see what happens."

And my professor, Doctor S.K. Saxena, who loved me so much, just like a son, and cared for me in every possible way... He would even go out of his way to take care of me. For example every morning when the examinations were on, he would come to the university, to my hostel room, to pick me up in his car and leave me in the examination hall, because he was not certain – I may go, I may not go. So for those few days while the examinations were on... And it was very difficult for him to get up that early.

He lived four, five miles away from the hostel, and he was a man who loved drinking, sleeping late. His classes never began before one o'clock in the afternoon because only by that time was he ready. But to pick me up, because the examination started at seven-thirty, at seven exactly he was in front of my room. I asked him, "Why do you waste thirty minutes? – because from here it is just a one-minute drive to the examination hall."

He said, "These thirty minutes are so that if you are not here then I can find where you are – because I am not certain about you. Once you are inside the hall and the door is closed, then I take a deep breath of relief, that now you will do something, and we will see what happens."

So Doctor Tripathi was there, and he was continually hitting my leg, reminding me that that man was really… So I asked Sir Saiyad, "One thing: first prevent my professor, who is hitting my leg again and again, telling me not to be outrageous, not to be in any way mischievous. He told me before, 'Whenever I hit your leg, that means you are going astray, and this will be difficult.' So please first stop this man. This is a strange situation that somebody is being examined and somebody else is hitting his leg. This is inconvenient. What do you think?"

He said, "Certainly this is inconvenient," but he laughed.

And I said, "My vice-chancellor has told me the same: 'Be very careful.' But I can't be more careful than I am. Just start!"

He asked me a simple question, and my professor thought my answer was mischievous. The vice-chancellor thought it was mischievous, because I destroyed the whole thing. He asked, "What is Indian philosophy?"

I told him, "In the first place philosophy is only philosophy. It cannot be Indian, Chinese, German, Japanese – philosophy is simply philosophy. What are you asking? Philosophy is philosophizing; whether a man philosophizes in Greece or in India or in Jerusalem, what difference does it make? Geography has no impact; nor have the boundaries of a nation any impact on philosophy. So first drop that word *Indian*, which is wrong. Ask me simply, 'What is philosophy?' You please drop it and ask the question again."

The man looked at my vice-chancellor and he said, "You are right; the student is also hard! He has a point, but now it will be difficult for me to ask any questions because I know he will make a mockery of my questions." So he said, "I accept! What is philosophy? – because that question you have put yourself."

I said to him, "It is strange that you have been a professor of philosophy for many years and you don't know what philosophy is. I really cannot believe it." And the interview was finished.

He said to Doctor Tripathi, "Don't unnecessarily let me be harassed by this student. He will simply harass me." And to me he said, "You have passed. You needn't be worried about passing."

I said, "I am never worried about that; about that these two persons are worried. They somehow are forcing me to pass; I am trying my best to undo what they are trying to do, but they are pushing hard."

If you take anything as mischief, you have a certain prejudice. Once you understand that whatsoever I have done in my life… It may not be part of the formal behavior, it may not be the accepted etiquette, but then you are taking your standpoint from a certain prejudice.

All things – and so many things have happened in such a small life that sometimes I wonder why so many things happened.

They happened simply because I was always ready to jump into anything, never thinking twice what the consequences would be.

I had won my first inter-university debate; it was an all-India debate, and I had come first and brought the shield to my university. The professor in charge, Indrabahadur Khare, was a poet and a good man, but a very proper gentleman

– just like proper Sagar – everything closed. Buttons, coat, everything had to be proper – and I was very unproper.

He took me to a photo studio. Because I had won the shield for the all-India competition, the newspapers needed a picture, so he took me. For my whole university career I was wearing a kurta, a kind of robe without any buttons at all. So when I stood there by the shield, Indrabahadur said to me, "Wait, where are your buttons?"

I said, "I have never used buttons. I love the air, I enjoy it – why buttons?" And he was completely closed up with so many buttons. He was using a Mohammedan *sherwani*, which is the national dress in India, a long coat with many buttons; even the collar is closed with a button.

So he said, "But without buttons... This picture will be reprinted in all the newspapers; I cannot allow this."

I said, "I cannot allow buttons. I can bring the buttons, and you can take a picture of the buttons for the copy – I have no objection. I have no interest in the picture. Has it to be my picture – or your picture? You stand up, you are absolutely proper; the picture will look good. But if you want my picture, it has to be without buttons, because I have lived without buttons for almost four years.

"I cannot change just for the picture – that will be phony, a lie. And how can I put on buttons, because there are no holes on the other side; even if I want to put on buttons, it will need holes and I don't want to destroy my dress at all. So please forgive me – either my picture has to be without buttons, or it is not going to be at all."

He said, "But this is mischievous of you."

I said, "It is not mischievous of me, it is too much of a mannerism on your part. And who are you to decide? In these four years, every professor has tried to insist that I should use buttons, and I have asked them, 'Where in the university code is it written that you should have buttons? Just show me the law, bylaw, any amendment, anything that proves that you should have buttons, and I will have buttons.' But nobody has thought about buttons, that this question will arise one day, that you should have it printed in the university code. So they all became silent to show that it's okay, nothing can be done about it."

I used to walk in an Indian sandal which is made of wood. It has been used by sannyasins for centuries, almost ten thousand years or perhaps longer. A wooden sandal, because it avoids any kind of leather, which is bound to be coming from an animal who maybe has been killed, killed only for this purpose – and the best leather comes from very young children of animals. So sannyasins have been avoiding that, and using a wooden sandal. But it makes so much noise when the sannyasin walks, you can hear from almost half a mile away that he is coming. And on a cement road or walking on the verandah in the university... The whole university knows.

The whole university used to know me, know that I was coming or going; there was no need to see me, just my sandals were enough. Now, one of my professors, Awasthi, a very loving man asked me, "Why do you choose strange things? Now, there are thousands of students, hundreds of professors – and I have been to many universities as a professor – but I have never come across a single student using wooden sandals and disturbing the whole university."

I said, "That's not right. If you are disturbed that means you don't have any control of your own mind. My wooden sandals, what can they do to you? Otherwise there are so many noises around, you will be continually disturbed: the car is passing by, the bus is passing by, somebody's horn – and in India you have continually…

Here I have not used the horn at all, but in India you have to use it every minute. There is no other way, otherwise you cannot move: a cow is standing there, a buffalo is standing there, a few people are standing and gossiping in the middle of the road… Particularly in places like Varanasi, where people go on leaving bulls as a religious thing – it is thought to be a great virtue.

The bull is Shiva's devotee, his symbol. So in a Shiva temple you will find a bull outside the temple. Shiva is inside, and the bull is sitting outside. He is Shiva's bodyguard, servant, devotee – everything. And whenever Shiva wants to move around, he rides on the bull.

So it has become a convention for hundreds of years that people bring bulls and leave them in Varanasi, because Varanasi is thought to be Shiva's city. And according to Hindu mythology it is the ancientmost city in the world. Perhaps it is true; it seems to be. The whole structure of the city, particularly the old city, seems to be really ancient.

So in Varanasi there are thousands of bulls, and to feed those bulls is a religious thing. A man may be dying, starving, but you will not bother about him: the bull has to be fed. If a bull comes to a vegetable shop and starts eating you cannot prevent him. No, he has a license from Shiva, he has simply to be allowed. When he goes, he goes. You cannot disturb him. He can eat sweets in a sweet shop, he can eat vegetables, fruits, whatsoever he wants; and he is completely free.

The only free being in India is the bull, particularly in Varanasi.

And nobody can beat the bull, nobody can do any harm to him. In Varanasi it was such a trouble. You go on honking the horn, but the bull does not care – and the bull is sitting just in front of your car. Unless you get out, push him, persuade him to move… And they are well fed because they are free, nobody can prevent them. Just to travel a small distance you have to start one hour earlier, because on the way everything is possible.

I used to speak in the Theosophical Society in Varanasi, and the place where I stayed was just five minutes' walk away. But it took one hour to drive, so I told my host, "It is better if we can walk and reach there without this trouble and without troubling so many of Shiva's devotees – because they are everywhere and they are resting and sitting. They have no other work – eating, walking, sitting, fighting."

I told Awasthi, "All these disturbances are going on around you."

He said, "I know all those disturbances are going on, but still your sandal stands separate. It is impossible to forget that you are around, even in all this noise. Why have you chosen this sandal? Just to annoy people, or…?"

I said, "No, not to annoy anybody. This keeps me alert. And my feeling is that they were not chosen to avoid leather, because Hindus are not against killing animals; they sacrificed animals. But they *have* chosen it. Jainas, who are vegetarians – nonviolent, against sacrifice – they have not chosen even the wooden sandal. They walk without anything, just naked feet; Buddhists also, just naked feet. So this reasoning, that wooden sandals have been chosen so that leather can be avoided, is nonsense – because you see the same sannyasin sitting on the leather of a lion. That is the traditional seat for a Hindu monk: the full leather of a lion, even with the head!

"So for a man who is sitting on the lion's leather, or a tiger's leather or a deer's leather, what problem has he to make shoes? That reason is not applicable. My reason is that when you walk on a wooden sandal you cannot fall asleep once. You can walk miles, you cannot fall asleep; that noise will keep you continually waking up, like an alarm. And it does keep you alert.

"If you start watching it, observing it, it is far better than breathing and watching the breath, because breath is a subtle thing, so you will miss it very soon: within a few seconds your mind will wander. But that click-clock, click-clock, click-clock hits you continually, as if somebody is hitting you on your head – click-clock, click-clock... How can you go astray? It has been of immense help for meditation."

Awasthi said, "You are simply impossible. It is just mischief. But you are now making a philosophy out of it."

I still say that I was not making a philosophy out it. It was not mischief If somebody is disturbed, that simply means that the man is not very centered. Otherwise somebody walking on the wooden sandal... If you are disturbed, then you will be disturbed by anything: a dog will start barking, a crow may be sitting on the roof calling you; you will be disturbed by anything. Sometimes, if there is nothing happening, *that* may disturb you: "What is the matter? – no noise, nothing is happening?"

But he insisted, "Whatsoever you say, I know that this is mischief."

I said, "If you already know, then there is no question of disputing the fact. I have explained it to you. If you want to refute me, I can bring a pair for you; I have a spare pair. Just start and you'll see."

He said, "You will make a buffoon out of me too! You are notorious for your sandals; now you want to play the trick on me."

I said, "No, just do it in your house, there's no need to go outside. Just do it in your house and see how it keeps you alert."

He seemed interested – just a little more persuasion... His wife came out and she said, "You are spoiling my husband. I will not allow these wooden sandals in my house. If you want wooden sandals and this meditation, do it anywhere else in the university, but not in my house. I have been tolerating even this boy's sandals for two years, and now he is persuading you."

Awasthi said to me, "This is true. I was almost on the verge of telling you to bring them. I have been trying meditation, but I have never been successful, because with breathing it is so subtle that the mind moves away easily. Your idea is good, but my wife..."

I said, "You can try them outside; others' wives will get disturbed" – because he was living in the professors colony. "You can walk on the verandah of other people's houses, so why should you be worried? Nobody can prevent me. I have already established the precedent – just go."

He said, "Let me think about it."

The next day I came with a pair. He said, "No, because I inquired of my neighbors. They said, 'Awasthi, if you do this then we are all going to complain against you that you should be removed from this colony to another colony; this is too much. This boy is enough. When he comes to meet you he wakes every-body. And a strange time he chooses – three o'clock in the morning! – and we cannot do anything against him. We have reported it to the vice-chancellor. The vice-chancellor says that he says it is a meditation.'"

Now, in India you cannot prevent anybody from any kind of meditation. That word is enough! When I started teaching people Dynamic Meditation, there was trouble everywhere, even in my own house. My uncle started doing it, and the neighbor filed a case against him in the court. My uncle told me, "This is a difficult meditation. That neighbor was my friend, and he would not normally do such a thing, but he is so angry that he says, 'unless you stop this meditation I am going to fight the case, because you disturb me early in the morning; when one really feels like falling into a deep sleep, that is the time of your Dynamic!"

But I told my uncle – and he is our sannyasin; he was here just a few days ago – "Don't be worried. You just say that this is our religion, and this is our med-itation." Once you say "meditation" in India, there is no problem.

When he came here, I asked, "What happened to the case?"

He said, "We have won the case, because I said, 'This is our meditation,' and I produced the book.

"The judge read the description and he said, 'If it is a meditation, then... The court has no power over religion.' So he told the neighbor, 'You have to accept it, there is no other way. This is his meditation. If you want to do it, you can also do it. Why get unnecessarily boiled up and angry in your bed? – better you also start.'"

The neighbor was very irritated with the court.

He said, "This is strange – the court suggesting, 'You also start, why waste time? And if it is meditation, we have no jurisdiction over religion.'"

It may appear as mischief – it was not. My mischief was the same shape as now; my shoes are still the same shape.

This is the shape of the wooden one I dropped because now it would disturb my meditation! Now I don't need any help from it; rather, it is a disturbance. That's why I changed it!

the distillation of rebellious spirits

Osho,
You have been speaking about the importance of being oneself. Could you
talk about the paradox of being an individual and melting into the commune?

There is no paradox as such, as far as the individual and his melting into the commune is concerned. The question has arisen out of a confusion between two words: *individuality* and *personality*.

Yes, with personality there is trouble. The personality cannot melt into anything – into love, into meditation, into friendship. The reason is that the personality is a very thin mask given to the individual by the society. And every society's effort has been, up till now, to deceive you and everybody, and to focus your attention on the personality as if it is your individuality. The personality is that which is given by others to you.

Individuality is that which you are born with which is your self nature: nobody can give it to you, and nobody can take it away.

Personality can be given and can be taken away. Hence, when you become identified with your personality you start becoming afraid of losing it. So anywhere when you see that a boundary has come beyond which you will have to melt, the personality withdraws. It cannot go beyond the limit it knows. It is very thin, an imposed layer. In deep love it will evaporate. In great friendship it will not be found at all.

In any kind of communion the death of the personality is absolute.

And you feel identified with the personality: you have been told that you are this by your parents, teachers, neighbors, friends – they have all been molding your personality, giving a shape to it. And they have made something of you which you are not and which you can never be. Hence you are miserable, confined in this personality. This is your imprisonment. But you are also afraid to come out of it because you don't know that you have anything more than this.

It is almost a situation like this: you think your clothes are you. Then naturally you will be afraid to stand naked. It is not a question only of the fear of dropping the clothes, but the fear that if you drop the clothes there will be nobody, and everybody will see that there is emptiness, you are hollow within. Your clothes go on giving you substance. The personality is afraid, and it is very natural that it should be afraid.

As far as individuality is concerned, once you know your individuality... And my religion is nothing but a process of individuation, finding, discovering your individuality. And in that finding – this is the most important step – you discard personality, you take away the identity; you withdraw from the personality and you start looking at it from a distance.

Create that distance between you and personality.

You have come so close that you cannot see the separation. Once you have understood that you are somebody other than your personality... You have been thinking up to now that you were somebody else: You are A, and you have been thinking up to now that you are B. That fallacy is bound to be afraid, that fallacy cannot be in love – there is no possibility.

That's why lovers are constantly in conflict. It is not their individualities conflicting, it is their personalities in conflict. Both want the other to melt, and both are afraid that if they melt they are lost, they are gone.

Friendship has disappeared from the world just as love has disappeared, because friendship is possible only when you meet naked, as you are – not as people want you to be, not as you should be, but simply just as you are. When two persons open up to each other just as they are, friendship grows.

When two persons are ready to drop their masks, they have taken a tremendous step towards religiousness. So love, friendship, anything that helps you to drop the mask, is taking you towards religion.

But the pseudo-religions have done just the opposite. They are against love. You can understand now, why they are against love: because love will destroy the personality, and the pseudo-religion depends on your personality. The pseudo-religions have made a great effort – all these churches and priests and sermons – and what are they doing? Their whole work is to create the personality. They manufacture personality – of course, different kinds of personality: a Hindu personality, a Christian personality, a Mohammedan personality. These are different models of personalities. All these religions are just like factories creating different models of cars, but the function is the same.

The pseudo-religions are all afraid of love. They talk about love, and they teach you marriage. They talk about love and they say marriages are made in heaven. It is not something that you have to find out; God has already found the person for you. The astrologer will help you, the palmist will help you, the priest will help you, the parents will help you to find them – because God has already created the person for you, you are not to find the person on your own.

They prevent you from loving, and they go on saying great things about love. But their great words about love are bogus; they have no substance in them.

Jesus says, "God is love." There *is* no God – then what about love? So as far as Jesus' love is concerned, there is no love. If God is love, then with God's disappearance love also disappears.

And to make God synonymous with love is a beautiful strategy. He has raised love to such a high pedestal – do you think it can happen between a man and a woman? God is going to happen when you fall in love? That is sin!

God is love when you love humanity, when you love words which don't mean anything. Have you ever met humanity anywhere? Can you imagine that some-day you will encounter humanity? You will meet only human beings. Humanity is simply a word.

"Love humanity" – it gives you the idea of something abstract. "Love God, love truth" – the sentences seem to be linguistically right, but existentially they mean nothing.

And you have to remember it: that most of our beautiful words are only words. You can play with them, you can create poetry, but you cannot live them because words cannot be lived. There is nothing living in them.

Now, just think of the idea: "Love God." What does it mean? How does one fall in love with God? You have not seen God. You don't know him. How are you going to recognize that this fellow is God?

I was watching a film, *The Difficulties of an Ordinary God*. It is a beautiful film. A man starts seeing a very ordinary God, just like an old hobo, with a hat cricketers use. Now, God in a hat which cricketers use! And he looks also like a cricket player. He is very old, but must have been in his young days a cricket player. And when God declared to this man, "You don't recognize me: I am God, I created the world," the man said, "My God! You created the world! Don't say it to anybody otherwise people will think you are mad."

But the old man insisted, he said, "You want some proof?"

The young man said, "I don't want any proof. Just seeing you is enough to know that you are no God. This is not the way – that God suddenly stops you on the way; that you are going somewhere and he wants a lift! This is a strange meeting. I have heard about the God Moses met on the mountain and Jesus heard from the sky, and Mohammed – but God asking for a lift?"

But the old man was stubborn, he said, "I will give you proof." And he gives him proof: he simply disappears.

The young man looks all around – he was in the car sitting by his side – he is not there! He says, "My God! Perhaps he really was God, but what a funny God! And I missed the opportunity."

The old man appeared again, he said, "Look, when I was gone you started thinking you had missed an opportunity."

But seeing him again the young man said, "You did some trick, you must know some magic. But I cannot accept you as God. Your clothes seem to be purchased from a secondhand place, or you have stolen them. They don't fit you, they are too loose and too dirty – as if you have not taken a bath for many years."

But the old man said, "God is so pure that he does not need any bath or anything. And of course the clothes are very old, because I am very old. I have told you that I created the world; at that time I created these clothes. Since then I have not created anything, so they are very ancient."

The young man said, "What to do about you? Where do you want to get out?"

He said, "Anywhere, because I am everywhere."

The young man said, "Then why did you want a lift?"

He said, "Just because I see a potential in you, that you can become my messenger."

The young man said, "My God! Your messenger? If I say to anybody that you are God they will think I am mad!"

But God said, "Try," gave his picture to him and disappeared.

The young man looked at the picture and said, "It is better to keep silent about the whole thing. Either I am hallucinating, dreaming…"

He came home. His wife looked at him and said, "You look very worried."

He said, "No, nothing, there is nothing."

She said, "But you look very worried and pale and afraid, as if you have seen some ghost or something."

He said, "My God! You think I have seen something?" He took out the picture and showed the wife: "Can you recognize this man?"

She said, "He looks like a hobo – perhaps an old cricket player, or maybe he just got a hat from some old clothes store. And what kind of clothes…? Where did you find this picture, and why did you bring it home?"

He said, "Can you keep this thing secret? I have something to tell you. Close the door. This man is God. He asked for a lift."

His wife looked at her husband and said, "Wait, I will phone the doctor. What are you saying? – God asking for a lift in your car? And he has given this picture to you?"

He said, "Yes, he has given this picture to me so that I can become his messenger. He wants me to become his messenger."

The wife said, "The first thing is, meet the doctor."

He tried hard: "I am perfectly sane, there is no problem."

But the wife said, "If you think this man is God, it is certain that there is some problem!"

So she takes him to the doctor, and the doctor is also puzzled. He said, "I have seen many ideas about God but this is an absolutely novel idea. Where did you get this picture?"

He said, "From God himself. He himself gave it to me by his own hand; and he has shown a miracle too." And he told them about the miracle.

The wife, the doctor, the nurses, they all laughed; they said, "This is…!"

So he said, "Wait." He raised his eyes upwards and said, "God, now please help me – because these are all my friends. The doctor is my friend, the family doctor; my wife, the nurse – there is nobody from the outside, we are all like family. Please appear, otherwise they are all going to think that I am mad."

And suddenly the man came out from the ceiling!

They all looked at him, and he said, "Wherever you need me I will be present; you just go on spreading the word."

But he said, "This is a very difficult word, just because of your picture. Can't you dress a little better?"

But he said, "No, this are my clothes, and this is the way I am."

Now, four or five people had seen him and they were all shocked: "This man is not mad, there is something in it." The whole town became agog with the rumor that five people had seen God. And the thing became so hot that the church became immediately annoyed and irritated thinking that this was a joke. "This man, and God!" The picture was printed in the newspapers and everybody was laughing: "If this is God, then everything is finished."

The problem became so much that the church had to call a meeting of the elders and force this man who was the messenger to appear before the council and prove that this was God. He tried, he told them, "Many times he has showed me miracles. Just this morning when I was shaving in my bathroom, a doubt arose in me that perhaps something was wrong with me; it was possible that I was simply fantasizing. And he immediately looked at me from the mirror. My picture disappeared and his picture was there in the mirror, and he said, 'Again I go on giving you proof, and you are again doubting.'"

And then at the church, the young man appeared before the church council. The high priest was there, and they were determined to punish this man if... And they said, "You say that this man is God?"

He said, "I have to say it. I have seen him many times. He has shown me many miracles. This morning he appeared in my mirror."

Everybody laughed, and this poor man said, "He has chosen me as his messenger."

They said, "This time he has really chosen a great messenger! Moses, Mohammed, Buddha, Jesus – they were some people – but this man is just a clerk in a railway station. Now what qualities have you got that he would choose you as the messenger?"

He said, "I don't know. I don't have any qualities, and I have never dreamed in my life that God would choose me. But he has chosen me and he has promised that if there is a need he will come to support me."

So the church council asked, "Then let him appear."

And they all were amazed that the door behind the priest opened, and God appeared. There was silence for a moment. Seeing God, the priest gathered courage and said, "You think you are God?"

He said, "I don't think, I am. And this is my messenger. But," He said, "you can understand the difficulties of an ordinary God. I am an ordinary God, that's why I have chosen an ordinary messenger, because to find an extraordinary messenger would be very difficult for me. You can see I am an ordinary, poor God. So don't be angry with this poor clerk; what he is saying is absolutely right."

How are you going to recognize God if he meets you in a cricketer's hat?

– and of course he will be wearing some kind of hat – or without a hat. If he is like me, bald, then he will be using a hat, some kind of hat.

This reminds me of the man I have been talking to you about: my geography teacher, Chotelal Munde. He had cursed me because I made him famous as "Munde"; so much so that once he had to sign himself as Chotelal Munde. That day he was just fire... I had asked the whole class for a collection. Twenty rupees were collected, and we made a money order in Chotelal Munde's name. And we arranged with the postman, "Come into his class when he is taking our class" – we gave him the time. So he appeared exactly on time, with a twenty-rupee money order, sender anonymous.

Chotelal Munde was a poor man with a big family. He could not lose twenty rupees. In those days twenty rupees was a lot of money. In India, in those days, a man could live on two rupees for the whole month, things were so cheap. Before the First World War things were so cheap that servants used to get one rupee, two rupees, three rupees a month at the most. And that was enough. Twenty rupees...

But the postman said, "You will have to sign 'Chotelal Munde', because it is in the name of Chotelal Munde." He thought for a moment, and he said, "I know who this anonymous sender is. He is here, and I will teach him a lesson because now he has forced me even to sign 'Munde.'" And he had to sign; he signed "Chotelal Munde." Then he came to me and he said, "I curse you, that one day you will become bald headed just like me."

I said, "That's perfectly okay. There is no harm in it."

And he said, "Anonymous!"

I remembered him just a few days ago when Sheela brought a newspaper which said that in Oregon people have found a new word for a rascal: *Rajneeshee*. That was Chotelal Munde's second curse, that "You will be known as 'the rascal.'"

I said, "This is perfectly good." Both his predictions have come true.

If you meet God in any dress, in any form, you will not be able to accept him, because there is no way for you to recognize him. There has never been any way to recognize him. That's why I say Jesus and Moses and Mohammed were all hallucinating. They had no grounds to declare that that was God's voice because they had never heard it before. So what evidence was there that this voice was God's voice? If they saw somebody standing before them, how did they recognize that this person was God? There was no way.

Jesus says, "God is love." But God is unproved, just a vague word. He makes *love* also a vague, meaningless word. Between you and God, what kind of love will happen? What will be the relationship between you and God? All the religions have tried to find some kind of relationship with God. Many religions call him father. There are a few which call him mother. There are a few which call him the beloved; for them he is a she, not a he.

In India there is a religion which believes that he is a lover and they are his beloveds. These people who believe God to be their lover and themselves to be his beloveds – in the day of course they are ashamed so they cannot move about in women's clothes, but in the night they do wear women's clothes, because the lover will be coming to meet them. And they sleep with a statue of Krishna, their lover.

Now what kinds of foolishness have been going on for centuries? And it is not that these people are idiots. Very scholarly people are among them, very learned, but there is a blind spot. In every religious – so-called religious – person's mind there is a blind spot. Everywhere else is light, but on that spot is complete darkness. Just as there are people who are color-blind, these people, in a certain way, in a certain aspect of their mind, are blind.

Bernard Shaw was color-blind. He came to know it when he was sixty. For sixty years such an intelligent man was not aware that he was color-blind. On his sixtieth birthday somebody sent him a present, a suit, but the person forgot to send him a matching tie. So with his secretary he went to the market, because he liked the coat, the pants – everything was really the best available. So he went with his secretary to find a matching tie for it. And when he was looking for the tie – the suit was yellow – he looked at a green tie.

The woman secretary nudged him and told him, "This won't look right: a green tie on a yellow suit. It will look odd."

The shopkeeper also said, "Yes sir, she is right. I was also worried about that."

He said, "But isn't it the same color? – my suit and this tie?"

They said, "No, this is green and this is yellow."

He said, "My God! I have never in my whole life thought that these are two different colors." He was blind to green; it appeared to him as yellow. Green did not exist for him at all.

Many people remain color-blind their whole life and never come to know about it. It was just a coincidence... If he had passed sixty years he could have passed forty more; there was no problem in it. It was just a coincidence.

In the same way, every pseudo-religion creates a blind spot in your mind, and from that blind spot it goes on manipulating you. That blind spot creates your personality; and because the blind spot creates your personality you can't see anything wrong in it.

It is all wrong for the simple reason that it is not you; it is something glued over you. It fulfills other people's needs – it destroys you completely. And naturally when you are covered by a painted paper you will be afraid to go in the rain. You know that you will start disappearing.

The question is: on the one hand I teach you individuality, on the other hand I teach you to melt with the commune. There seems to be a paradox; there is none.

The personality is afraid; hence the personality will prevent you from melting in all the situations where melting is needed. And it seems absolutely logical that the personality should be afraid. But individuality is never afraid of melting, because it is your nature; there is no way to lose it.

You can melt in the commune, and by melting you will simply be more authentically individual than you were before. The very step – that you dared to melt – is going to throw away your personality, and only the individuality will remain.

Individuality is your intrinsic nature. Nobody can take it, nobody can steal it. If it were possible to take it away, society would have taken it away already; they would not have taken any chances. They would have taken the individuality from every child as he was born. But because it cannot be taken away, there is no way, they have tried another strategy: cover it. It can only be covered or uncovered.

I teach you to melt in the commune because that will uncover you. It will destroy your personality. If you are too attached, you will find excuses for not melting, but those excuses are coming from your personality, not from your individuality. And the sooner the personality melts the better, because out of that melting you will find for the first time who you are. And you will be surprised that all along you have been playing a role which was prompted by the society, by the educationist, by the priest, by the parents. They were all prompting you, manufacturing you for a certain career.

I was staying in a friend's house in Amritsar. Early in the morning I went into the garden. My friend's young child, not more than eight years old, was also there picking flowers. Seeing me, he came to me and we started talking. I asked him, "What are you going to become in life?"

And he said, "My mother wants me to become a doctor, my father wants me to become an engineer, my uncle wants me to become a scientist, my younger sister wants me to become the prime minister; and as far as I am concerned, nobody asks me. And I don't know either. If somebody asks the way you have asked, I don't know who I want to become."

But this is the situation of every child. He is being dragged by others, forced by others this way and that. Of course he lands somewhere, he becomes something, but he loses his being. In this becoming, he has lost his most precious treasure.

Hence, I teach you melting with the commune. The commune is only a device for you to melt. What will be melting will not be really you, only your personality. And what will emerge out of that will be you.

But right now you don't know who you are. And the one you think you are, you are not. That which you are not is going to melt, certainly. And that which you are is going to be a revelation, to you and to everybody. That is going to be a finding; and it brings tremendous joy, ecstasy.

In just coming to know who you are, all your fears, phobias, and mind problems simply disappear, evaporate, because they were part of the personality.

All your inner conflicts are no longer there.

There is only harmony and a silence which is so profound that there is no way to imagine it. And to see one's original being is to see all that is worth seeing, because from there the door opens towards existence.

So I am teaching you everything that will help you to melt. I teach you love, not marriage. I teach you friendship, or even better, friendliness. I teach you melting with the commune.

The commune is not the family. You are born in a family... You have to understand a little bit about the family. The family is a very strange institution, and one
of the most poisonous institutions. The parents think they own you. The mother
thinks she has given birth to you, the father thinks he has given birth to you: you
are his blood.

It was a continual problem in my childhood with my parents. I would object
whenever they would mention or indicate indirectly that I belonged to them.
I said, "That's absolutely wrong. Forget the idea of possessing me. Yes, I have
come through you, but just because of that you don't become my possessor;
I am not your possession. A child comes through you: you are a passage. If
passages started possessing, then any road you pass by will call to you, 'Where
are you going? I possess you, I have brought you here.'"

My parents would say, "You can say anything you want to say to us, but such
things, not in front of others. If anybody hears that you are telling your father, 'You
are just a road'..."

I said, "But I have to say these things because you provoke me; the whole
fault lies in you. You start – of course unconsciously, but you start thinking that
you possess me."

He wanted me to become a scientist, and I told him, "You should leave it to
me. I am now mature enough to decide in what direction to go. And I am thankful that you have brought me up to this point; but now, leave me alone. And this
I am not saying out of any ungratefulness; I am grateful that you have made me
capable of choosing my path. But one day I have to tell you: 'Now, leave
me alone.' It is shocking, it hurts, but what to do? You are the cause because
you have raised the expectation that this is what you would like."

He was rarely angry with me, but on that point he was very angry; and he
was right in everybody's eyes. The whole family was in agreement with him. The
neighborhood was in agreement with him, "What is the point in going to an arts
college and studying philosophy? You will be good for nothing."

In India many universities have closed their philosophy departments, and
other universities which still have a philosophy department only get girls as their
students. I myself was with two girls – only three students. And girls join it for
a different purpose: because in the philosophy department the professors are
continuously in need of students, they are afraid to fail anybody. If people don't
come then their department is closed, and they will be unemployed; so they
persuade students to come. And for girls in India, a degree is only for marriage. A
postgraduate girl will get a rich husband, a cultured family. She will move in the
highest circles immediately. She has nothing to do with philosophy.

One of my professors was a Bengali, and he believed in celibacy – fanatically.
In departments of philosophy you will find all kinds of strange creatures. Whether
it was raining or not, whether it was hot or not, sun or not, he would walk with his
umbrella just covering almost his face so he did not have to see any woman. The
university was full of girls, and in his class there were two girls. Because of those
two girls, he used to teach with closed eyes.

For me that was a great opportunity; I used to sleep. For six months it went perfectly well. One day the girls didn't turn up, but that was my time to sleep, so I went to sleep. That day he was teaching with open eyes – I did not think that he would teach with his eyes open. So he said, "You can open your eyes. I know you also believe in celibacy."

I said, "For six months you were thinking this? I was simply sleeping. I believe in sleeping, not in celibacy."

He said, "This is strange; I was thinking you are just like me, and I was feeling great respect for you. You deceived me for six months."

I said, "I will deceive you in future too. It is not a deception, this is just my time to sleep. And it was good that you were teaching with your eyes closed, so there was no trouble, no conflict – because nobody was listening.

"Those girls are not interested in philosophy in any way, and what you are teaching is so much crap that once in a while in my sleep when I hear it, I just throw it out. And those two girls have nothing to do... You can teach, you are paid for it. But those girls are just earning a degree so that they can get a good marriage partner.

"I come here just to sleep, and you come here to teach; our ideas are different. I don't say to you, 'Don't disturb me,' and I don't disturb you either. I am sound asleep and I don't snore. Have I ever snored?"

He said, "You are strange, you drive me nuts! You take the question in such a direction where I have nothing... Now you are asking about snoring. Come to the point."

I said, "I am exactly on the point. I am saying, have I ever disturbed you? If I have not disturbed you then what is the complaint against me? I could have not listened to you with open eyes. That's what those two girls are doing, but they are not interested in philosophy at all. While you are teaching with your closed eyes, they are talking about clothes, about their saris, and inquiring where to get this from, and how much...? That's what they are doing.

"Am I such a fool that I should listen to those two girls and you? Only I am caught in between. So I simply sleep; that's the only way to escape from all this. And you know perfectly well from now on that I am not deceiving you. If you had asked before I would have told you; it was just your assumption. You presumed that I am also a celibate, you projected that idea."

But he was so afraid of seeing a woman. And I said. "Now that you have raised the question I would like to say to you that your celibacy is not worth anything. You can't even look at a woman? Are you so afraid? Your umbrella is nothing but your cowardice. You are continually carrying it all around the university, and everybody is laughing. People can't see your face, you can't see people's faces." He would walk so fast that nobody could start walking with him or talking with him. And he had a really good walking pace – fast, covered with his umbrella.

"How long is this umbrella going to protect your celibacy, you tell me. And have you heard of any scripture that says an umbrella can help you to remain celibate? Have you seen any pictures of Mahavira, Buddha, Krishna carrying an umbrella? You are the first celibate in the world who is trying to be celibate by using an umbrella. And I know perfectly well that you must be looking; here in class also you must be looking sometimes, just opening your eyes a little bit."

He said, "But how do you know, because you are fast asleep?"

I said, "How do you know that I am fast asleep? You must be looking. How long can you keep your eyes closed? And then to teach…"

The family tries to make something of you.

My family wanted me to become a scientist; they saw a potential. I said, "I do understand that as a scientist I will be paid more, I will be respected more. As a philosopher perhaps I may remain unemployed. But the time has come that I should choose my own path. If it leads into the desert at least I will be happy that I have followed my own path; there will be no grudge against anybody. Following your path, even if I become the greatest scientist, I will not be happy because I have been forced; it is a kind of slavery. And you have the power to force me, but remember that I will not in any way allow anything to be imposed upon me."

That time my father became angry. He said, "Okay, go to the arts department but I am not going to give you any money."

I said, "That's settled. Money is yours; I am not yours. If you don't want to give me money, that I can understand. And I can understand that if I go to the science department, you are ready to give me money because then I am following your desire. You are ready to give money to me only if I remain under your control.

"So that's perfectly clear: you are using money to force me in a certain direction which I refuse. But," I said, "you will suffer repentance just because you mentioned money. Do you think you can force me by threatening that you are not going to give me any money?"

I left the house. For two years he was continually coming, saying, "Forget that and forgive me. I am really sorry that I mentioned the money. I can see your trouble, and I am the cause of it" – because at night I used to work as an editor in a newspaper just to earn money so that in the day I could join the university. But I said, "How can I accept money from you?"

One day, when tears came to his eyes, I said, "Okay, if you insist, just put the money on the table. I will not take it from your hand. From the table I can take it because with the table I have no problem, no trouble, no conflict." So that's the way it continued the remaining four years. He would put it on the table and I would take it from the table, but not from him – "because," I said to him, "that strategy is ugly."

But the family exploits every child because it has the power of money, prestige, the power of numbers. And a child is just a child; how can he revolt? And the family poisons the child: you are a Hindu, a Muslim, a Christian. It poisons the child: you are a republican, you are a democrat, you are a socialist, you are a communist. It goes on poisoning him. And this whole poisoning piles up and becomes your personality.

The commune is not your family… Or it is your *real* family.

Strangely enough, every boy hates his father, every girl hates her mother; but nobody says so. On the surface everything is polite and nice, just goody-goody. Deep down there are wounds. All the wounds that have been inflicted upon you in your childhood you will carry your whole life. And those wounds will work upon you in such a way that they will spoil your whole meaning.

For example, I see that the girl who hates her mother will behave exactly like the mother – because from where is she going to learn? The mother was the first woman she knew. She hates her because the mother forced her to be someone who she is not, and now she has to carry that burden.

So on the one hand she hates her; on the other hand that was the woman she came to know most intimately. So in her gestures, in her language, in her reactions, in everything she will repeat her mother. She will be just a carbon copy: the personality that she is carrying is her mother's personality.

No wonder that people hate themselves too. It is for the simple reason that the personality they think they are, is the personality given by the people whom they wanted to rebel against, but against whom they were helpless.

Sigmund Freud has made a significant point about it: that the idea of God as father must have arisen as a compensation. Somewhere back in primitive prehistory days, some young man must have killed his father because that was the only way to be himself. But then the repentance for killing the father...

Sigmund Freud has no historical facts about it, there is no history available, but his deduction is psychological, not historical. He says that every boy is going to hate his father. He will go on hating him.

But in hating one's own father, the conscience is disturbed. To console the conscience, he starts worshipping the father.

In India particularly – because I know India more than any other country – the son has to touch the feet of the father, of the mother, of everybody who is older than him. This is just a way to help him: by touching the feet of the father, he balances his hate with respect, and he feels at ease that he respects his father.

If you don't hate your father, I don't think there is any need to touch the feet of the father. Perhaps once in a while, out of gratitude, you may touch them; but that cannot be a formality, it can only be an informal happening. Right now, people touch the feet, but there is no feeling in it. How can there be feeling in it? There is hate inside: this is the man who has spoiled your life.

The family becomes your basic unit; so if your family is in conflict with the neighbor, then it is your family – right or wrong, you will fight alongside your family.

In front of my house lived a goldsmith – he was a little eccentric. One of his eccentricities was that whenever he would go to the market or to the river, he would lock his house – even if his wife was inside, his children were inside. He would lock the house from the outside and would pull the lock two or three times to see whether it was really locked. And if anybody created suspicion – and I was continually... I would stand just a few houses away when he was going to the river, and I would say, "Soniji" that means "goldsmithji" – "have you forgotten to check your lock?"

He would say, "Have I forgotten?" and back he would go.

Once when he was taking a bath in the river, I told him, "Today you have forgotten."

He said, "Really?" I said, "I was sitting in front of you."

And half-bathed he ran back first to check.

He was in some conflict with my father – a legal case about some land. The land really belonged to him, but my father had paid his younger brother for it. The younger brother had pretended that it belonged to him, so my father paid him. And on the registry day, it was found out that the man was deceiving: the land belonged to the other brother. He would not return the money, and my father would not give up control of the land to the other brother to whom it belonged; so there was a legal case.

I told my father, "I will be coming to support the eccentric goldsmith."

He said, "What! You will be a witness against me?"

I said, "Of course. I know that you have paid, but that was your fault. You should have found out to whom the land belonged before you paid. And that poor eccentric goldsmith, what fault is it of his? – the land belongs to him. And anyway he is far poorer than you; so even if you lose the money, it is better than if he loses the ground, because he is really poor."

My father said, "But you don't understand a simple thing: being against your own father...?"

I said, "It is not a question of being against my own father. I don't believe in this 'right or wrong, my family...' And I know that your claim is right, but it is your mistake; you should suffer. And I have been harassing that poor goldsmith, so it is a chance to help him. I will be helping him."

The family wants you to be with it. I have seen families, generations after generations fighting in the courts, destroying each other, killing each other, for generations. Because your forefathers were against somebody – you have nothing to do with these people who are living now, they have not done anything wrong to you – somewhere in the past, four, five, six generations ago... You may not even know the names of the people who fought, but the enmity goes on.

The family tries to disconnect you from the whole society, just as the nation divides you from other nations. It is the same strategy of division. A commune is not a family. Nobody here is father, nobody here is mother. Nobody here is brother or sister. Nobody here is husband or wife.

Here are only individuals, and these individuals have decided to live in freedom, and to support each other in living the way of freedom. Nobody possesses anybody. Nobody has any hold on anybody. Everybody is supportive of whatsoever you are, of whatsoever you can be.

The family is dictatorial. A commune is simply supportive. I don't give you even guidelines, because even guidelines may become dictatorial in your mind, because your mind has been made by the society. Even if I give you guidelines you may think these are commandments.

Guidelines are not commandments. You are not to follow them, just under-standing them is enough. Then follow your path. Perhaps on your path something that I had said may be of use, or perhaps nothing will be of any use. So there is no need to have faith in it.

A commune is a gathering of free individuals – undemanding, non-forcing, non-dictatorial – just supporting and helping. Because alone it will be difficult; you will find it almost impossible to be yourself in the so-called society, because that society is not supportive. Yes, if it supports, it supports conditionally; it is always a bargain, a business. The society will do this for you if you are ready to do that for the society: a simple contract.

A commune is not a business, a relationship. There is no contract: just a few people who feel imprisoned in the society drop out and create a gathering of similar rebels. They are all rebels, and they are all supportive of each other. Whatever one's rebellion, and whatever one wants to be, the commune's support is unconditional. But the commune can exist only if you merge with it. If you keep yourself aloof, there is no commune because there is no communion. Hence I say, dissolve yourself in the commune.

And remember that you will become an individual by this dissolving. You will not lose your individuality, you will find it – that's the only way to find it. In the society you can go on changing your personality, but you will never find your individuality. You can change from a Catholic to a communist, but that will not make any difference at all. You will not go any longer to the Vatican, but now to the Kremlin – those red stars will be holy. Now Russia will become your holy land.

You have simply changed from one ditch and you have fallen into another ditch. Maybe they have a little different shape, but ditches are ditches. From one jail you move into another jail. Of course, while you are moving from one jail to another, just in between you will have a little taste of freedom. Don't think that this is going to be the taste of the other jail. That is only in between.

Escape! Don't go to the other jail; escape from any jail. And never go again into the same structure, because all structures are the same.

A commune is an immensely spiritual phenomenon: you are with people and yet you are alone. Nobody trespasses on your aloneness. Everybody respects your aloneness. You are with many people, you are together, but nobody tries to impose any condition, any relationship, any bondage. Nobody takes from you any promise for tomorrow, because tomorrow you will be different, the other will be different. Who knows about tomorrow? When tomorrow comes we will see.

The commune has no tomorrow, it lives here and now. And it lives totally and intensely, because we are not living as a means to some other life. We are living as an end to itself.

Catholics are living for some other life; this life is only a ladder. And the same is true with all the religions: this life is to be sacrificed. They all teach you sacrifice – they really sacrifice you. You are all butchered – on different altars, in different temples – but you are all butchered.

The only way to save yourself from these butchers who are all around is to join together with similar kinds of rebels, so the way of revolution becomes strong, grounded, self-supporting. And then you find everybody is living intensely.

We are not living for another world, so why should we live lukewarm?

We should live real hot!

In Ahmedabad I used to go often on a bridge where there was a very big advertisement. I liked that advertisement; just one word was not right. It was an advertisement for a certain cold drink. The advertisement said, "Livva little hot, sippa Gold Spot" – Gold Spot is something like Coca-Cola. But they have found a really good slogan: "Livva little hot" – but why a little? That was my trouble. Sippa anything, but why a little?

Jayantibhai used to drive me over that bridge, and he would go fast when the board was there. And I would say, "Jayantibhai, wait!"

He said, "That is why I was going fast; otherwise you will see that board again..."

And I told him, "That board is really very philosophical – just a little mistake, but all philosophers have been making mistakes. A *little* hot? – that hurts. Be really hot, because there is nothing to sacrifice for."

All religions teach you to be martyrs. All families teach you to be martyrs. All nations teach you to be martyrs. It is a strange world. Why are people being taught to be suicidal? – because to be a martyr is just a good word for committing suicide. Nobody teaches living. Nobody encourages living. Nobody teaches you that you can be a little more hot – why are you just smoking with no fire? Many people are just smoking with no fire.

How long have you been smoking, and how long are you going to smoke? Create some fire!

And when there is real fire, there is no smoke. When it is really hot there is no smoke. Burn like a flame without any smoke! But everybody is telling you to keep a low profile. Why? Such a small life, why keep a low profile?

Jump as high as you can.

Dance as madly as you can.

Melt as totally as you can.

And out of that burning, living, melting, you will find your authenticity, your individuality. Individuality is never afraid.

In front of my house there was a tall tamarind tree. Now the tamarind tree is not very strong, its branches can break very easily. It was so tall, and I was always going and climbing it. My whole family would gather around and they would say, "Now stop, no further!" I would continue going higher, and they would shout, "Do you hear or not? No further."

I would say, "Till you stop shouting 'No further' I am going to climb. At the most I can fall – perhaps a few fractures; but the height is so challenging, it is calling me up. You shut up completely, then I will stop." When they saw that I had reached a place from where a fall was certain then they would shut up. And that was a condition: "Unless you stop trying to stop me, I will go on and on."

Only my grandfather used to say, "Don't be worried about anything. These people are all cowards. I would have loved to come with you but I am too old, but you should remember always that I am with you. So let them shout 'Stop!'"

Even neighbors would come and start shouting, "Stop!" But I had made it a condition again and again: "Unless you stop shouting, I will go still higher. And now it is getting really dangerous, so be quiet." They had to be quiet. But again, next time I would... And they would shout again, and I would say, "You don't understand. Just leave me alone! At least trust that I can also see that the branch is now getting thinner, and the wind is stronger, and the tree is swaying. I can also see it. Let me see and let me feel. And let me decide; don't decide for me. I hate that."

But every family goes on deciding for you.

A commune does not decide for you. At the most it helps you. So with the commune there is no paradox between individuality and melting. It is not a society, not a family. It is a gathering of rebels of all kinds. So there is no need to fit with each other and be like each other. All are rebels of different kinds. One thing is common, that they are rebels.

The rebellious spirit is the common factor that joins the commune and makes it one whole – without destroying anybody's individuality, without destroying anybody in any way.

conscience: a coffin for consciousness

Osho,
Is there any point in living?

Man has been brought up by all the traditions in a schizophrenic way.

It was helpful to divide man in every possible dimension, and create a conflict between the divisions. This way man becomes weak, shaky, fearful, ready to submit, surrender; ready to be enslaved by the priests, by the politicians, by anybody.

This question also arises out of a schizophrenic mind. It will be a little difficult for you to understand because you may have never thought that the division between ends and means is a basic strategy of creating a split in man.

Has living any meaning, any point, any worth? The question is: Is there some goal to be achieved by life, by living? Is there some place where you will reach one day by living? Living is a means; the goal, the attainment, somewhere far away, is the end. And that end will make it meaningful. If there is no end, then certainly life is meaningless; a God is needed to make your life meaningful.

First create the division between ends and means. That divides your mind. Your mind is always asking why? For what? And anything that has no answer to the question, "For what?" slowly, slowly becomes of no value to you. That's how love has become valueless. What point is there in love? Where is it going to lead you? What is going to be the achievement out of it? Will you attain to some utopia, some paradise? Of course, love has no point in that way. It is pointless.

What is the point of beauty? You see a sunset – you are stunned, it is so beautiful, but any idiot can ask the question, "What is the meaning of it?" and you will be without any answer. And if there is no meaning then why are you unnecessarily bragging about beauty?

A beautiful flower, or a beautiful painting, or beautiful music, beautiful poetry – they don't have any point. They are not arguments to prove something, neither are they means to achieve any end.

And living consists only of those things which are pointless.

Let me repeat it: living consists only of those things which have no point at all, which have no meaning at all – meaning in the sense that they don't have any goal, that they don't lead you anywhere, that you don't get anything out of them.

In other words, living is significant in itself. The means and ends are together, not separate.

And the strategy of all those who have been lustful for power, down the ages has been that means are means, and ends are ends. Means are useful because they lead you to the end. If they don't lead to your end, they are meaningless. In this way, they have destroyed all that is really significant. And they have imposed things on you which are absolutely insignificant.

Money has a point. A political career has a point. To be religious has a point, because that is the means to heaven, to God. Business has a point because immediately you see the end result. Business became important, politics became important, religion became important; poetry, music, dancing, love, friendliness, beauty, truth, all disappeared from your life.

A simple strategy, but it destroyed all that makes you significant, that gives ecstasy to your being. But the schizophrenic mind will ask, "What is the point of ecstasy?"

People have asked me, hundreds of people, "What is the meaning of meditation? What will we gain out of it? First, it is very difficult to attain – and even if we attain it, what is going to be the end result?"

It is very difficult to explain to these people that meditation is an end in itself. There is no end beyond it.

Anything that has an end beyond it is just for the mediocre mind. And anything which has its end in itself is for the really intelligent person.

But you will see the mediocre person becoming the president of a country, the prime minister of a country; becoming the richest man in the country, becoming the pope, becoming the head of a religion. But these are all mediocre people; their only qualification is their mediocrity. They are third rate and basically they are schizophrenic. They have divided their life into two parts: ends and means.

My approach is totally different: to make you one single whole.

So I want you to live just for life's sake.

The poets have defined art as for its own sake, there is nothing else beyond it: art for art's sake. It will not appeal to the mediocre at all because he counts things in terms of money, position, power. Is your poetry going to make you the prime minister of the country? – then it is meaningful. But in fact your poetry may make you just a beggar, because who is going to purchase your poetry?

I am acquainted with many kinds of geniuses who are living like beggars for the simple reason that they did not accept the mediocre way of life, and they did not allow themselves to become schizophrenic. They are living – of course they have a joy which no politician can ever know, they have a certain radiance which no billionaire is going to know. They have a certain rhythm to their heart of which these so-called religious people have no idea. But as far as their outside is concerned, they have been reduced by the society to live like beggars.

I would like you to remember one great, perhaps the greatest, Dutch painter: Vincent van Gogh. His father wanted him to become a religious minister, to live a life of respect – comfortable, convenient – and not only in this world, in the other world after death too. But Vincent van Gogh wanted to become a painter. His father said, "You are mad!"

He said, "That may be. To me, you are mad. I don't see any significance in becoming a minister because all I would be saying would be nothing but lies. I don't know God. I don't know whether there is any heaven or hell. I don't know whether man survives after death or not. I will be continually telling lies. Of course it is respectable, but that kind of respect is not for me; I will not be rejoicing in it. It will be a torture to my soul." The father threw him out.

He started painting – he is the first modern painter. You can draw a line at Vincent van Gogh: before him painting was ordinary. Even the greatest painters, like Michelangelo, are very small compared to Vincent van Gogh, because what they were painting was ordinary. Their painting was for the marketplace.

Michelangelo was painting for the churches his whole life; painting on church walls and church ceilings. He broke his backbone painting church ceilings, because to paint a ceiling you have to lie down on a high stool while you paint. It is a very uncomfortable position, and for days together, months together… But he was earning money, and he was earning respect. He was painting angels, Christ, God creating the world. His most famous painting is of God creating the world.

Vincent van Gogh starts a totally new dimension. He could not sell a single painting in his whole life. Now, who will say that his painting has any point? Not a single person could see that there was anything in his paintings. His younger brother used to send him money; enough so that he did not die of starvation, just enough for seven days' food every week – because if he gave him enough for a whole month he would finish it within two or three days, and the remaining days he would be starving. Every week he would send money to him.

And what Vincent van Gogh was doing was for four days he would eat, and for the three days in between those four days he was saving money for paints, canvasses. This is something totally different from Michelangelo, who earned enough money, who became a rich person. He sold all his paintings. They were made to be sold, it was business. Of course he was a great painter, so even paintings that were going to be sold came out beautifully. But if he had had the guts of a Vincent van Gogh, he would have enriched the whole world.

Three days starving, and van Gogh would purchase paints and canvasses. His younger brother, hearing that not a single painting had sold, gave some money to a man – a friend of his not known to Vincent van Gogh – and told him to go and purchase at least one painting: "That will give him some satisfaction.

The poor man is dying; the whole day he is painting, starving for painting but nobody is ready to purchase his painting – nobody sees anything in it." Because to see something in Vincent van Gogh's painting you need the eye of a painter of the caliber of van Gogh; less than that will not do. His paintings will seem strange to you.

His trees are painted so high that they go above the stars; stars are left far behind. Now, you will think that this man is mad: trees going up higher than the stars? Have you seen such trees anywhere? When Vincent van Gogh was asked, "Your trees always go beyond the stars…?" he said, "Yes, because I understand trees. I have felt always that trees are the ambition of the earth to reach the stars. Otherwise why? To touch the stars, to feel the stars, to go beyond the stars – this is the desire of the earth. The earth tries hard, but cannot fulfill the desire. I can do it. The earth will understand my paintings, and I don't care about you, whether you understand or not."

Now, you cannot sell this kind of painting. The man his brother had sent came. Van Gogh was very happy: at last somebody had come to purchase. But soon his happiness turned into despair because the man looked around, picked one painting and gave the money.

Vincent van Gogh said, "But do you understand the painting? You have picked it up so casually, you have not looked; I have hundreds of paintings. You have not even bothered to look around; you have simply picked one that was accidentally in front of you. I suspect that you are sent by my brother. Put the painting back, take your money. I will not sell the painting to a man who has no eyes for painting. And tell my brother never to do such a thing again."

The man was puzzled how he managed to figure it out. He said, "You don't know me, how did you figure it out?"

He said, "That's too simple. I know my brother wants me to feel some consolation. He must have manipulated you – and this money belongs to him – because I can see that you are blind as far as paintings are concerned. And I am not one to sell paintings to blind people; I cannot exploit a blind man and sell him a painting. What will he do with it? And tell my brother also that he also does not understand painting, otherwise he would not have sent you."

When the brother came to know, he came to apologize. He said, "Instead of giving you a little consolation, I have wounded you. I will never do such a thing again."

His whole life van Gogh was just giving his paintings to friends: to the hotel where he used to eat four days a week he would present a painting, or to a prostitute who had said once to him that he was not a beautiful man. To be absolutely factual, he was ugly. No woman ever fell in love with him, it was impossible.

This prostitute out of compassion – and sometimes prostitutes have more compassion than your so-called ladies, they understand men more – just out of compassion she said, "I like you very much." He had never heard this. Love was a far away thing. Even liking…

He said, "Really, you like me? What do you like in me?"

Now, the woman was at a loss.

She said, "I like your ears. Your ears are beautiful." And you will be surprised that van Gogh went home, cut off his ears with a razor, packed them beautifully, went to the prostitute and gave his ears to her. And blood was flowing...

She said, "What have you done?"

He said, "Nobody ever liked anything in me. And I am a poor man, how can I thank you? You liked my ears; I have presented them to you. If you had liked my eyes, I would have presented my eyes to you. If you had liked me, I would have died for you."

The prostitute could not believe it. But for the first time, van Gogh was happy, smiling; somebody had liked at least a part of him. And that woman had just said jokingly – otherwise who bothers about your ears? If people like something, they like your eyes, they like your nose, your lips – you won't hear lovers talking about each other's ears, that they like them.

Only in ancient Hindu scriptures on sexology: the *Kamasutras* of Vatsayana... That is the only book I have been able to find that can be connected to this incident five thousand years afterwards with Vincent van Gogh, because only Vatsayana says, "Very few people are aware that ear lobes are tremendously sexual and sensitive points in the body. And lovers should play with each other's ear lobes" – and this is a fact, although unknown.

If you start playing with the ear lobes of your lover, she or he may think that you are a little crazy – what are you doing? Because people have become fixed on certain ideas: kissing is okay... But there are tribes where nobody has ever heard about kissing; they rub noses with each other, and that is thought to be the most loving gesture. Certainly it is more hygienic, far more medically supportable than the French kiss. Those people who rub noses think of people giving French kisses to each other as just dirty, simply dirty.

But this prostitute perhaps was aware – because prostitutes become aware of many things which ordinary women and men don't become aware of, because they come in contact with so many people. Perhaps she was aware that ears have a sexual significance. They certainly have. Vatsayana is one of the greatest experts. Freud and Havelock Ellis and other sexologists are just pygmies before Vatsayana. And when he says something, he means it.

Van Gogh lived his whole life in poverty. He died painting. Before dying he went mad, because for one year continually he was painting the sun: hundreds of paintings, but nothing was coming to the point he wanted. But the whole day standing in the hottest place in France, in Arles, with the sun on the head – because without the experience how can you paint? He painted the final painting, but he went mad. Just the heat, the hunger... But he was immensely happy; even in madness he was painting. And those paintings which he did in the madhouse are now worth millions.

He committed suicide for the simple reason that he had painted everything that he wanted to paint. Now painting was finished; he had come to a dead end. There was nothing more to do. Now to go on living was occupying space, somebody's place; that was ugly to him.

That's what he wrote in his letters to his brother: "My work is done. I have lived tremendously – the way I wanted to live. I have painted what I wanted to paint. My last painting I have done today, and now I am taking a jump from this life into the unknown, whatever it is, because this life no longer contains anything for me."

Will you consider this man a genius? Will you consider this man intelligent, wise? No, ordinarily you would think he is simply mad. But I cannot say that. His living and his painting were not two things: painting was his living, that was his life. So to the whole world it seems suicide – not to me. To me it simply seems a natural end. The painting is completed. Life is fulfilled. There was no other goal; whether he receives the Nobel Prize, whether anybody appreciates his painting...

In his life nobody appreciated his work. In his life no art gallery accepted his paintings, even free. After he died, slowly, slowly, because of his sacrifice, painting changed its whole flavor. There would have been no Picasso without Vincent van Gogh. All the painters that have come after Vincent van Gogh owe him, incalculably, because that man changed the whole direction. Slowly, slowly, as the direction changed, his paintings were discovered. A great search was made.

People had thrown his paintings into their empty houses, or in their basements, thinking that they were useless. They rushed to their basements, discovered his paintings, cleaned them. Even faked paintings came onto the market as authentic van Gogh. Now there are only two hundred paintings; he must have painted thousands. But any art gallery that has a Vincent van Gogh is proud, because the man poured his whole life in his paintings. They were not painted by color, but by blood, by breath – his heartbeat is there.

Don't ask such a man, "Is there any meaning in your painting?" *He is* there in his painting, and you are asking, "Is there any meaning in your painting?" If you cannot see the meaning, you are responsible for it.

The higher a thing rises, the fewer the people who will recognize it.

When something reaches to the highest point, it is very difficult to find even a few people to recognize it. At the ultimate omega point, only the person himself recognizes what has happened to him; he cannot find even a second man.

That's why a buddha has to declare himself that he is enlightened. Nobody else can recognize it, because to recognize it, you will have to have some taste of it. Otherwise, how can you recognize it? No recognition is possible because the point is so high.

But what is the meaning of buddhahood? What is the meaning of becoming enlightened? What is the point? If you ask about the point, there is none. It itself is enough. It needs nothing else to make it significant.

That's what I mean when I say that the really valuable things in life are not divided into ends and means. There is no division between ends and means. Ends are the means, means are the ends – perhaps two sides of the same coin inseparably joined together – in fact, they are a oneness, a wholeness.

You ask me, "Is there any point in life, in living?" I am afraid that if I say there is no point in living, you will think that means you have to commit suicide, because if there is no point in living, then what else to do? – commit suicide! I am not saying commit suicide, because in committing suicide also there is no point.

Living: live, and live totally. Dying: die, and die totally. And in that totality you will find significance.

I am considerdly not using the word *meaning*, and using the word *significance* because meaning is contaminated. The word *meaning* always points somewhere else. You must have heard, you must have read in your childhood, many stories... Why are they written for children? – perhaps the writers don't know, but it is part of the same exploitation of humanity.

The stories are like this...

A man is there whose life is in a parrot. If you kill the parrot, the man will be killed, but you cannot kill the man directly. You can shoot, and nothing will happen. You can swing your sword and the sword will pass through his neck, but the neck will remain still joined to the body. You cannot kill the man – first you have to find where his life is. So in those stories the life is always somewhere else. And when you find out you just kill the parrot and wherever the man is, he will immediately die.

Even when I was a child, I used to ask my teacher, "This seems to be a very stupid kind of story because I don't see anyone whose life is in a parrot or in a dog or in something else, like a tree." It was the first time I heard that story, that type of story; then I came across many. They were written specially for children.

The man who was teaching me was a very nice and respectable gentleman. I asked him, "Can you tell me where your life is? Because I would like to try..."

He said, "What do you mean?"

I said, "I would like to kill that bird in which your life is. You are an intelligent man, wise, respected. You must have put your life somewhere else so nobody can kill you. That's what the story says – that wise people keep their life somewhere else, so that you cannot kill them, so that nobody can kill them. And it is impossible to find where they have kept their life unless they tell the secret, nobody can figure it out. This world is so big, and there are so many people and so many animals, and so many birds, and so many trees... Nobody knows where that man has put his life.

"You are a wise man, respected, you must have kept it somewhere; you can just tell me in private. I will not kill the bird completely; just give him a few twists and turns, and see what happens to you."

He said, "You are a strange boy. I have been teaching this story my whole life, and you want to give me a twist and turn. This is only a story."

But I said, "What is the point of the story? Why do you go on teaching this story and this kind of things to children?"

He could not answer. I asked my father, "What can be the meaning of this story? Why should these things be taught, which are absolutely absurd?"

He said, "If your teacher cannot answer, then how can I answer? I don't know. He is far more educated and intelligent and wise. You harass him, rather than harassing me."

But now I know what the meaning of the stories is and why they are being taught to the children. They enter in their unconscious and they start thinking life is always somewhere else – in heaven, in God, always somewhere else – it is not in you. You are empty, just an empty shell. You don't have meaning in your life herenow. Here you are only a means, a ladder. If you go up the ladder, perhaps someday you will find your life, your God, your goal, your meaning, whatever name you give to it.

But I say to you that you are the meaning, the significance, and living itself is intrinsically complete.

Life needs nothing else to be added to it.

All that life needs is that you live it to its totality. If you live only partially, then you will not feel the thrill of being alive. It is like any mechanism when just a part is functioning… For example in a clock: if only the second hand is working but neither the hour hand nor the minute hand moves – only the second hand goes on moving – what purpose will it serve? There will be movement, a certain part is working, but unless the whole works and works in harmony, there cannot be a song out of it.

And this is the situation: everybody is living partially, a small part. So you make noise but you can't create a song. You move your hands and legs but no dance happens. The dance, the song, the significance comes into existence immediately your whole functions in harmony, in accord. Then you don't ask such questions as: Is there any point in living? – you know.

Living itself is the point. There is no other point.

But you have not been allowed to remain one and whole. You have been divided, cut into several parts. A few parts have been completely closed – so much so that you don't know even that they belong to you. Much of you has been thrown in the basement. Much of you has been so condemned that although you know it is there, you cannot dare to accept it, that it is part of you – you go on denying it; you go on repressing it.

You know only a very small fragment in you, which they call conscience, which is a social product, not a natural thing, which society creates inside you to control you from inside. The constable is outside, the court is outside controlling you. And the conscience is inside, which is far more powerful.

That's why even in court they will first give you the Bible. You take the oath on the Bible because the court also knows that if you are a Christian, putting your hand on the Bible and saying, "I swear to tell the truth, the whole truth, and nothing but the truth," your conscience will force you to speak the truth, because now you have taken the oath in the name of God, and you have touched the Bible. If you speak a lie you will be thrown into hell.

Before, at the most, if you were caught you would be thrown into imprisonment for a few months, a few years. But now you will be thrown into hell for eternity. Even the court accepts that the Bible is more powerful, the Gita is more powerful, the Koran is more powerful than the court, than the military, than the army.

Conscience is one of the meanest inventions of humanity. And from the very first day the child is born we start creating a conscience in him; a small part which goes on condemning anything that the society does not want in you, and goes on appreciating anything that the society wants in you. You are no longer whole.

The conscience continuously goes on forcing you, so that you have to always look out – God is watching. Every act, every thought, God is watching, so beware!

Even in thoughts you are not allowed freedom: God is watching. What kind of peeping Tom is this God? In every bathroom he is looking through the keyhole; he won't leave you alone – even in your bathroom?

There are tribes in the world where even in your dream if you do something wrong, in the morning you have to go to the person... For example you have insulted somebody in your dream – in the morning you have to go to apologize: "Forgive me, last night I insulted you in a dream; I am so sorry." Even dreams are controlled by the society. You are not allowed even in a dream to be yourself.

They go on talking about freedom of thought – that's all nonsense because from the very beginning they put the base in every child for unfreedom of thought.

They want to control your thoughts. They want to control your dreams. They want to control everything in you. It's through a very clever device – conscience. It pricks you. It goes on telling you, "This is not right, don't do it; you will suffer." It goes on forcing you: "Do this, this is the right thing to do; you will be rewarded for it."

This conscience will never allow you to be whole. It won't allow you to live as if there is nothing prohibited, as if there are no boundaries, as if you are left totally independent to be whatsoever you can be. Then life has meaning, then living has meaning – not the meaning that is derived from ends, but the meaning that is derived from living itself. Then whatever you do, in that very doing is your reward.

For example, I am speaking to you. I am enjoying it. For thirty-five years I have been continually speaking for no purpose. With this much speaking I could have become a president, a prime minister; there was no problem in it. With so much speaking I could have done anything. What have I gained? But I was not out for gain in the first place – I enjoyed.

This was my painting, this was my song, this was my poetry.

Just those moments when I am speaking and I feel the communion happening, those moments when I see your eyes flare up, when I see that you have understood the point... They give me such tremendous joy that I cannot think anything can be added to it.

Action, any action done totally, with every fiber of your being in it... For example, if you bind my hands I cannot speak, although there is no relationship between hands and speaking. I have tried.

One day, I told a friend who was staying with me, "Tie both my hands."
He said, "What?"
I said, "Just tie them, and then ask a question."
He said, "I am always afraid to stay with you, you are crazy. And now if somebody sees that I have tied your hands, and now I am asking a question and you are answering it, what will they think?"

I said, "Forget all that. Close the door and do what I say."

He did, because he had to do it; otherwise I would have thrown him out, saying, "And being my guest, you cannot even do this simple thing for me? Then don't bother me at all, just get lost."

So he tied my hands to two pillars, and he asked me a question. I tried in every possible way, but my hands were tied; I could not say anything to him. I simply said, "Please untie my hands."

He said, "But I cannot understand what this is all about."

I said, "It is simply that I was trying to see whether I could speak without my hands. I cannot."

What to say about hands... If I put this leg on the other side, and the other leg on top of it – which is the way I sit in my room when I am not speaking... If I have to put it under the other leg, then something goes wrong, then I am not at home. So the way I am sitting, the way my hands move, is a total involvement. It is not only speaking from a part of me; everything in me is involved in it. And only then can you find the intrinsic value of any act. Otherwise you have to live the life of tension, stretched between here and there, this and that faraway goal.

The pseudo-religions say, "Of course, this life is only a means so you cannot be involved in it totally; it is only a ladder you have to pass. It is not something valuable, just a stepping-stone. The real thing is there, far away." And so it always remains far away. Wherever you will be, your real thing will be always far away. So wherever you will be, you will be missing life.

I don't have a goal.

When I was in the university I used to go for a walk in the morning, evening, anytime... Morning and evening absolutely, but if there was another time available, I would also go for a walk then, because the place and the trees and the road were so beautiful, and so covered with big trees from both sides that even in the hottest summer there was shadow on the road.

One of my professors who loved me very much used to watch me: that some days I would go on this road, some days on that road. There was a pentagon in front of the gate of the university, five roads going in five directions, and he lived just near there; his were the last quarters near the gate. He asked me, "Sometimes you go on this road, sometimes on that road. Where do you go?"

I said, "I don't go anywhere. I just go for walking." If you are going somewhere then certainly you will go on the same road; but I was not going anywhere, so it was just whimsical. I just came to the pentagon and I just used to stand there for a little while. That was making him more puzzled: how do I figure it out, what do I figure out standing there?

I used to figure out where the wind was blowing. Whichever way the wind was blowing I would also go; that was my way. "So sometimes," he would say, "You have been going on the same road for a week continually; sometimes you go only one day, and the next day you change. What do you do there? And how do you decide?"

And I told him, "It is very simple. I stand there and I feel which road is alive – where the wind is blowing. I go with the wind. And it is beautiful going with the wind. I jog, I run, whatsoever I want to do. And the wind is there, cool, available. So I just figure it out."

Life is not going somewhere.

It is just going for a morning walk.

Choose wherever your whole being is flowing, where the wind is blowing. Move on that path as far as it leads, and never expect to find anything.

Hence I have never been surprised, because I have never been expecting anything – so there is no question of surprise: everything is surprise. And there is no question of disappointment: everything is appointment.

If it happens, good; if it does not happen, even better.

Once you understand that moment-to-moment living is what religion is all about, then you will understand why I say drop this idea of God, heaven and hell, and all that crap.

Just drop it completely because this load of so many concepts is preventing you from living moment to moment. Live life in an organic unity. No act should be partial, you should be involved fully in it.

A Zen story:

A very curious king, wanting to know about what these people go on doing in the monasteries, asked, "Who is the most famous master?" Finding out that the most famous master of those days was Nan-in, he went to his monastery. When he entered the monastery he found a woodcutter. He asked him, "The monastery is big, where can I find Master Nan-in?"

The man thought with closed eyes for a few moments, and he said, "Right now you cannot find him."

The king said, "Why can't I find him right now? Do you understand that I am the emperor?"

He said, "That is irrelevant. Whoever you are, that is your business, but I assure you, you cannot find him right now."

"Is he out?" asked the king.

"No, he is in," replied the woodcutter.

The king said, "But is he involved in some work, in some ceremony, or in isolation? What is the matter?"

The man said, "He is right now cutting wood in front of you. And when I am cutting wood, I am just a woodcutter. Right now where is Master Nan-in? I am just a woodcutter. You will have to wait."

The emperor thought, "This man is mad, simply mad. Master Nan-in cutting wood?" He went ahead, and left the woodcutter behind. Nan-in again continued to cut wood. The winter was coming close, and wood had to be stored. The emperor could wait, but winter wouldn't wait.

The emperor waited one hour, two hours – and then from the back door came Master Nan-in, in his master's robe. The king looked at him. He looked like the woodcutter, but the king bowed down. The master sat there, and he asked, "Why have you taken so much trouble to come here?"

The king said, "There are many things, but those questions I will ask later on. First I want to know: are you the same man who was cutting wood?"

He said, "Now I am Master Nan-in. I am not the same man; the total configuration has changed. Now here I am sitting as Master Nan-in. You ask as a disciple, with humbleness, receptivity. Yes, a man very, very similar to me was cutting wood there, but that was a woodcutter. His name is also Nan-In."

The king got so puzzled that he left without asking the questions he had come to ask. When he went back to his court, his advisers asked what happened. He said, "What happened it is better to forget about. This Master Nan-In seems to be absolutely insane! He was cutting wood; he said, 'I am a woodcutter and Master Nan-In is not available right now.' Then the same man came in a master's robe and I asked him, and he said, 'A similar man was cutting the wood, but he was the woodcutter; I am the master.'"

One of the men in the court said, "You have missed the point of what he was trying to say to you – that when cutting wood he is totally involved in it. Nothing is left which can claim to be Master Nan-In; nothing is left out, he is just a woodcutter."

And in Zen language, which is difficult to translate, he was saying not exactly that "I am a woodcutter," he was saying, "Right now it is wood cutting, not a woodcutter – because there is not even space for the cutter." It is simply wood being chopped, and he is so totally in it, it is only wood cutting: wood cutting is happening. When he comes as a master, of course, it is a different configuration. The same parts are now in a different accord. So with each action you are a different person, if you get totally involved in it.

Buddha used to say, "It is just as the flame of the candle looks the same, but is never the same even for two consecutive moments. The flame is continuously becoming smoke, new flame is coming up. The old flame is going out, the new flame is coming up. The candle that you had burned in the evening is not the same candle that you will blow out in the morning. This is not the same flame that you had started; *that* has gone far away, nobody knows where. It is just a similarity of the flame that gives you the illusion that it is the same flame."

The same is true about your being. It is a flame. It is a fire.

Each moment your being is changing, and if you get involved totally in anything then you will see the change happening in you – each moment a new being, and a new world, and a new experience. Everything suddenly becomes so full of newness that you never see the same thing again.

Then naturally, life becomes a continuous mystery, a continuous surprise. On each step a new world opens up, of tremendous meaning, of incredible ecstasy.

When death comes, death too is not seen as something separate from life. It is part of life, not an end of life. It is just like other happenings: love had happened, birth had happened. You were a child, and then childhood disappeared; you became a young man, and then the young man disappeared; you became an old man, and then the old man disappeared – how many things have been happening! Why don't you allow death also to happen just like other incidents?

And actually the person who has lived moment to moment lives death too, and finds that all the moments of life can be put on one side and the one moment of death can be put on the other side, and still it weighs more. In every way it weighs more because it is the whole life condensed; and something more added to it, which was never available to you. A new door opening, with the whole life condensed: a new dimension opening.

Okay, you can ask your second question...

Osho,
On the face of American money is the phrase, "In God we trust." the priests have lied and said that there is a God. The politicians have lied and said that the American constitution and civil rights would ensure social justice for all. How can I now trust in a religionless religion?

I have never asked you to trust in a religionless religion. How can I ask you? – because that very asking has been religion up to now. To boycott it I am calling it religionless religion, using an obvious contradiction. But the reason is clear. Calling it religionless means that I will not ask you for any faith, any belief, any trust.

If trust arises in you, that is a totally different thing.

The religions ask that you believe in one God, one messiah, one book. I do not ask you; but how can I prevent you if trust arises in you? Then trust is nothing but a kind of love. It is not belief, it is not faith, because belief has to be forced to repress doubts; faith has to be continually indoctrinated in you. You hear it so many times that slowly, slowly you start forgetting that you have only *heard* it, that you don't know anything about it.

You have a tendency – and a comfortable tendency – to forget your ignorance and cling to your knowledge. Faith is conditioned knowledge given by others to you, forced upon you. But slowly, slowly, it goes so deep in your mind, it becomes part of you. You start thinking it is "my faith." Trust is neither.

Nobody can ask for trust, just as nobody can ask for love. Can I ask any-body, "Love me"? The person will say, "But how?" If love arises, it arises; if it does not arise then what can be done? Yes, you can pretend, as the whole world is pretending. Trust can also be pretended if asked for. I am not asking. I want you to be completely saved from any kind of pretension, hypocrisy. But if trust arises I cannot help it, you cannot help it. Nobody can do anything about it if it arises. You suddenly feel a new heartbeat in you – what can you do?

In my religionless religion, trust is not required. Trust is not demanded, not ordered, not commanded. It happens. And we are all helpless about it; nothing can be done about it when it happens. It is so beautiful that who would like to miss it when it happens?

Yes, the politicians have deceived people, the religions have deceived people.

And I have lived my whole life condemned by all the religions and all the politicians, for the simple reason that I was exposing them.

This is very strange. The question says that on the American dollar it says, "In God we trust." My God! On the dollar you say, "In God we trust" – then what is this attorney general of Oregon doing by trying to declare our city illegal? He should declare America an illegal country! – because this is mixing state and religion.

If Rajneeshpuram is declared an illegal city… And we have not done anything like that: saying, "In God we trust" on the dollar, you are mixing God with money, mixing state with religion. This attorney general of Oregon can make history. He should declare the whole American nation illegal.

They use the Bible in the courts for taking the oath – that is mixing law with religion, state with religion – or they ask, "In the name of God…" All this mixing is happening, except in Rajneeshpuram, where there is no mixing happening. In fact, we don't have any God to mix!

These people are strange, and it looks as if they don't think about what they are doing, what they are saying. There seems to be no coordination in their mind; otherwise… The president of America goes to a certain church; before he takes the oath of the president he goes to be blessed by the priest of his church. Now what business has a priest to bless the president, and why? The president should start from the very beginning mixing church and state?

Why does the president of America go to the Vatican to meet the pope? As president he should not go. He can go as Ronald Reagan, but then he should not have any facility that is provided for a president. But he goes as the president. And still *we* are blamed that we are mixing religion and state. We don't have anything that can be mixed with the state!

I am against politics. How can you mix it with politics? I condemn politics. My whole life I have been condemning the politicians. I see them as criminals who are clever enough not to be caught, clever enough to cheat people by giving them false hopes, phony utopias. We don't have any politics here. And we don't have any religion that they think is religion.

My religion is a way of life. It is not a way of prayer, it is a way of living.

Can you mix love with state? How will you mix them? They are unmixable. And this phenomenon that is happening here is of the same quality as love. We love life, and we want to live it in its fullness. Who cares about your politics and your state?

The mayor of Rajneeshpuram is not a politician. It is just because of your stupid categories, that a city should have a mayor, that we have a mayor. If you allow us to be a city without a mayor, we will be immensely happy; and our mayor, K.D., will be immensely happy, because whenever I look at him, he feels ashamed, he looks downwards because the poor man has to be in the position of a politician – just a necessary evil. And it is just because of your constitution and your legal structure.

We can't change your constitution and your legal structure, so we decided: okay, let one sannyasin fall into the gutter. Let him become the mayor, what else to do? K.D. is suffering in the gutter, and we will pull him out. We will not leave him there forever, because he has not come here to become a mayor! Nor is anybody concerned in becoming the attorney general of Oregon or the governor of Oregon or the president of America. Nobody is interested at all.

We are interested simply in being left alone.

But these people are strange, they cannot leave us alone. They are afraid, they are worried. They are suspicious: what is happening, what is going on? They are not even courageous enough to come here and see; just on rumors – public opinion – and that public has also not come here. And *these* people go on deciding things!

The city of Rajneeshpuram the attorney general has declared illegal. This is a unique situation; in fact a unique city in the whole world, because there is no city in the whole world which is illegal, and there never has been before. Either a city is a city, or it is not a city. But an illegal city, that's something that is absolutely unique!

But leave all this nonsense to these people. They should also create a post in Oregon: the Idiot General of Oregon, and he should be given all these kinds of things to do. Then one can understand that it is just humor; one can laugh at it and enjoy it. And they are very serious people; they are not doing things out of a sense of humor. And my religion has a basic quality: a sense of humor. If out of sheer being with me, with my people, a trust is born... And it is not trust in God, it is not trust in somebody particular; it is just a quality, unaddressed.

There is no address on the envelope: "In God we trust." Who are you to trust in God? On what authority do you trust in God? – you don't know God. You are dragging God also to the same status as a dollar, making him a thing of the marketplace. And you cannot find anything more dirty than currency, because it moves in so many hands.

I have not touched any note for thirty-five years. It is the dirtiest thing. Not that I am against money but it is the most dirty thing. All kinds of people...somebody may have cancer, somebody may have tuberculosis, somebody may have AIDS, and who knows what he has been doing with his notes? Anything is possible, because people are so perverted, they can do anything with bank notes. I said, "I am not going to touch them" – and I stopped touching them. And on that note you write, "In God we trust"? Please forgive God and forget all about him.

The trust that arises in my sannyasins is simply a quality of their heart; they just start trusting. It is not trust in something. They start trusting; even when they are deceived, they trust: knowing that this man has deceived them, they trust. It is not a question of whom, it is just their aroma.

In the university I had to live for a few days with a roommate. I had never lived with anybody but there was no space and the vice-chancellor said to me, "For a few days you manage and I will find some other place for you. I can understand that you will not like anybody to be in the room, and it is good for the other fellow also that he is not in your room, because you may drive him crazy. I will arrange it."

But it took four, five months before he arranged it. And that man was a very good boy; he just had one problem – just one, so you cannot say that it was a big trouble – he was a kleptomaniac. Just for sheer joy he would steal my things. I had to search for my things in his suitcases, and I would find them, but I never said anything to him.

He was puzzled. He would use my clothes. When I was not in the room he would just take anything. He would take my shawl and go for a walk, so when I came back the shawl would be gone. I would say, "It will come back, soon it will return." To save money from being taken by him I used to deposit it with him and say, "Keep this money, because if I keep it you will take it anyway. And then it will be difficult to know how much you have taken and how to ask you for it. It looks awkward. Just take it. It is this much: you take it!"

He said, "You are clever. This way I have to return all the money whenever you need it."

But after four, five months...because whenever and wherever he was, with whomsoever he lived – his family or friends, or in the hostels – everybody was condemning him. But I never said anything to him – instead of looking in my suitcases I just looked into his. It was simple! It was not very different; my suitcases were in this corner, his suitcases were in that corner.

He said, "You are strange. I have been stealing your things and you never say anything."

I said, "It is a very small problem. It can't create distrust in me for a human being. And what trouble is there? Rather than going to my suitcase, I simply go to your suitcase, and in your suitcase I find whatsoever I need."

He said, "That's why I was wondering... I go on stealing from you, you never say anything, and those things disappear from my suitcases again! So I was thinking that perhaps you also are a kleptomaniac."

I said, "That is perfectly okay. If you stop taking from my suitcases, I will stop taking from your suitcases. And remember, in this whole game you have been losing."

He said, "What do you mean?"

I said, "I take a few things that are not mine" – because he was stealing from everywhere, other rooms, professors' houses; anywhere he would find any window open, he would jump in. And there was no intention of stealing, just the joy of it, just the challenge; an opportunity and challenge that nobody could catch hold of him.

I said, "I will never prevent you. You can go on moving my things, you can move my whole suitcase under your bed; it doesn't matter. In fact I am perfectly happy with you. I am worried now that soon the vice-chancellor is going to give me a single room. Where will I find a person like you? – because you provide so many things which I need. And I trust you perfectly!"

imitation is your cremation

Osho,
You have been saying that disobedience is a religious quality. It suddenly
means I have to disobey you, the commune and the discipline of sannyas.
I cannot even participate in our prayer, the *gachchhamis*.

The questioner is certainly an Oregonian, a born Oregonian, not just twenty days resident in Oregon. As far as I am concerned it is enough to breathe Oregon's air for twenty minutes to become an Oregonian!

I have said that disobedience is a religious quality, but to be disobedient you need to be very intelligent. To obey...an idiot can do it. All that he has to say is "Yes sir." To disobey is not just saying no; that too can be done by an idiot very easily.

Disobedience needs tremendous intelligence because you are deciding your life, your future, your destiny.

I have said disobey anything that is imposed on you, against you, against your will, against your intellect, against your reason, against your being. Then risk everything and disobey it – because in fact by disobeying it, you are obeying your inner self. By disobeying it, you are obeying existence.

In other words, by disobeying it you are disobeying the personality and obeying the individuality.

I have not said that you have to disobey everything – you will go nuts, unless you are already nuts. I have emphasized disobedience because all the religions have been emphasizing obedience. Obedience to whom? Obedience to their God, which is their creation; obedience to the commandments, which are their creation; obedience to society, convention, tradition – which are all their vested interests – obedience to the parents, to the teachers, to the priests.

All the religions have been teaching you obedience; hence, just to emphasize it clearly before you, I had to say disobey, rebel.

That does not mean that I am against obedience. But the obedience I am for is a very different phenomenon. It does not come as an imposition on you, it comes as a flowering of your being. It is your intelligence, your maturity, your centeredness, your aliveness, your response. You are the source of it; not Moses, not Mohammed, not Jesus, not me, but you, just you.

But do you know who you are? You know you are a Jew, and you are not. You know you are a Christian, and you are not. You know you are a Hindu, and you are not. These are all impositions.

People have been painting on you as if you are a canvas. They are making your face according to their idea. They want to become in some way ideals for you, and they want to reduce you to imitators.

There is a great Christian classic, *Imitation of Christ*, which is respected by the Christians almost next to the Bible. But it is an ugly book. The very title of the book shows what it is: *Imitation of Christ*. You may imitate Christ for millions of lives; still you will not be a Christ, you will be only an imitation. And the imitation is not your original face.

The more you succeed in imitating, the more you are failing as far as your being is concerned. The deeper you go into imitation, the farther away you are going from yourself; and the return journey is not going to be easy.

It is going to be immensely difficult, because when you were continuously imitating a certain pattern, you were becoming identified with it. The return journey means you will have to start killing all that identification. It will look like committing suicide, as if you are cutting off your own limbs. It is not going to be just like dropping your clothes, not that easy. It is going to be like peeling your skin.

It is so difficult that even a very intelligent man like Bertrand Russell confessed, "My reason says that Gautam Buddha is certainly the greatest figure in the whole of human history, but although I am not part of any Christian congregation, although I have completely disassociated myself from Christian mythology, religion, theology, somewhere I cannot put Buddha above Christ. With my reason I understand, but as far as my feelings are concerned Jesus remains higher – and I know he is not."

Now, a man like Bertrand Russell cannot get rid of a certain conditioning. He has been told from his very childhood that there has never been anybody like Jesus. Although he has renounced Christianity consciously, publicly... He wrote a very famous book, *Why I Am Not a Christian*, and gave all his reasons, very valid reasons. Anybody who has a little bit of intelligence can understand that if what Bertrand Russell is saying is the case, then you cannot be a Christian either. And that is the case; he has exposed Christianity completely.

But even after that... And this confession was long after he had written that book. He had written the book some twenty years before, and this confession came when he was nearabout eighty-five, absolutely mature. He remained intelligent to the very last moment of his life. He lived almost a century; he never became senile. Even at the last moment of his life he was as intelligent and alive as ever.

He confessed: "As far as my feelings and emotions are concerned, Jesus somehow hangs above everybody else. And I know perfectly well there is no comparison of Gautam Buddha with Jesus; Gautam Buddha is far superior. But that is only intellectual; emotionally Christ still has the grip." Although he has said that he is not a Christian, he is still a Christian.

That's why I say it is very difficult to come back. Going is difficult, but coming back is far more difficult. Imitation is going to be a difficult thing: you are trying to be something which you are not meant to be, which is not your destiny. You are going against the very nature of your being, you are trying to swim against the current. Yes, it is difficult to imitate – but not so difficult as when you start coming back to your natural self.

You have lost it somewhere far back. You can't remember even where you lost it. You can't remember where you deviated from yourself. You deviated in such moments when you were not even aware.

If you remember your past, you will at the most go back to the age of four, on average. Not all people can go back to the age of four. A few people, very rare people can go to the age of three. And rarely, once in a while, you can find a person who can go back to the age of two. It happens only once in a century that a person can go back to the age of one. And it happens only once in many centuries that a person can go into the memories of his mother's womb.

But your deviation starts even when you are in your mother's womb, because whatsoever your mother is doing is affecting you. When you are in your mother's womb, your mother's mind is your mind, her feelings are your feelings, her emotions are your emotions. If she is angry, something in you gets angry. If she is happy, something in you rejoices.

In the East, psychology is one of the most ancient sciences; in the West it is just a hundred years old – not even a hundred years old. The oldest name in Western psychology, the ancientmost, is Sigmund Freud, who was alive just a few years ago. But in the East, in India, psychology goes as far back as Patanjali – five thousand years. And Patanjali cannot be said to be the source because he quotes more ancient sources. In China it goes as far back as Lao Tzu. But Lao Tzu quotes at least five-thousand-year-old sources: five thousand years before Lao Tzu, who is twenty-five centuries before us.

Eastern psychology says that when the mother is pregnant, those nine months are the most important period in the life of the child who is not yet born. In these nine months as much care as possible should be taken. The mother should not become angry, should not become sexual, should not become worried, should not become irritated, annoyed. She should be kept in such a way that the child is not affected at all by her emotions. She should be almost in a meditative state for all those nine months.

That's the recommendation of Eastern psychology, that the mother for nine months should be continuously in a meditative state; that's the only way to save the child from becoming an imitator. Otherwise neither the mother knows the child, nor the child knows himself, and he becomes an imitator. This is the situation in the womb – what to say about when the child comes out of the womb.

Then, at every step everybody is determined to give a certain shape, a certain color, a certain character, a certain career to you – and with all good intentions. The path to hell is paved with good intentions. Nobody is your enemy, but they all prove to be your enemies.

There is one statement of Gautam Buddha which Buddhists try to avoid because they don't have the understanding to explain it. And it is so clear, they cannot even explain it away. The statement that Buddha makes is, "Unless you hate your father, your mother, your brother, you cannot follow me." Now, what kind of statement is this? – "Unless you hate your father, your mother, your family, you cannot follow me."

The Buddhists don't quote it. In no Buddhist monastery does anybody even give a sermon on it. Monks just pass it by quickly. How to explain it? A man like Buddha who teaches love, nonviolence, is saying to hate your mother and father.

Then Jesus certainly seems to be far superior: "Love your enemy; not only the enemy, love your neighbor" – which is certainly far more difficult. The enemy is far away and once in a while maybe there is some trouble, but the neighbor is a twenty-four hour trouble, and just a pain in the neck continually, twenty-four hours a day. And Jesus says, "Love your neighbor just like yourself."

Naturally if you compare these statements Jesus will look far more religious than Buddha. But before I say anything else, let me quote Bodhidharma, who defeated his own master, Buddha, in every possible way. And that is the only joy of a real master, that he should be defeated by his disciple. Of course, they were not contemporaries; there was at least eleven hundred years' difference between Buddha and Bodhidharma.

Bodhidharma says: "First go and kill your father and mother, then come to me. First, be finished with your father and your mother and then come to me. Otherwise go somewhere else – I am not for you." How you are going to explain it? And I say to you that what Jesus says is just hocus-pocus.

What Bodhidharma is saying is pure psychology. He is not saying that you should kill your father and mother, but in a certain way you have to kill the father that has entered you, and the mother that has entered you. That is your family inside, which is surrounding your being, which won't allow any ray of light to reach your innermost corner. The crowd has gathered there, and because of that crowd the inner center is in darkness.

Bodhidharma brings Buddha's statement to its logical conclusion. Why just hate? – be completely finished, because hating is again a relationship, just like love. If you love somebody, you remember him; you cannot forget him – you are not supposed to forget the person you love. Sometimes you may forget the person you love, but you cannot forget the person you hate. Although all the so-called moral teachers have been telling you to forgive and forget, you can neither forgive nor can you forget. Perhaps you can forgive, with effort, but how can you forget? Then you will remember two things: first, that you hated him and second, that you have forgiven him – now you will remember even more. So what have you done?

You cannot forget your enemy. It is a relationship, a very close, very intimate relationship. And that's why it is very easy for lovers to become haters, friends to become enemies, enemies to become friends. It is very easy because both are relationships: just a little turn, a little change in the situation...

For example, in the Second World War America and Russia became friends, great friends, fighting together hand in hand. They were enemies before, they are enemies afterwards. Strange! But the situation took such a turn... Adolf Hitler did a miracle, he was a man worth counting. All the miracles of Jesus are nothing compared to what Adolf Hitler did: he turned Americans and Russians into friends. Both flags flying together by courtesy of Adolf Hitler! And the moment Adolf Hitler was finished, the friendship evaporated immediately, instantly. They were enemies again.

You could see the Berlin wall... Half of Berlin remained with the Russians – they could not even wait for Berlin to become whole again. Adolf Hitler gone, the friendship finished. When the magician is gone, the magic is finished; the enemies are again enemies. But enemies can become friends, and without becoming friends you cannot become enemies. First you have to be friends, that is the first step; then only can you become enemies – that is something higher, more evolved. Perhaps you have brought your friendship to its logical conclusion.

So Buddha, by saying hate your father and mother, also does not mean your father and mother, but the father and mother that have penetrated you, that have become like a thick layer of personality in you. But he was a very sophisticated man, the son of a king, very educated. Bodhidharma is very raw; he simply calls a spade a spade. Why bother about sophistication, hate, and this and that – simply kill. And I say to you, without killing you cannot get out of the prison.

So when I say disobey, I mean disobey everything that is not coming from your own self.

Obey that which is your nature.

Now, this man is saying that this means he cannot obey me. That's why I called him a born Oregonian, because if listening to me say disobey, you disobey, that is obedience – can't you see it? Before listening to me you were obeying; now because I have said disobey, you have to disobey. This is disobedience? Then what is obedience? This will be obedience!

You have not understood me at all. You have just heard that I am saying disobey, so now you have to disobey me, disobey the commune, disobey the discipline of sannyas. This man may be representing parts in all of you, because I have been receiving letters continually: "Osho, you are teaching disobedience, and in the commune we have to follow a certain discipline." To them it seems contradictory.

Disobey me, or the commune, or sannyas, if it is not from you. Who has forced you to be part of the commune? It is your choice. You were not born in the commune. It is your choice, and a difficult choice, because by being part of my commune you are going against everybody else around you. You are taking a risk.

It is dangerous to be part of my commune. It is dangerous to be in association with me. You have chosen it. I don't convert anybody; I try my best to dissuade you from becoming a sannyasin – what more can I do? I give you no consolation.

There is one question: "Osho, you have taken God away, now there is only existence. Existence means nature; it is harsh, it is indifferent, it doesn't care. If there is no God then I feel very much afraid."

Naturally, you will feel very much afraid because your God was nothing but a way to hide your fear. It was fear-oriented. It was just to keep your fear suppressed. Take God away and fear springs up. It is there; even when you are putting the rock of God on the spring, it is still there. You know perfectly well that it is there, alive, ready to burst forth any moment – just waiting for its chance, an opportunity.

Your whole life you have believed in God, and I have just said that there is no God – and that's enough! Perhaps for fifty years you have believed in God, found consolation in it, then just an ordinary man like me says there is no God, and fifty years of conditioning disappears and fear arises! Whom are you trying to deceive?

If I can do this, anybody can do this. Just anybody meeting you on the road can whisper in your ear, "There is no God" – finished! Your God is dead! Your fear is more alive than ever. Hence all the religions teach, their scriptures teach, "Don't listen to anybody who does not belong to your faith."

In India, Jaina scriptures say that if you are being followed by a mad elephant and you come close to a Hindu temple – although you could be saved if you take refuge in the temple and close the doors – don't go inside the temple. It is better to die on the road under the mad elephant's feet, because who knows? – in the Hindu temple you may hear something which will spoil your faith. And the same, exactly the same, is repeated in the Hindu scriptures: "Don't go in a Jaina temple, because sometimes a single sentence coming from an antagonistic religion may spoil your whole life's effort." But this is strange.

Just a few days ago an old man was here because he wanted to sit close to me at least once. He has been coming here for almost one year, has been doing all kinds of therapy groups, meditations, and is immensely interested in becoming a sannyasin – but unfortunately he is a billionaire. The family, the company of which he is the chairman… He is afraid of all those people – the board members, the company, the family.

They give millions of dollars every year in donations, but of course those donations go to the faith in which he was born. This time he was wavering between to be or not to be. Finally he decided that it was better, before he takes sannyas, to go and tell the family and the whole board of directors. Rather than afterwards, it was better to say it before. So he went. Now, he must be at least sixty, not less than that – not somebody immature who can be easily converted, programmed, deprogrammed. But you will be surprised: his family immediately went to a deprogrammer. The first thing, hearing his ideas they were shocked, they were angry; they could not believe that a man of sixty years old who earns one thousand million dollars per year can be so easily converted by a cult. He has to be deprogrammed.

These people are not special; it's just the common mind. And the deprogrammer suggested, of course, the right thing to do. He said, "He is not a child so you have to be very careful. You are not to be angry, you are not to show that you are against his new ideology, because your anger and your clear disappointment in him will take him farther away from you. You have to be very supportive, very loving."

The deprogrammer is really cunning but he understands one thing, that a sixty-year-old man cannot be treated like a child, that you deprogram him in two days. And we have not programmed him at all. We have not tried to make him become a sannyasin, he was asking to become a sannyasin. Now the family is pretending to be loving and very supportive. And the old man finds it very strange. The message has come, "Very strange things are happening. My family has never been so loving."

But deep down they are all boiling inside. I don't think that by their lovingness and supportiveness, which is all phony and American, the man can be prevented from coming here. In fact he will think – which the deprogrammer has not thought about – that my ideology is so beautiful that just hearing about it the family has become so loving and so supportive. It would have been perfectly right to go as a sannyasin. And next time he is going to become a sannyasin.

But they will make every effort: this is just trying the first deprogrammer. If it doesn't work they may try saying, "This man is mad, he cannot be in a responsible post like the chairman of a company. He should be put into a mental asylum or into some nursing home where he needs to be treated psychiatrically." They will not leave him so easily. That's why I said unfortunately he is a billionaire. If he were a poor man, the family would have been happy: "Get lost. Who cares! It is good that we get rid of you. Why have you come back? You should have become a sannyasin there."

I have not given you any discipline. The questioner says, "...the discipline of sannyas." Can't you understand a little bit of humor? What discipline of sannyas have I given to you? That you have to wear red clothes – does that mean anything? It is simply to annoy the old traditional sannyasins, just to give them a good headache. And that's what we were doing in India, because I had thousands of sannyasins and it was becoming difficult for people to decide who was my sannyasin, and who was the old traditional sannyasin.

They would even touch the feet of my sannyasins. But when they looked at my picture on the *mala*, they were shocked! That *mala* and picture are just to shock people. What discipline have I given to you? You don't know discipline. You should go and look in a Trappist monastery and then you will understand what discipline is.

I am reminded of a story:

In a Trappist monastery you enter for ever; you cannot get out unless you are thrown out. Unless you become a nuisance and the monastery decides to throw you out, you cannot get out on your own. That freedom is not allowed; about that, you have to decide before you enter. You can take your time, but once you enter the monastery it is for your whole life, it is lifelong. Only your dead body will come out of the monastery.

This man entered the monastery, perhaps the most orthodox in the whole world. The monks remain absolutely silent. Only one time can they speak, after three years. After each three years they have the right to speak once, if they have any complaint or any difficulty or any problem.

This man was suffering continually for three years because he had no mattress, so he was just sleeping on the naked floor, and it was really cold. Even his bones started hurting. But you had to wait three years before you could say, "I need a mattress."

After three years all the monks of the monastery gathered and the chief abbot asked them, "If anybody has anything to say, he can say it. For three years again there will be no meeting; nothing is to be said."

This man waited, then he said, "I need a mattress." Now, do you think for three years he was thinking of Jesus Christ? – only the mattress. And waiting and waiting, looking at the calendar for three years.

The chief abbot said, "Okay. For three years, now, no more complaints. In three years time you can speak again. A mattress will be provided."

The mattress was provided but it was too big, and his cell was too small, so that while they were bringing in the mattress they broke the glass of the door. The mattress was in but the glass was broken so the wind started coming in, the rain started coming in, and now three years... The poor man. At least before he could stretch his body; now he was sitting in a corner, the rain was coming in, the snow was coming in.

And what do you think? – that for these three years he was praying? Yes, he was praying that these three years should pass, "And if I am still alive..." It looked as if it would be difficult to be able to survive three years, but he survived. Man has an immense capacity to adjust to any kind of circumstances. Even in a Trappist monastery people survive. He survived.

And after three years, again the gathering. He came running to the gathering, and even before the chief abbot had asked, he raised his hand. The chief abbot was very angry. He said, "You are the same man again! Any complaint?"

He said, "For three years I have been suffering rain, wind, snow. My glass was broken when the mattress was brought in. The mattress was big, and the door was small."

The chief said, "Okay. Now for three years be silent. Your door will be mended."

The door was mended. The three years he had survived, but the mattress had not survived. It was stinking, and because the door had been open the stink was not so much. Now the door was closed and no air was coming in... And the mattress had become utterly rotten because for three years every kind of hazard that had been possible... Now the man could not breathe! It became so... And for three years!

He said, "Now these are my last days. I will not be able to raise my hand again." But he survived. Again he survived, because the adjustment capacity of man is really tremendous. If you are living in a stinking room, sitting on a rotten mattress, soon you will not smell it because your sensitivity to smell will be dulled, will be killed by the stink, the continuous stink. Your nose is not so strong, it is not made of steel, and very small parts in your nose have the capacity to smell. If there was this continuous warfare against your capacity to smell your nose would become dead.

He survived, but when three years had passed he ran as fast as he could. And before he could raise his hand, the abbot said, "Stop! Since you have come I have never heard anything but complaints. Get out! I don't want to listen anymore."

He said, "But I have not said anything yet. Just please listen to me."

The abbot said, "This type of people are not acceptable in a Trappist monastery. I have not heard anything from you in nine years except complaints, complaints, complaints."

They threw the poor man out.

And you say that you cannot follow the sannyas discipline? I have not given you any discipline. Yes, three things I have done...

I have given you a new name so that you can start disidentifying yourself from your old personality, and you can begin anew, as if a new child is born.

I have given you red clothes to wear just to destroy the monopoly of traditional sannyasins on red clothes – they are nobody's monopoly. And it was just a mockery of the sannyas that has existed in the East for thousands of years. I was saying that just by changing your clothes to red you don't become a sage.

I have given you a *mala*, because all the ancient sannyasins of all religions have used a rosary for prayer. I have not given it to you for any prayer.

It was an old method of counting. For example in Hinduism: how many times you take God's name is your account in the other world. But to remember "Ram, Ram, Ram..." You will forget. But to continue to remember, "One Ram, two Ram, three Ram" will be a disturbance. And "one, two, three, four, five" will grow to "one thousand and four...one million, two million, three million..." You are going to get lost somewhere and forget the counting. Then it will be a real loss because God will ask, "How many times...?"

So the rosary was a method: you count, you just go on, you say "Ram" and you slip one bead down. You needn't say "One." You say "Ram," and you slip the second bead down. You don't say "Ram two, Ram three," you just go on slipping the beads down. And it was good also because you could say it inside with nobody knowing about it. In India they have a small bag hanging around the hand, and the rosary is inside; so even walking on the road they can go on counting.

You will see shopkeepers selling things, and their hand is in their rosary bag: they are counting. With the customer they are talking but deep down they are saying, "Ram, Ram, Ram, Ram," and with the rosary they are counting. In between they will say to the wife: "The beggar!" and their rosary continues.

It was just to mock all these idiots that I put the rosary around you. It is not a prayer method for you, it is just a mockery of the whole tradition. And then I put an ordinary man's picture – anybody's picture will do. That annoys them even more.

But this world is strange. Sometimes things can happen which you had never expected or even dreamed of. Just the other day Sheela brought a letter from the Punjab – because in the Punjab there has been great trouble, with Hindus and Sikhs continually fighting and killing each other. Thousands of people have been killed.

In one small village there were two Sikhs, both our sannyasins, but the whole village was Hindu. These two Sikhs were teachers in the school. The principal suggested to them, "Don't come out of your home; and be careful, very careful because the whole village is mad. The whole of the Punjab is in madness, and you are only two – the crowd can kill you."

And that day, the whole day the crowd was moving around the city to find some Sikh to kill. They knew those two Sikhs were there, but where had they disappeared to? By the night as the sun set and darkness came over, those two Sikhs thought the crowds must have disappeared. The whole day they had been hiding in the house, so they thought to just come out for a little bit and breathe fresh air.

When they came out, immediately – as if the crowd had been waiting, hiding just nearby, knowing that they were hiding in the house – from both sides the crowd rushed towards them. One of them escaped into a nearby forest; in the darkness it was difficult to find him. But the other one was caught. He has written the letter to thank me, because when the crowd took hold of him, somebody n the crowd said, "This is not a Sikh, this is an Osho sannyasin!" So they said, "It is useless to kill this man – he is no longer a Sikh."

He writes to me, "Osho, you saved me; otherwise they would have cut me into pieces."

I have never thought that somebody would be saved by me, but strange things in this world always happen! This is simply a strange thing. You can be killed in my name, but you cannot be saved. It was a strange situation: they were going to kill a Sikh, but seeing his orange clothes and the *mala* with my photo, they said, "This man is already no longer a Sikh. To kill him is pointless." And they left.

But basically I had put that picture there so that it hangs around your neck and irritates everybody, and you cannot go anywhere without being noticed.

One of my sannyasins in Mumbai... He took sannyas, and after two, three days he came back and said, "I am in a real trouble. Will you give sannyas to my wife too? I have brought her."

I asked, "Why?"

He said, "The problem is, wherever I go with her people say, 'What kind of sannyasin is this? Sannyasins are not supposed to move around with women.' And I cannot say that she is my wife, because if I say that, they will kill me. A sannyasin having a wife? So it is very awkward; what to do? It is better you give sannyas to her."

I said, "I will give sannyas to her but this won't solve the problem. Try it." I gave sannyas to his wife. After two days he was back. He said, "You were right. Yesterday in the train..." It was a local train; he takes the train to work in his office and goes back. It was a holiday so he had come with his wife and child. A crowd gathered, and they asked, "Whose child is this?" – because in Mumbai children are being stolen. In all the big cities of India children are being stolen. Then they are crippled, blinded, and they are made beggars. And there are gangs: a certain man who feeds them and takes all their earnings in the evening. He feeds them, he gives them clothes, he gives them shelter. But unless they are blinded, crippled, their legs cut off or their hands cut off, who is going to give them money? The more crippled and the more miserable they look, the better are their chances for begging, and the more money they bring in.

So in every big place children are being stolen. And they end up in some gang where there are hundreds of children. The police know; the police take their own part of the money. The police do not prevent the children from begging on the streets; rather, they protect them. In fact they help the owner of these children so that these children cannot escape anywhere.

In fact these children cannot escape because they have been blinded, crippled – where can they escape to? Who will look after them? They don't know where their father is, their mother is, from where they have been brought – because if they were caught in Kolkata, they would be used in Mumbai. If they were caught in Mumbai, they would be used in Chennai. So they don't know where they come from or where they are right now.

They cannot escape, but the police still keep an eye out so that nobody tries to escape. Everybody has his share, except that child. And if he comes back from begging one day without any money, then he gets beaten. So he has to come with it. He cannot try to hide some money from the owner, because he knows how much a child earns.

The owner goes on walking around and looking to see how much this child will have earned by the end of the evening. So tentatively he knows that this boy is bound to come with ten rupees, fifteen rupees. And if he comes with only two rupees then he gets beaten. And where can he hide the money? That money is found immediately.

So a crowd gathered and they asked, "You are both sannyasins; this woman is a sannyasin, you are a sannyasin. In the first place, why are a woman and a man sannyasin together? That is not allowed. In the second place, this child – from where did you get this child?"

They said, "This is our child." They had to say it. And people started getting ready to beat them: "This is your child? You are a sannyasin and you have a child."

Somehow they tried to explain, showed the *mala*, and said, "We are not old, traditional sannyasins."

Somebody in the crowd knew about me. He said, "Leave them. They are not your type of sannyasins. They belong to a different kind: neo-sannyas."

From the station they came directly to me. They said, "Give sannyas to our child also, because without it we will be caught again. We are poor people and anybody can start beating us and can create trouble for us." I had to give sannyas to the child too!

It was not a discipline; it was simply a revolt. I wanted to show the sannyasins of India, who are in millions, that just by changing the clothes or having a rosary it does not mean that you have become a saint. I can create millions of saints like them without any trouble. And I have created them!

The only thing that you can call a discipline is meditation. And it is not an order from me that you have to meditate. I explain to you what meditation is. If it appeals to your reason, if something clicks in you, if a desire arises in you to explore this dimension of meditation, then it is not that you are following my idea, you are following your own intelligence. And if it does not appeal to you, of course you should not do it.

And saying, "I cannot even participate in the *gachchhamis*," the person has used the words "our prayer." It is not prayer. A prayer is always to beg for something. That's actually the meaning of the word *prayer*, praying for something: "Give us, Lord, our daily bread," or whatsoever it is, but "Give us something. You are the giver, and we are the beggar. You are compassionate, and we are in need of your compassion; save us. This life is miserable, this existence is suffering, take us out of this wheel of life and death." Different religions, different prayers... But everybody is asking for something.

You cannot call our *gachchhamis* "prayer." It is not; because what do you say in the *gachchhamis*? "I go to the feet of the awakened one; I go to the feet of the commune of the awakened one; I go to the feet of the ultimate truth of the awakened one."

You are declaring something, you are not praying. It is a declaration, and a determination – "I go the feet of the awakened one" – a determination to drop the ego, a declaration, "From now on, to be awakened is going to be my whole effort, my whole involvement, my whole commitment; I am not going to live an unconscious life anymore." It is not a prayer.

In my vision there is no place for prayer because there is no place for God. To whom can you pray? – there is no one. The sky is absolutely empty. You are simply wasting your time and throwing nonsense words into the atmosphere, crowding the atmosphere with meaningless words.

You must remember: these words never die. Once uttered, a word goes on resounding just like a pebble thrown in a lake: waves start moving towards the farther away shore. But this existence has no shores, no banks, no boundaries. Once you say something it is going to remain forever. It will go on resounding farther and farther away. It will touch other planets, it will touch other stars; it will go on moving and moving.

Now we know – before the invention of radio we had no idea – that something said in Washington is passing just by your side. Now you know because we have discovered how to catch hold of it. Whatsoever they are creating is already passing all the stations of the world. Of course they are creating very strong vibrations. They go on moving around you; you just have to attune your radio to a certain wavelength, then on that wavelength whatsoever is uttered will be caught.

It is true about us too. Whatsoever we are saying is not very strong, but it never dies, the sound continues. One day we will find a way to catch hold of sounds which were uttered by different people in the past – because each person has a different vibe, a different frequency. If we can get hold of the frequency of Krishna, then what he really said in the Gita five thousand years ago, and whether it was said at all or not, will be caught again. And I am certain that this big book, the Gita, could not possibly have been written in the situation in which it was said to have been.

Two armies facing each other – they are just waiting for the signal and they will start slaughtering each other. And Arjuna says to his charioteer, Krishna, "Take me in front." He is the chief warrior of one side. Seeing all the people there, his friends, his relatives... The other party was nobody else but his cousin-brothers, and they had all grown up in the same house, in the same palace, they were taught by the same man. Dronacharya, the man who had taught both parties the art of archery, was there on the other side: his own master.

On this side everybody was related to those on that side. On that side everybody was related to those on this side: it was a family quarrel. Arjuna freaked out. He simply said to Krishna, "I will not fight this war. This is not war, this is simply suicide. These are all our people. Whosoever dies will bring tears to my eyes. My father's father, my grandfather, is standing there. My master who has taught me, who has brought me up to be the greatest archer in the world, he is on the other side. No, I cannot fight. I would rather renounce the world and become a sannyasin and go to the Himalayas."

Now, this is the situation. This big book is a dialogue in which Arjuna goes on asking questions and Krishna goes on answering them. For me to comment on it took almost – Taru, how many years? – perhaps three years: twelve volumes, one thousand pages each. In this situation it doesn't seem to be likely that this big sermon... In eighteen days the whole war was finished; in eighteen days the whole Gita cannot be finished! So perhaps he had spoken a few words and later on it is just elaboration, and more and more was added to it to clarify and simplify and to make it understandable.

But one day it is possible that we may catch hold of Krishna – or Jesus giving his sermon on the mountain – because no sound ever dies; once it is uttered it remains forever. Yes, it will become weaker and weaker and weaker and weaker, and you will need more and more forceful, forcible, stronger receivers to catch hold of it. And of course it will be a tower of Babel, because millions of people have been speaking for millions of years and all their words will be mixed.

But there is a possibility... It is just as your fingerprints are yours alone: they have never existed before and there never will be a possibility for them to exist in the future. You fingerprints are simply your fingerprints. Your sound prints are also simply your sound prints; sooner or later we will be able to sort them out. And once we get your sound print, your frequency, then whatsoever you have said in your whole life can be reproduced.

You will be surprised to know that Mahavira is the only man in the whole of history who has said, "Don't say anything which you would not like to be associated with you forever, because whatsoever you say is going to be eternal." He is the only man, but what he is saying certainly has a tremendous insight. His reason for not saying bad words, ugly words, is very scientific, not religious. He is saying it because those words will remain always; they will be your footprints in time. Don't leave anything ugly behind you.

When you declare, "*Buddham sharanam gachchhami* – I go to the feet of the awakened one," you are not saying a prayer. You are simply declaring to existence, to yourself, your intention: "I want to drop my ego."

Hence, *gachchhami* – *gachchhami* simply means "going." The English word *go* comes from the Sanskrit word *gachchh*. You will be surprised that the Sanskrit word for cow is *gau*, because the cow was very much loved by the Hindus, worshipped as a mother, thought to be holy. The movement of the cow – cow is pronounced gau – his movement is called "Gachchh." And from *gachchh* comes the English word.

"Going to the feet" needs one absolutely necessary condition: that you drop the ego. With the ego you cannot go to the feet of the buddha, the awakened one. And by "the awakened one," we are not saying any particular person. We are simply saying that because the quality of awareness is the same, all the awakened ones become the same when they are awakened: there is no difference at all. Awakening is simply awakening. So we go to the feet of whosoever is awakened, wherever he is awakened – in the past, in the present or in the future.

It is a decision to drop the ego. It is a declaration that: "Existence, remain my witness, I am going to the feet of the awakened one. Let me be reminded if I forget." That's why it has to be repeated. The more you repeat it, the better, because the more it becomes a determination, the more it becomes a clear perception of what it means.

But to go to the feet of the awakened one is not very difficult. It is very easy. The very presence of the awakened one will create in you the desire to go to his feet. It is not something literal, that you have to go to his feet. It simply means that you start feeling a kind of surrender. The surrender is not asked; if it is asked, disobey. If the surrender happens to you, obey; it is your own feeling, your own authentic experience. But it is easy, hence the second *gachchhami*: "*Sangham sharanam gachchhami.*"

It is easy to go to the feet of the awakened one, it is a little difficult to go to the feet of the commune of the awakened one, because in the commune all will not be awakened. Many will be fast asleep and snoring; many will be even deeper in sleep than you. Now, the ego will feel it more difficult to go to the feet of these people. That means you will have to drop the ego now even more determinedly. Perhaps in the first *gachchhami* you had only dropped a few leaves of your ego. In the second you will have to drop the whole tree.

The third is even more difficult, but for a different reason. "*Dhammam sharanam gachchhami* – I go to the feet of the ultimate truth of the awakened one." What it is that the awakened people have experienced, they have not said; it is inexpressible. They have all remained silent about it.

Where are you going to find the feet of the ultimate truth? And in your state of unawareness, in your state of unconsciousness, in what direction are you going to search? And not knowing where to surrender, to whom to surrender, what to surrender, it becomes even more difficult for the ego. You will even have to bring the roots of the tree out from the ground; they are hiding underground. Even if the tree has fallen, the tree can again grow from the roots. These are simple declarations – and they have to be your declarations, they can't be my declarations.

But listening to me saying that disobedience is a quality of religion, immediately the desire to disobey arises in you. And you have listened to many things from me, but never before has any desire like this arisen. Certainly deep down you want to disobey.

Perhaps you have forced yourself into obedience. Then you have done wrong; then this is not the place for you. Then you have simply trapped yourself in something which has not come out of your decision. Perhaps you have imitated some other people – perhaps your friend was becoming a sannyasin, and you became a sannyasin. Perhaps you were impressed by my words, impressed by my reasoning. But your sannyas has not arisen from your deepest core; otherwise after listening to me say that disobedience is a religious quality, you would have waited a little and thought about it.

You should have asked, "Then what is obedience? Is not obedience also a religious quality?" That would have been the right question. I am continually giving you the right answer to the wrong question, but nothing else can be done. I can understand you can't ask the right question and I can't give you a wrong answer; so what to do? This way it goes on. You go on asking the wrong question. But I don't care much about your question: I go on answering what I want to answer. Your question is just an excuse.

Obedience is a greater religious quality than disobedience.

Disobedience is only for the beginners who are just starting to learn how to walk – wobbling. Disobedience is a religious quality for those who are much too attached to their personality, their conditioning, their programming. Disobedience is a technique for you to deprogram yourself, so that you become clean of all Christianity, Judaism, Hinduism, Mohammedanism. You simply come clean out of all that. You come out just simple, yourself, innocent. Then obedience is the quality of religion.

Then comes the time to obey; but first learn to disobey. Disobey is a negative word. It is simply to cut all the crap from you, to burn all the rubbish in you. It is a negative process. But it is only the beginning. When this negative process is complete and you have burned all the crap, and you are unburdened and free and ready to fly, then obedience is the quality of religion. But that is a higher quality, a far more conscious quality.

But you don't obey anybody else. You now simply obey your being. Wherever it leads you, go fearlessly, in freedom.

To be with me you have to disobey all that has been taught to you. I have not taught you anything. I have not said to you, "Do this, don't do that." I am not bothered about details, I am simply concerned with the fundamentals; to make clear to you that these are the fundamentals. Now it is up to you what you want to do with these fundamentals. You can turn your back and go anywhere you like, and it is perfectly okay with me. But when you understand the fundamentals you cannot turn your back on them. It is not possible; in the very nature of things it is impossible.

Once you see a certain truth you cannot do anything other than obey it. But it has to be your seeing, your perception, your realization.

Begin with disobedience. It is always necessary to begin with the negative, with the no. If you want to reach the yes, you will have to say a thousand no's to find one yes in life. Because your whole life has been ruined by so many people, you will have to say no to all those people. And after a thousand no's, perhaps you may find yourself in a state where you can say yes.

But that yes will come from the deepest core of your being, and it will bring out a fragrance in you.

jesus: the only savior
who nearly saved himself

Osho,
Yesterday we were met by five bible-packing Christians who had come to
save us. What do you say? Can we be saved?

These idiots are all over the world, perhaps more so in Oregon. The very idea
of saving somebody is violent. It is interfering, trespassing on somebody's
life. Nobody has the right to save anybody.

He can save himself... But there is a psychological reason why these Bible-
packing people start saving others: they are not confident that they are saved. To
gain that confidence they have to shout loudly, make a noise, make efforts to save
others. And certainly they will find a few fools who are ready to be saved. That will
give them tremendous confidence, but there is no base. Their very life is just the life
of a fanatic who thinks he is saved because he believes in Jesus Christ.

Life needs transformation, and transformation is a great work upon oneself. It
is not a child's play: "Just believe in Jesus Christ, go on reading the Bible again
and again, and you are saved." Saved from what? Saved from transformation!

So if you meet these people again, please tell them, "You have come to the
right place. Here we unsave people who have fallen into the mistaken idea that
they are saved. We unsave them again. We pull them back to the earth from their
foggy mind."

But the responsibility is not with these poor people – they are pitiable – the
responsibility goes back to Jesus himself. He was trying to save people. And
what signs was he providing them? No signs, no idea how they can change their
lifestyle, how they can find their true being, how they can discover the truth that
they are carrying within themselves. No structure, no process, no methodology is

given. All that is required is: "Believe that I am the only begotten son of God, that I am the Messiah," and that's enough.

Is transformation of life so cheap that you believe in anybody and just by believing…? You are not losing anything, and Jesus is not giving you anything but a sort of hallucination that you are saved.

Not a single person has been saved by Jesus. And I don't think he was able to save himself. The way he behaves, the way he talks all show that it is not the flavor of an awakened being; something is missing. His ego is tremendously strong. Yes, it has a religious jargon about it, the "only begotten son of God" – but any madman can say that.

What evidence does he bring? It is because of this that the Christians go on emphasizing the miracles of Jesus, because without those miracles what evidence has he got? And those miracles were never performed, because if such things were performed, it is impossible that Jewish sources would not have mentioned them. He would have been accepted as the messiah.

The Jews never accepted him, not even today. His contemporaries have to be asked why not a single authoritative source even mentions his name. And if such a miracle man was around he would be the only news for centuries, but not even his contemporaries bothered about him. And his contemporaries have given a clear-cut indication by crucifying this man. Why did they crucify him?

People have not inquired into the incident, why the Jews crucified Jesus. They crucified him for the simple reason that this man is mad, and is pretending something which will misguide millions of people. It is better to be finished with him. He is not the messiah because the Jews have criteria for who is the messiah, who will save the whole world from suffering, from misery, from anguish. The same idea that Jesus gives to the Christians, *he* has got from his ancestors. He is a perfect Jew.

What the Jews were saying was about some messiah somewhere far away, happening in the coming history, in the future. Jesus' fault was only this: he started saying, "I am that man you have been waiting for. I am that hope you have been desiring. I have come." And they really laughed at him – anybody would have laughed at him.

The hope of the Jews has to remain a hope. Whenever anybody will try to say, "I have come to fulfill the hope," he will be crucified, for the simple reason that he is taking away the hope of a whole race. They are living on that hope; that is their only light, their only guiding star. And this carpenter's son – ignorant, illiterate, good-for-nothing – wants to prove that he is that hoped for messiah: "This man has to be finished off!"

And there was one more reason why they crucified him: "If on the cross he can manage to provoke God to help him, then we will be able to see whether he is the messiah or not – God will save him." If God is not even bothering about saving his own son on the cross, then what to say about others? And if Jesus cannot provoke God to save him, how can he provoke God to save others?

The crucifixion was going to be a criterion. Thousands of people had gathered; it was not an everyday thing. Only once in a while a madman declares such a thing. And they were laughing and joking and throwing stones at him and spitting on him.

They had put a crown of thorns on him, they had forced him to carry his own cross. Three times he fell on the way; the cross was too heavy. He could not carry his own cross and he was trying to carry the crosses of the whole of humanity, trying to save the whole of humanity, taking all their miseries, their anguishes, their sufferings. And whenever he fell people laughed, and they said, "You can't carry even your own cross, how you are going to carry the crosses of everybody else?"

And on the cross they had written "King of the Jews," just as a joke, because this man was constantly talking about the Kingdom of God, and saying, "Those who believe in me will be saved. At the judgment day, I will be there with God indicating the people who are my people: sorting out people into those who have to be saved, and those who have not to be saved. And I am going to be your witness. The judgment is in my hand."

On the cross he himself feels shaken up. He cries to God, "Have you forgotten me? Have you forsaken me?" – because he sees that the crucifixion is happening and there is no miracle. He looks upwards towards the sky...that God will be descending on a white cloud, angels will be coming, singing "Alleluia, Alleluia."

But no angels are coming, no God is seen anywhere; the sky is completely clear, not even a cloud. And the crowd is shouting and rejoicing and dancing. They are hilarious, saying, "Look at the fool! He was going to save the whole world!"

And he feels thirsty, obviously. Walking a long way, carrying a heavy cross in the hot sun – and the crucifixion happened on a hill, Golgotha – he was thirsty, and on the cross as blood started oozing out from his hands and feet...

The Jewish crucifixion was the most cruel way of killing a man that has been practiced anywhere. It took sometimes thirty-six to forty-eight hours for a man to die. An electric chair is far more nonviolent. You simply sit in it and you are gone – just a switch. Perhaps you may not even hear the click. By the time you hear the click, you are no more.

Every country has its way, but the Jews had the most torturous. Death is not a torture; death may be a relief from a torturous life, but on the Jewish cross you will be praying, "Kill me, God, kill me; I cannot wait anymore" – because you are hungry and thirsty, and as the blood goes out of your body, you feel more thirsty, more thirsty, because you are losing liquid. You are still alive, and the pain is tremendous. Such a slow death. It is not just death. Death can be very simple: you cut the head off the person; it's not much of a problem. It does not need forty-eight hours, forty-eight hours of dying.

He started asking for water. Now, this is the man who used to walk on water. This is the man who used to turn water into wine. This is the man who raised the dead from their grave. But he cannot stop his blood flowing out of his body. He cannot make his blood flow backwards into the body. He cannot even manage a glass of water – and he was able to change stones into bread!

Why can't he change the air into water? Why can't he arrange a cloud to shower just on him so he can have a good shower and drink the water? He proved absolutely impotent on the cross.

But the Christians go on, all over the world, saving people. They don't even understand what it means to save.

In the East, no religion has ever proclaimed that anybody can save you except yourself; and the East knows far more deeply about man's life and its transforming forces. It has been working on the human psyche for thousands of years. Still much has to be discovered – perhaps that is not the right word: rediscovered will be the right word – by the West, which the East has already discovered long before.

For example, when Sigmund Freud, Jung and Adler and other great psychologists of the beginning of this century started talking of the unconscious mind, the subconscious mind, the conscious mind, it was Freud's rediscovery. But he never came to know that it was a *rediscovery*, that in India for thousands of years we have known all these divisions are there.

But the West was shocked, could not believe there was an unconscious. "If there is an unconscious then why is it not mentioned in the Bible? – because anything which is not mentioned in the Bible certainly does not exist. God has given the whole message entirely about everything: the unconscious mind is not mentioned."

Jung went a little deeper and found the collective unconscious mind. But you will be surprised that Buddha talks about not only these minds but a few more minds, because this is only one way... For example, Freud goes downwards: the conscious mind is of course acceptable to everybody because that's where we are, but Freud goes downwards and finds the subconscious mind. That's when you dream. A boundary line between the unconscious and the conscious, it is just the middle part that joins the unconscious with the conscious.

Jung goes a little deeper and finds that if you go deeper into the unconscious, you suddenly find a depth which is not individual, which is collective. It is as if on the surface you see many icebergs, but as you go deeper you find only a big iceberg with many peaks above the surface of the water – but underneath it is only one big iceberg.

Buddha goes upwards too. He goes downwards – and farther than Jung. After the collective unconscious mind he says there is a cosmic unconscious mind, because the collective unconscious mind means the unconscious mind of the whole humanity – but what about the animals and the trees and the mountains and the rivers and the stars? Go a little deeper and you will find a cosmic unconscious mind.

And Buddha goes upwards too. So going downwards, the conscious mind is just in the middle, where we are. Below it are the subconscious mind, unconscious mind, collective unconscious mind and cosmic unconscious mind. He also moved upwards, which in the future psychology has to do. He says, "Above the conscious mind is again the same ladder that goes downwards. Just as below there is a subconscious mind; above there is a superconscious mind."

If you move upwards then above the superconscious mind you will find, in Buddha's language, the super-superconscious mind. Then you will find the collective conscious mind, and then you will find the cosmic conscious mind. Then you have traveled the whole journey, downwards and upwards.

Now, before Sigmund Freud, people thought that Buddha was just imagining. But Freud was not a religious man in any sense. He had a scientific mind: he proved the subconscious, the unconscious. Jung was not a religious man; he proved the collective unconscious. Now some other scientist is needed to prove the cosmic unconscious.

And he will be coming soon, because if it is a fact – and it must be, because if this man Buddha goes about finding the fourth absolutely correctly, there is no reason to doubt that he is correct about the fifth. And if he is correct about the downward ladders, then why should he not be correct about the upward ladders?

But to move upward you will need the religious mind. The scientific mind will not be enough.

The scientific mind can go more towards things. And this is how you are going to move towards things: from the conscious mind you have to come to the cosmic unconscious mind. Perhaps things have a cosmic unconscious mind, absolutely dormant, but it must be there. Otherwise how is it possible that you eat food, which is dead, which is a "thing," but it feeds your brain, your mind, and keeps them functioning. Somewhere, some part of the things you eat is releasing some consciousness, some mind quality to you. Otherwise from where do you get your mind?

They say if you don't breathe for six minutes, and oxygen does not reach the brain, the brain starts deteriorating. Its cells are so delicate that at the most they can survive without oxygen only six minutes.

It happened in the Second World War that a few people had heart attacks, just a psychological heart attack: a bomb fell just in front of them, exploded and killed many people. When you see so many people dying – suddenly an explosion and so many people dying – it is possible to have a psychological heart attack. You may fall dead. You are not dead, but amongst so many dead how can you stand alive? You can't be an exception. You are not the only begotten son of God; you are just an ordinary human being, and when everybody is dying what are you doing here? Just the shock may stop your breathing.

They revived many people like this in Russia in the Second World War. If the person was revived after six minutes had passed, he became alive, but he never became conscious. He remained in a coma because already the brain had broken, but the rest of the body came back; everything else started functioning.

I have seen one woman who had been for nine months in a coma, with everything functioning. She was breathing, her pulse was normal, everything was good, just somehow her brain had gone into nonfunctioning. The doctors said she could live years. If you went on supporting, helping, feeding her, she could live for years, but there was no hope that her brain could be restored. And we don't yet have banks for brains, to put somebody else's brain in your skull.

But somebody else's brain will bring somebody else's personality, not your personality. That is a difficult problem. Even if one day we can manage to have banks of brains for transplant, those brains will be carrying memories of somebody else, his education... Perhaps he was a mathematician, a poet, a painter; perhaps he was a beggar or a very rich man: he will have different kinds of memories.

His brain could be fixed into your skull, but it will not be you who comes back to consciousness, he will come back: he will use your body. He will speak his language: if he was French, he will speak French, if he was Russian, he will speak Russian. He will not take any notice of who you are, whether you have been somebody who had not even heard a single word of Russian.

That's a problem. First, to have transplant banks is a problem because the brain cells die so quickly. But perhaps we can find some way that when a person is dying, before he dies the brain is taken out and put into a tank where enough oxygen is available, so the brain can go on functioning. He will be dreaming there in the tank – making love to a woman, or if he is a pervert then doing something else. Still, certainly he will be dreaming and doing his thing – what he was doing inside his original body.

Now he will be doing it in the tank – perhaps far better because more oxygen and more pure oxygen will be available. And he will not be able to know that he has been taken out, because one strange thing about your skull is that inside the skull there is no sensitivity.

So if you take the brain out, the brain will not feel as if it has been taken out, removed from its original place, placed into something else. It could simply live on its own. It could function on its own. And whenever it is put back again into a body, the body will start following the orders of this brain.

Buddha goes upwards too. He says this brain… And there are certain facts about the mind and the brain to be known, which scientists have discovered that half of the brain is non-functioning. Only fifty percent of your brain is functioning, and the other fifty percent of the brain, towards the back, is almost completely non-functioning.

Now, nature never creates anything for nonfunctioning. It only creates things to function, and such a valuable thing as the brain… If half the brain is non-functioning it simply means that we don't know its uses yet. We have not discovered for what it is meant to be used.

That gives me a clue. The half of the brain that is functioning is being discovered by our psychologists, and the half of the brain that is not functioning starts functioning with meditation. And slowly, slowly you start becoming aware of something higher than you, beyond you, and beyond, and beyond. The cosmic conscious mind is your ultimate truth.

Unless you know it you are not saved, because then you will be moving in the labyrinth of the unconscious, the collective unconscious, the cosmic unconscious; you will be moving in this labyrinth of darkness which creates all your misery.

Now, what does Jesus know about it? Just by his telling people, "Believe in me," I don't think that the other half of their brain will start functioning. These Bible-packing people – do you think that their other half is functioning? Most probably their whole mind has stopped functioning; they are in a coma.

Faith is a kind of coma. You stop reasoning, you stop doubting. You stop questioning. Naturally, because these are the functions of your mind, and when those functions disappear, by and by your mind stops. If it is not used it gathers junk; it becomes more and more dull, because doubt is not allowed. Strange things are expected from you...

Just the other day, Sheela brought me the latest message to humanity from pope the Polack, a message of one hundred and thirty-nine pages. Naturally it has to be one hundred and thirty-nine pages because he has not left a single stupid thing unsaid. You will be surprised that he has found some new sins which are not mentioned in the Bible. Only a Polack can do that; otherwise what were all those Old Testament prophets, and then Jesus, doing?

The Polack has found new sins, but those sins are worth consideration. One of the sins that he speaks of is the idea of class struggle: to believe in the idea of class struggle is a sin, a major sin. Now whether you believe in the class struggle or not, the class struggle is there. There *is* a struggle between the rich and the poor. It is not a question of your belief.

In India there is a struggle between castes, a double struggle: class struggle *and* caste struggle. Hindus have divided their society into four major *varnas*. The word *varna* is significant; it means color. Perhaps in the beginning the division was done by color. The whitest were the Aryans, whom Adolf Hitler claimed to be the Germans, the Nordic Germans, the purest Aryans. He used the word *Aryans* for Germans, and he used the Aryan symbol of the swastika for his flag. That is a Hindu symbol, an ancient Aryan symbol. They were the highest, and as your color became darker, you became lower and lower and lower.

South India is almost black. If you cut Africa and India from a map and put them side by side, you will be surprised – they fit absolutely. It is a very recent finding that once South Africa and India were connected, then slowly they drifted away. So South India is really of Negro blood. And it is strange in many ways that the color of the South Indians is black and their languages are the only languages in India which are not Sanskrit-oriented, while all the European languages are Sanskrit-oriented. For example, thirty percent in English, forty percent in German, thirty-five percent in Russian, seventy percent in Lithuanian, forty percent in Italian...

So in Europe the roots have come from Sanskrit, but the South Indian languages – Tamil, Telugu, Kannada, Malayalam... Not a single percent of their language has been borrowed from Sanskrit. This is a very strange thing. It indicates something: these people are not Aryans. Germans and Russians and Swiss and French and English are offshoots of the Aryans, but the South Indians are not Aryans.

So perhaps in the beginning just on the basis of color... That's why they call them the four *varnas*; but later on, slowly the color got mixed. When you live with people... Even in America, you will find a person who is half Negro and half Caucasian, half Negro, half Italian, half Negro, half English. When people live together they go on mixing. It is very difficult to keep blood separate. So slowly the *varnas* got mixed, the colors got mixed, but the castes remained.

There is a certain struggle between the brahmin and the sudra. The brahmin is the highest caste, and the sudra is the lowest caste. There is a struggle, a five-thousand-year-old struggle. Thousands of sudras have been killed, murdered, butchered, burned alive; even today that continues for small excuses.

For example, in a small Indian village you will find two wells. One well is for the higher castes, the three higher castes: the brahmins, the priest class; the kshatriyas, the warrior class; and the vanikas, the business class. And the sudras, the untouchables, have a second well. Untouchables are not allowed to take water from the same well as the three higher classes.

And sometimes it happens that those poor people cannot manage to have a deep enough well – and they are the poorest of the poor. In summer their wells dry up, so they have to go miles to a river or to a lake to bring water, but they cannot go to the well in the city. If they are found... Sometimes it happens in the night, when somebody is thirsty. The river is so far away, everybody is asleep, and nobody will come to know... He goes silently and tries to take a bucket of water – and he is caught. That is enough. That well has become impure, and that will create a riot.

These poor untouchables, the sudras, live outside the town. They don't live inside the town, hence their other name is *antyaja. Antyaja* means "those who live outside the town." And they have the poorest huts made of grass and bamboo. You can go with just one burning torch in your hand and set fire to the whole of their village. Just a single man within five minutes can set the whole untouchables village on fire.

Their children will be burned, their animals will be burned, their old men who cannot escape in time will be burned. And if a whole village is trying to burn the sudras, then with torches, burning torches, they will not allow anybody to escape; they will force them back into their burning huts. This happens even today on any small excuse.

A rumor that a high-caste girl is being seduced by an untouchable young man – just a rumor is enough! It may not be true; most probably it is not true, because in an Indian village it is very difficult to have any love affair, it is such a close-knit society.

And the women are not free to move outside the house. They don't go to school, they don't go to college, they don't go to the university; there is almost nowhere they can go. The only places they go are the water well and the temple. In both places, the sudra is not allowed. So where will a high-caste girl meet an untouchable? To fall in love you have at least to be introduced.

And the sudras are so impure, so dirty in the minds of the higher classes that even their shadow is dirty. Great imagination! Now, a shadow has no existence. A shadow is simply there because you are standing in the way of the sun rays so the sun rays cannot pass you; hence you create a shadow. There is nothing like a shadow. You cannot catch hold of it, you cannot put it in a bag and take it home; you cannot escape from it, it will follow you. It does not exist; it is just an absence of rays because you are blocking them.

But Hindus have condemned those poor people so much that even if their shadow passes over you – you are sitting and a sudra passes by, not touching you but his shadow touches you – it is enough to create a riot! A few people may be murdered, because: "Why was he so arrogant? He should be more careful."

In the old days, and in very remote corners even today, the sudra first has to declare, "I am a sudra and I am coming; so please, if anybody is on the road, move away." In the past a sudra used to have to do two things... There were streets which were not open for him, he could not go on them. But for certain purposes it was impossible not to, so at certain hours he was allowed.

For example, he was to clean the latrines of the higher classes, so at certain hours, early in the morning before anybody gets up, he would come and quickly clean the latrines. But even then – perhaps somebody may have gone for a morning walk – he had to go on doing two things. He had to shout, "I am coming – I am a sudra. Please move away if you are somewhere on the way."

And the second thing – you will be surprised – he had to keep something like a brush made of a certain kind of grass that is used in India for cleaning the floors. That brush, that grass brush, used to hang behind him just like a tail; he had to keep it tied to his waist. That was to clean the path behind him. As he was moving, automatically the brush was cleaning the path after him, his shadow, any dirt that he is leaving behind – so nobody becomes impure. This is a caste struggle.

Now, no sudra was allowed to study or be educated. If he was found studying, perhaps secretly, then it was enough of a crime for him to be killed; that was the only punishment.

And this pope, the Polack, says, "The idea of class struggle, the very idea is a sin." This is a great discovery! And why does he say it? The fear of communism – he is not courageous enough to say that to believe in communism is a sin because the whole philosophy of communism is based on the idea of class struggle. Cunning. Why not be clear that to be a communist is a sin? He must be afraid that when he goes back to Poland, then those communists there will kill him. And what will happen to communists in Poland? Poland now is a communist country; the whole of Poland will become sinners.

You see the trickiness of these priests? So he calls it class struggle: the idea of class struggle, to spread the idea of class struggle, is a great sin.

And another thing, even more marvelous: he says that nobody can have a direct contact with God; that is a sin. You have to go via the Catholic priest; you cannot confess directly, that is not possible. God is not going to hear you. Your confession is useless.

Can you see the strategy? The strategy is very complicated, but simple to understand. The Catholic priest lives on your confessions. The whole function of the priest disappears if you can have a direct contact with God; then what is the need of the priesthood?

The pope is not interested in saving you, he is interested in saving the priesthood. He is the head of the priesthood class, and he is worried about the thousands of Catholic priests if people start a direct communication with God. You have to go to the Catholic priest to confess; only then will you be forgiven. The priest will persuade God to forgive you. You cannot ask directly.

The implications are many. The Catholic priest knows about every Catholic: with whose wife he is flirting, who is a homosexual; he also knows with whom his wife is flirting. He knows about every Catholic – that is his power. No Catholic can go against him. He has all the keys in his hands; he can expose you at any moment.

Confession is a strategy of power politics. Hence the Catholic is the most imprisoned religious man in the world, because the priest knows every wrong thing that you have done. The court does not know, the police do not know, your wife has not any knowledge of it, but the priest knows everything. That is his power over the flock: he can expose you any moment in front of the society. The police will be after you, the government will be after you, your wife will be after you, your father will be after you – you will be crushed.

He knows all the sins that you have committed; but you have not been caught, so they are not crimes. And you yourself had gone to confess. In fact, that is his only joy in life. The Catholic priest, what else has he got? There is no need for him to go to the movies or to see the television: just sitting in his confession box and listening to all the groovy things is such a joy. And he goes on giving the punishment also. He says, "Go out in the church and do this prayer ten times."

One day it happened…

A rabbi who was a friend of a Catholic priest was visiting the priest; it was a confession day. Suddenly a man came running. The Catholic priest had just finished one confession and given the man a punishment of ten prayers because he had raped a woman. The rabbi was also sitting in the confessional box. They were friends so he was just listening to what was going on.

The man came running and said, "Somebody is very sick, almost dying and you are needed to bless him for the journey."

So the priest said to the rabbi, "I will have to go. I will come back as quickly as possible. But meanwhile somebody may come to confess, so you just sit here."

The rabbi said, "But what am I to do?"

The priest said, "You just have to listen to so many confessions; just give them some punishment. And you can't see them face to face – there is a curtain – so nobody feels awkward." Otherwise confessing one's sins feels awkward. And the priest, inquiring more about it and going more and more into your sin – how you committed the rape, and what happened; what you did and what she did – would feel awkward asking these things… "So the curtain is there so nobody will know who is inside – a rabbi or a Catholic priest."

So the rabbi said, "Okay, go, but come back quickly because I am not accustomed to this business – we do things differently."

A man came, and by chance he had also committed a rape. The rabbi felt at ease, he said, "Don't be worried, son." Exactly in the tone of the minister: "Don't be worried, son. You just go and do ten prayers."

But the man said, "The last time I committed a rape you asked only for five prayers."

The rabbi said to himself, "This is a difficult problem." So he said, "Don't be worried; you can commit one more, but do ten prayers." What else to do? "For the future, you have five in advance."

Now these people are gathering details of your underground life, which is very dangerous because that man now has every power over you. Whatsoever he says, you have to do it. Now, the pope is trying to save the priesthood and its power, and its hold over you. It has nothing to do with saving you, because what is the problem in confessing directly to God? What can this priest do? But no, you have to go via the right channel, the proper bureaucracy. Even with God there is a bureaucracy: you have to go through the priest. You cannot contact God directly.

This is his great message to humanity: disconnecting you from God completely; your only approach is the priest. It is none of your affair to think of having any direct contact with God. Now is this a religion? True religion teaches you that you are part of this existence, already connected with it, already one with.

The pope is teaching that you are not connected, that you are a lost soul; only through the priest can you be saved.

So when these Bible-packing Christians come to you, tell them, "In the first place we are not lost, so don't waste your time. In this place nobody is lost, we have never been lost, so the question of saving does not arise. And for your sake, we advise you, don't come near here because our whole effort is to unsave people who believe that they are saved. If you go on coming here, we will unsave you again."

In India I have come across these kinds of people; they are the most stupid type. And perhaps if they are Oregonians – and they must be – then they have an even better chance of being idiotic. In fact, listening to the question I thought that it would be a good idea to have a special election on the first of April every year.

All Oregonians would be eligible candidates and eligible voters. The only hearing process would be that before the polling booth they would have to do twenty minutes' deep breathing. That is enough to prove that they are Oregonians. A simple process, not a difficult process – I believe in simple things. Just breathe for twenty minutes and that is enough proof that you have lived in Oregon. And twenty minutes are enough to contaminate anybody.

This election will choose three persons: The Idiot General for Oregon, the Idiot General for America, and the Idiot General for the whole world. But all the three can only be Oregonians. If nobody stands then you can fill in the name of anybody you feel is the right person. And the polling booth will only be in this unique illegal city of Rajneeshpuram.

So each April I now give this work to poor K.D., the mayor of the illegal city of Rajneeshpuram: he has to listen to the breathing, the twenty minutes' breathing, and then everybody... And there will be no age limit, because children are more capable of seeing who is an idiot. By the time you become older, you become duller. And living with idiots, and dealing with idiots, you start, by and by, speaking their language. So even children, anybody who wants, man, woman, living, dead... Just the breathing process will decide who can vote. The dead person of course will be in difficulty, but he need breathe for twenty minutes only.

Every April first we will declare three Idiot Generals: Idiot General of Oregon, Idiot General of America, Idiot General of the world. And you cannot fill in the name of anybody who is outside Oregon because those idiots are lukewarm idiots. Here you will find real hotcakes.

Okay, you can ask one more question. My hands are not tired yet.

Osho,
Were you not punished for your mischievous acts in childhood?

I have been punished, but I have never taken any punishment as punishment. From my very childhood that has been my attitude: that how you take a thing makes all the difference. Nobody can punish me if I don't take it as a punishment.

One of my teachers in the primary school when I was in the fourth grade... It was my first day in his class, and I had not done anything very wrong, I was just doing what you do in meditation: "*Aum, aum...*" but inside, with closed mouth. I had a few of my friends, and I told them to sit in different places so he could not figure out from where the sound was coming. One time it was coming from here, another time it was coming from there, another time it was coming from here; he went on looking from where the sound was coming. So I told them, "Keep your mouths shut, and do the *aum* inside."

For a moment he could not figure it out. I was sitting at the very back. All teachers wanted me to sit in the front so they could keep an eye on me, and I always wanted to sit at the back from where you can do many more things; it is more feasible. He came directly to me. He must have heard from the third grade teacher, "You keep an eye on this boy!" So he said, "Although I cannot figure out who the people are who are doing it, you must be doing it."

I said, "What? What am I doing? You have to tell me. Just saying, 'You must be doing it' does not make sense. What...?"

Now it was difficult for him to do what I was doing, because that would have looked foolish, and everybody would have started laughing. He said, "Whatsoever it is, hold both your ears in your hands and sit down, stand up, sit down, stand up – five times."

I said, "Perfectly okay." I asked him, "Can I do it fifty times?"

He said, "This is not a reward, this is a punishment."

I said, "This morning I have not done any exercise so I thought that this was a good chance, and you would be very happy. Instead of five I will do fifty. And always remember, whenever you give me any kind of reward" – that's exactly the word I told him – "whenever you give me any kind of reward, be generous." And I started doing fifty.

He went on, "Stop! It is enough. I have never seen such a boy. You should be ashamed that you have been punished."

I said, "No, I am doing my morning exercise. You helped me, you have rewarded me; this is a good exercise. In fact, you should do it too."

I never took any punishment as punishment. How can you punish a man who is ready to accept it as a reward?

In my high school it was an everyday affair that I was standing outside the classroom, because the moment the teacher would see me, he would say, "You better go out before you do something. I will have to send you out in any case. Please go out and leave us alone."

And I would say, "Thank you sir, because outside I enjoy it so much; it is so beautiful." And we had beautiful trees and birds and vast greenery for miles behind the school. "Standing on the verandah is such a joy and the air is so pure that I feel sorry for you all sitting in this dirty room." And I really enjoyed it outside.

They figured out that this was not a punishment, they were really providing a good opportunity and a chance for me to enjoy myself in complete freedom – because outside I was free to move anywhere or to just go into the thick forest that was behind. They figured out that this was not a punishment, this was a reward. They started stopping it.

I would ask them, "What happened, has the policy changed? I am no longer sent outside. Have I to do something before you send me? It saves me from the torture of you and your history. I am not interested in Alexander the Great, I am not interested in Emperor Akbar. What have I to do with these people? I am not interested in history at all. If I am interested then the only interest can be to *make* history. Only fools who cannot make history, read history. Read, and teach all these fools that are here, but throw me out.

The teacher of history took me to the principal. He said, "What am I supposed to do? You cannot give him any corporal punishment – he immediately threatens to go to the police station, and unfortunately the police station is just nearby, in front of the school, and he will create trouble. And he is so strange that he has found a legal expert to support him."

One of my friends' fathers was the best advocate in the city. Everybody called him Bachchubhaiya, I don't know what his full name was. Bachchu is just a nickname for small children. It means just a child; the literal meaning is "a child." He must have been loved by people; he was a very lovable person. He used to be called Bachchubhaiya. Bachchubhaiya means brother. He was almost sixty, still everybody called him Bachchubhaiya, and he was very friendly with everybody.

So I went to him and asked him, "They threaten me with corporal punishment. You have to support me, because I will report it to the police but the police may listen to me, may not listen to me. It is better I go with a legal expert."

He said, "Don't be worried. I will keep your case prepared. Whenever you want I will come along with you and I will see that what you want has to be done."

So this teacher of history told the principal, "Bachchubhaiya has promised him that he will go with him. That will create immediate trouble because the police inspector, the police commissioner, nobody can deny Bachchubhaiya: he is the most powerful advocate, and he has power over all police authorities, civil authorities, criminal authorities. And Bachchubhaiya has told him that if the police inspector does not listen he will go directly to the collector. So we cannot punish him.

"I asked him to sit down and stand up. He thinks this is exercise. And one day it became such a scene that he told all the students 'Why are you sitting?

You also do it. Exercise is exercise, it is good for the body.' And all those students – they listen to him more than to me – they all started doing the exercise. I looked like a fool standing there, and I started thinking why I punished him. And he won't stop. Then I started throwing him out of the class, but he enjoyed it so much that it is not a punishment any more."

The principal sent me back. He wanted to talk with the teacher in private. He suggested, "Give him a punishment such that his family comes to know."

There used to be a register in the principal's office – whenever somebody was doing real mischief, the teacher would go and write in it his name and the fine of ten rupees. Then I would have to collect the ten rupees from my family, from my father; I would have to ask them.

So he did that. He put a ten-rupee fine on me and came back and told me, "We have found the way: I have put a ten-rupee fine against your name."

I said, "Okay. Now I am going to fine you."

He said, "You are going to fine me?"

I said, "Of course, because in the register it is not mentioned anywhere that only teachers can fine the students. There is no condition like that." And I went and I put twenty rupees against his name.

The principal said, "Are you mad or what? You are a student!"

I said, "I know I am a student, but is there any prohibition that says I cannot fine a teacher if he is doing mischief? – and this *is* mischief. If I am doing anything wrong then I should be punished; this fine is punishing my father. Can you justify it? Why should my father be punished? He is not involved in it at all."

I wrote my teacher's name and the twenty-rupee fine and I said, "Unless he pays, I am not going to pay."

Still in that register those two punishments remain unpaid because he would not pay me what the principal asked: "You pay the twenty rupees."

And I told the principal, "Don't cross this out, otherwise I will fine you. And even crossing it out won't make any difference because when the inspector of the school comes I am going to report this, and I am going to show him what has been crossed out, and you will have to answer for it."

So he never asked for the ten rupees from me because my condition was: "First you get twenty rupees from that man, then I will consider it."

Punishments have been given but I enjoyed the whole thing. It was sheer joy. It is a question of attitude – how you take it – and that is something to be learned about your whole life.

I am reminded...

There was a world conference of psychologists, psychiatrists, therapists – people who are involved in the mind games. They are still games, they have not yet got to the point where you can call them a science. Although they are arriving slowly, and are on the right track, still they are playing games. It was a world conference of all the famous psychiatrists, psychologists, therapists.

While the president was inaugurating the conference, he was feeling very uneasy, very disturbed by something just in the front row. There was a beautiful woman, a famous psychiatrist, and an old psychologist, also very famous in his own way – the only surviving colleague of Sigmund Freud. He was playing with the tits of the woman; and just in the front row! Now, how could the president go on speaking?

He tried looking this way, looking that way, but you can't address a conference just looking this way or that way; you have to look in front too, at least once in a while. And it was too much. The old man was really something; he was not worried that the whole conference, everybody in the hall, could see what was happening. And the woman was even greater; she was sitting and listening to the lecture.

Finally it was too much, and the president said, "Please forgive me, but, lady, can I ask you a question?"

She said, "Of course."

He said, "Why don't you complain against this dirty old man?"

She said, "It is his problem, it is not my problem. His dirtiness or whatever he is doing, that is his problem. How am I concerned in it? – he is doing no harm to me. And if it gives him some consolation, some satisfaction, so far so good. He is a patient, that much I can say; he is not a therapist, he is a patient. But you don't complain against a patient – I feel sorry for him. Buy why are you disturbed? Continue. If I am not disturbed then why are you disturbed and why is everybody else disturbed?"

It is not a joke. The woman is saying something immensely meaningful: she is saying, "It is his problem, and he is suffering from a problem. He needs sympathy not complaint." But this woman must have been of immense understanding, really a therapist, not only playing games but moving to the very roots of man's psychic troubles.

The woman simply said that he is behaving like a child, and treating her like his mother, so what is wrong with it? He has not grown up, he is retarded. Now, to make a fuss about it, to disturb the whole conference about it, is meaningless. Let him. She told the old man, "Continue," and she told the president, "You also continue. I am undisturbed because it does not concern me at all. Just touching my skin, what does it matter?"

This woman can become awakened because she is behaving like a watcher, even about her own body. She is not identified with the body, she is far above, look- ing at the retarded old man but not feeling offended – because "I am not the body."

I have been caned, not by my teachers, because they were afraid I would go to the police station, but by my uncles. My grandfather was always favorable to me about anything. He was ready to participate if he could; of course he never punished me, he always rewarded me.

I used to come home every night and the first thing my grandfather would ask was, "What did you do today? How did things go? Was there any trouble?" We always used to have a good meeting in the night in his bed, sitting together, and he enjoyed everything. I used to tell everything that had happened in the day, and he would say, "It was really a good day!"

My father only punished me once because I had gone to a fair which used to happen a few miles away from the city every year. There flows one of the holy rivers of the Hindus, the Narmada, and on the bank of the Narmada there used to be a big fair for one month. So I simply went there without asking him.

There was so much going on in the fair... I had gone only for one day and I was thinking I would be back by the night, but there were so many things: magicians, a circus, drama. It was not possible to come back in one day, so three days... The whole family was in a panic: where had I gone?

It had never happened before. At the most I had come back late in the night but I had never been away for three days continuously, and with no message. They inquired at every friend's house. Nobody knew about me and the fourth day when I came home my father was really angry. Before asking me anything, he slapped me. I didn't say anything.

I said, "Do you want to slap me more? You can, because I have enjoyed enough in three days. You cannot slap me more than I have enjoyed, so you can do a few more slaps. It will cool you down, and to me it is just balancing. I have enjoyed myself."

He said, "You are really impossible. Slapping you is meaningless. You are not hurt by it; you are asking for more. Can't you make a distinction between punishment and reward?"

I said, "No, to me everything is a reward of some kind. There are different kinds of reward, but everything is a reward of some kind."

He asked me, "Where have you been for these three days?"

I said, "This you should have asked before you slapped me. Now you have lost the right to ask me. I have been slapped without even being asked. It is a full stop – close the chapter. If you wanted to know, you should have asked before, but you don't have any patience. Just a minute would have been enough. But I will not keep you continually worrying where I have been, so I will tell you that I went to the fair."

He asked, "Why didn't you ask me?"

I said, "Because I wanted to go. Be truthful: if I had asked, would you have allowed me? Be truthful."

He said, "No."

I said, "That explains everything, why I did not ask you – because I wanted to go, and then it would have been more difficult for you. If I had asked you and you had said no, I still would have gone, and that would have been more difficult for you. Just to make it easier for you, I didn't ask, and I am rewarded for it. And I am ready to take any more reward you want to give me. But I have enjoyed the fair so much that I am going there every year. So you can...whenever! ...Disappear, you know where I am. Don't be worried."

He said, "This is the last time that I punish you; the first and last time. Perhaps you are right: if you really wanted to go then this was the only way, because I was not going to allow you. In that fair every kind of thing happens: prostitutes are there, intoxicants are available, drugs are sold there" – and at that time in India there was no illegality about drugs, every drug was freely available.

And in a fair all kinds of monks gather, and Hindu monks all use drugs – "so I would not have allowed you to go. And if you really wanted to go then perhaps you were right not to ask."

I told him, "But I did not bother about the prostitutes or the monks or the drugs. You know me: if I am interested in drugs, then in this very city..." Just by the side of my house there was a shop where all drugs were available: "and the man is so friendly to me that he will not take any money if I want any drug. So there is no problem. Prostitutes are available in the town; if I am interested in seeing their dances I can go there. Who can prevent me? Monks come continually in the city. But I was interested in the magicians."

And my interest in magic is related to my interest in miracles. In India, before the partition, I have seen every kind of miracle being done on the streets by magicians, poor magicians. Perhaps after the whole show they may get a one-rupee collection. How can I believe that these people are messiahs? For one rupee, for three hours they are doing almost impossible things. Of course everything has a trick to it but if you don't know the trick then it is a miracle.

You have simply heard – I have *seen* them throwing a rope up, and the rope stands by itself. They have a boy with them they call "Jamura"; every magician has a *jamura*. I don't know how to translate it...just "my boy." And he goes on talking with the *jamura*, "Jamura, will you go up the rope?"

And he will say, "Yes, I will go." And this continual conversation has something to do with the trick; it keeps people's mind on the conversation, and the conversation is funny in many ways. I have seen that boy climbing up the rope and disappearing!

And the man calls from down below, "Jamura?"

From far above comes the voice, "Yes, master."

And he says, "Now I will bring you down part by part." Then he throws a knife up, and the head of the boy comes down! He throws the knife up, and a leg comes down! Part by part the boy comes down, and the magician goes on putting the parts together, covers them with a bed sheet and says, "Jamura, now be together."

And the *jamura* says, "Yes, master."

The magician removes the bed sheet and the boy stands up! He pulls down the rope, winds it up, puts it in the bag and starts asking for money. At the most he would get one rupee – because in those days sixty paise was equivalent to one rupee and nobody was going to give him more than one paise, two paise at the most; a very rich person would give him four paise. If he can gather one rupee for his miracle he is fortunate. I have seen all kinds of things, and the people who are doing them are just beggars.

So when I hear that your faith in Jesus will disappear if you know that he never walked on water, that he never turned water into wine, I cannot conceive of it, because in the twentieth century, the secrets of how to do all these magic tricks are available, even in books. And you can do them, you just have to learn a little strategy.

One sannyasin was with me; he lived with me in Mumbai. He was interested in magic, so I told him, "Have a press conference and give a show of your magic, but call them miracles, not magic." And he did it. Even my caretaker Vivek was one of the participants in his magic – miracles, not magic.

The miracle was that Vivek had to swallow a thread, a long thread which she goes on swallowing. And then he takes back that thread from her navel; he goes on pulling it and it all comes out. And the whole trick was just a small operation. A few days before, he just made a little cut near the navel and pushed a thread inside; and this was the thread that was coming out. The thread that she had swallowed was a different thread – but to the press it was a miracle. "The woman has taken the thread inside and he takes it out from her navel! – and it comes out, the same length and everything." But just a small trick...

He did many things there, and you know, just because he was my disciple many papers described how I had done these miracles. He drank some poison, enough to kill a man... But everything was a trick. He was just practicing there, in my own house and on my own people, and they all were saying, "What is happening?"

Vivek was saying, "This is cheating. I thought it was going to be a real miracle. It is nothing like a miracle, it is just a cheat."

I said, "Everybody has been a cheat; there has never been a miracle."

So I told my father, "I was interested only in the magic, because in the fair all kinds of magicians gather together, and I have seen some really great things. My interest is that I want to reduce miracles into magic. Magic is only about tricks – there is nothing spiritual in it – but if you don't know the trick, then certainly it appears to be a miracle."

I have been punished, but I have enjoyed every mischief so much that I don't count those punishments at all. They are nothing.

I have a certain rapport with women, perhaps that's why mischief – if it was Mister Chief or Master Chief, perhaps I would have avoided it, but Miss Chief! – the temptation was so much that I could not avoid it. In spite of all the punishment I continued it. And I still continue it!

watchfulness, awareness, alertness: the real trinity

Osho,
How does one explore the higher states of consciousness?

There are not many ways, there is but one: the way of awareness. Man is almost unconscious. I say "almost" – there are moments, situations where he becomes conscious, but they are momentary.

For example, suddenly your house is on fire. You will feel a flare-up within you, a sense of alertness that was not there before. You may have been tired, you may not have slept for a few days, you may have been traveling and you were hoping that as you reached your house, the first thing you were going to do was to fall asleep – but the house is on fire!

All tiredness disappears. You forget the whole nightmare of the journey, and inside you find something new which perhaps you will miss because the house is on fire; so you will become not alert of your alertness, but alert of the fire that is burning your house.

In ordinary life also, there are moments when people touch a higher state of consciousness, but miss because that higher state comes as an emergency, and they have to first tackle the emergency that is facing them. And that cannot be the circumstance where they can start exploring what is happening inside them.

But if you can remember – even as a memory – some moments in your life when suddenly you were more aware than you usually are, it will be a great help to understand what I am going to say to you.

I have told you that modern psychology has moved below the so-called human consciousness. And when people like Sigmund Freud found that just underneath your thin layer of consciousness there is another layer, it was a great discovery for him, and for the West. And his whole life he devoted to exploring the underground, the basement of your consciousness.

That's why he became interested in the analysis of dreams, because when you are conscious you can pretend, you can be a hypocrite. You can say something that you don't mean, you can do something that you never wanted to do. You can smile, and inside you want to cry, weep. You can cry and weep, and inside you are enjoying, you are rejoicing.

So your consciousness has been so polluted by the society, it is not reliable. This was one of the most significant contributions of Sigmund Freud: that your consciousness is not reliable. Strange, that he feels your unconsciousness is more reliable than your consciousness.

Nothing can be a greater condemnation of the whole human civilization, the whole human history of all the religions. What else can be a greater condemnation than this: that your consciousness is not reliable; that your society, your tradition, your religion, your convention, have made it unreliable.

In one of Kahlil Gibran's stories, the mother and her daughter are both sleep-walkers. The daughter one night walks in her sleep, goes into the garden and starts saying nasty things about her mother. And just by accident her mother also sleepwalks behind her and starts saying ugly things about her. But the cold wind outside suddenly wakes them both.

And the daughter says, "Mom, you don't have anything warm around you, you should not come out at your age. You make me so worried."

And the mother says, "My beloved daughter, in this whole world there is nobody except you whom I can call mine."

This much is the story, but it contains the whole discovery of Sigmund Freud: while they were asleep they were saying really what they feel about each other. When they wake up they are saying what they are supposed to say to each other. And they will not become aware of their two sides.

And if there were only two sides, things would have been far easier, but there are many more sides. I have told you – it will be good to be reminded – consciousness is a very thin layer where we are existing. Below it is the subconscious mind; that is half-conscious, half-unconscious. That's why you remember dreams only of the later part of the night. You don't remember all your dreams from the whole night because in eight hours of sleep, for six hours you are dreaming.

Now this is a scientifically proved fact. Only here and there for a few minutes you fall into deeper sleep where there are no longer dreams; the total is two hours. But the dream total is six hours. You don't remember in the morning six hours' dreams – almost the length of three movies. At the most you remember some fragment, or sometimes a whole dream, but that dream was the last dream when you were waking up.

The subconscious mind has two sides. One is connected with the unconscious, the bottom part. When you are deeply asleep, dreams are moving at the bottom part of the subconscious. The conscious is very far away. But when you wake up in the morning, you are coming closer to the conscious mind, then the top layer of the subconscious is dreaming.

That's why your consciousness can hear little bits and pieces of dreaming, and in the morning you can remember something. But that is only the tail of the elephant. The whole elephant has disappeared, you have no notion of it. And of course the tail makes no sense because the elephant is not there.

Hence the psychoanalyst is needed to find out the elephant: what kind of elephant it was, whether it was an elephant or a camel or a cow or a horse, because you have only a tail – perhaps not even the whole tail, a few hairs of the tail.

The whole function of psychoanalysis is to put those hairs together and to figure out whose tail this can be; to dig you from this corner and from that corner, and hit you from this point and that point, so something comes up which is there, but of which you are not aware. The psychologist makes almost the whole animal on the basis of a few hairs of the tail. That's why there are so many schools of psychoanalysis.

It was bound to be so. Sigmund Freud wanted psychoanalysis to remain one integrated movement. It was impossible, because the work of the psychoanalyst is more or less imagination: he has a few things in his hand but those things can lead to any conclusion.

If you go to Sigmund Freud then those same hairs will prove you are sexually obsessed: that is his elephant. And once he has found the elephant you will start seeing according to his vision, and you will find explanations that perhaps he is right. And perhaps he *is* right.

If you go to Adler, he has a different kind of imagination: will-to-power. For Sigmund Freud it is will-to-sex, will-to-reproduction. To Sigmund Freud it is more of a biological phenomenon than to Adler.

To Adler it is more of a political phenomenon: will-to-power. If you take the same hairs to Sigmund Freud he will manage to figure out and discover perversions of sex in you. And I am saying perhaps he is right, and I also want to say perhaps Adler is also right.

If you go to Jung then he will find through those same hairs some mythological phenomenon. It will not be biological, it will not be political, it will be mythological. And I want to say: perhaps he is also right.

All these three continually quarreled, not knowing that man's mind has multi-aspects, that it is not exhausted by one explanation, that not only are there these three, there are more possibilities. Just a few more Freuds, Jungs and Adlers are needed who have some poetic imagination, and some scientific way of explanation.

Man's mind is multidimensional. And every dimension is connected.

For example: sexuality is part of his will-to-power, it is not separate. Through sex also he is trying to be powerful, to be a creator, to give birth, to possess a woman or a man. And you can look at any couple: they are continually in a power conflict – who possesses whom?

The wife is trying in every possible way... And she has some natural capacity which she uses. If you are not allowing her to be more powerful than you then she will deprive you of sex, and she knows that you cannot starve as far as sex is concerned. You are going to beg her, you are going to persuade her: you are going to bring chocolates and ice cream and beautiful clothes. She understands that this is all bribery. You also understand it, that this is trying to make coexistence possible.

But your effort is also continuously to dominate her.

One of my friends was in love with a woman but was not ready to marry her. Now the woman was troubled; she came to me and she told me, "This is strange. Now my family is after me saying, 'If he loves you then he should marry you, otherwise you are passing the marriageable age.

"'And in India it is then difficult to find a young man of your age available. They will already be married. Then you will have to be married to somebody who is far older than you – perhaps once or twice married before, and whose wives fortunately went on dying and who is still a bachelor.' So, they are after me: 'Either he marries you or we choose somebody else.'"

I said, "Let me ask him what the problem is."

And he told me, "I cannot hide it from you. I really love her, but when the question of marriage arises, the trouble is, she is taller than me."

I said, "What kind of trouble is that? I don't see any trouble in it. If she is taller, you can stand up on a stool and kiss her – at the most a stool is needed!"

I showed him a picture – just that day it was in the newspaper and the newspaper was laying there – of Mountbatten, the last viceroy of India, who was a very tall man, with the first prime minister of India, Jawaharlal Nehru, who was only five feet five. So when he gave the oath to Jawaharlal it would have looked really bad: the prime minister would have looked very small, the viceroy really tall. He must have been six and a half feet, or even more, so they arranged it in the picture...

I showed him, "You see the management. Jawaharlal is standing on a step, the steps that lead to the throne. He is standing on a step, and Mountbatten is standing on the floor so they seem almost equal in size." I said, "Can you see the trick? It is not much of a problem. You can have a folding stool which you can always have in the back of your car, so wherever you need you take your stool."

He said, "You are making a laughingstock of me. I am serious, because wherever I go, she will be taller and I cannot continually walk with the stool. And in the marriage ceremony when I am taking the seven rounds around the sacred fire, she is so tall I will be ahead of her looking almost like her child. I love her, but I cannot marry her because everybody will laugh."

And in the marriage ceremony in India all the relatives and friends from faraway gather. It is a gathering of thousands of people. And they were rich people, so everybody would come and everybody would see only one thing: the tallness of the wife. Love had to fail before the power instinct.

I said, "What does it matter? You can tell them, 'I am not taller than my wife.'"

But you can look around the whole world, and you will find the husband always taller than the wife. How has it been managed? Why has the woman remained smaller than the man? It is simply a question that for millions of years that was the choice: the man will always choose a wife smaller than himself. Slowly, by sheer selection, the taller women went out of existence; it was difficult for them to find a husband. They became prostitutes, they became part of the marketplace, available to all. They could not live a respectable life unless they happened to meet a man taller than them.

But the man was always taller; slowly, slowly, this is how it happened. You can inquire of those people who crossbreed animals. After generations of this continual crossbreeding: taller husband-smaller wife, taller husband-smaller wife...

If the woman is so tall that she cannot find a husband, she becomes a prostitute, she goes out of the biological market, she is a dropout. She will not be creating children any longer, because a prostitute cannot afford children. So her line dies out; that branch grows no further.

It is not natural that women have to be smaller. It is the power instinct, the will-to-power.

But sexuality and the will-to-power are not two separate things, not as separate as Adler and Freud think. The people who become very much power-oriented start losing interest in sex because their whole energy moves into the will-to-power. The people who are very deeply interested in exploring their sexuality cannot go into politics; they don't have any energy left.

You can see it in actuality in many places. We don't allow soldiers to have their wives on the battlefield. The general can, because the general remains behind; he is not really fighting, he is simply ordering people to fight. And he is perfectly defended; if there is any danger, he will be the first to get out. He is far behind the forces. He is allowed to have a wife there because there is no problem, he is not going to fight. But the soldiers are not allowed to. Why? – for the simple reason that if their energy goes into sex, they don't feel like fighting.

You can observe it in yourself. If you are deeply in love with a woman, you don't feel like fighting with anybody. But if you cannot find any outlet for your sexual energy then you will become a criminal, you may kill somebody. You may be constantly searching for some excuse to fight.

It is not just a coincidence that all the religions have preached that their monks remain celibate, because once they are celibate then their whole energy starts moving towards an imaginary God – then God becomes their sexual object.

And you can see it in the songs of the devotees. They talk of God almost as if they are talking of a beloved or of a lover. Meera, one of the most famous mystics in India, must have been studied by Sigmund Freud. If he did not study her, he will have to be born again, because those two have to meet and come to an understanding. Freud never heard about Meera, otherwise he would have found all the great explanations that he needed and searched and looked for – and was unable to find.

Meera talks of Krishna almost in sexual terms. She sleeps with the statue of Krishna. She calls Krishna "my husband." And the words she uses are exactly those romantic words which lovers use for each other. The same is true about the Sufi mystics who think of God as a beloved, a woman. And you have to see their description of the beauty of God, the youthfulness of God.

When Fitzgerald, a very talented poet, translated Omar Khayyam, a Sufi mystic, he did something almost impossible, because Omar Khayyam, in the original, does not seem to be as impressive as he becomes in the translation of Fitzgerald. And the reason is, Fitzgerald had no idea that Omar Khayyam was talking about God, not about a woman.

The Sufis call God, *saki.* A *saki* is the woman in the pub who pours wine for the customers. Particularly in the Arabic and Persian nations, the *sakis* are chosen just as in the West you choose Miss World, Miss Universe, Miss America. The *saki* is chosen just like that. The most beautiful girl in the city will become the *saki.* The most beautiful women move into the profession of being the *saki.* And Sufis call God *saki.*

Fitzgerald had no idea that *saki* means, to a Sufi, God. He simply translated literally that *saki* is a woman, and when Omar Khayyam says, "Saki, fill my cup full," he thinks he is asking a woman to fill his cup full. And when Omar Khayyam says, "Even the wine is not so sweet as your kiss," he is thinking of a woman; hence, his poetry becomes more romantic, more colorful. One who understands the Sufi terminology will not find much in Omar Khayyam.

You will be surprised that in Persia, Omar Khayyam is not known as a great poet. But in the whole world, Omar Khayyam is Persia's most important poet, and this miracle has happened because of Fitzgerald. And you would not have enjoyed Omar Khayyam. He was a mathematician – the first mistake that he made was to be a mathematician. Now, a mathematician writing poetry, you understand, cannot be juicy. From where can a mathematician get juice? Then over and above that, he is a Sufi, a seeker of God. There is no place for any woman in his life; he lived a celibate life.

Fitzgerald never bothered about the man's life. Before he translated his poetry he should at least have looked to see whether this man was capable of writing poetry about women. He was a celibate mathematician! A Sufi. But Sufis, remaining celibate, think of God as a woman, dream of God as a woman, the most beautiful woman of course – there can be no comparison with God. So they pour all their sexuality onto the image of God, the beloved. He is not a man.

In Omar Khayyam's book – it is an illustrated book – naturally Fitzgerald saw the most beautiful pictures of women pouring wine. He thought that this was really a woman. And he looked at the poetry; it talks about the woman. Sufis are very angry: Fitzgerald made Omar Khayyam world famous, while their real poets of Persia are unknown to the world. This man was not thought to be a poet at all. Once you understand that this woman is not a real woman but God looked at through the eyes of a celibate Sufi... It is a hallucination.

Religions understood it: that if you stop sexual energy moving in its natural way, then the man can manage to see God, to meet Jesus, to talk to Krishna; anything is possible. The sexual energy is a kind of drug, the most powerful drug that nature has invented. That's why, when you fall in love with a woman, you start seeing in that woman things that nobody sees. It is your projection, it is your drug, your chemicals, your hormones which are creating the hallucination around the woman. The woman is just an object, a screen, on which you are projecting your picture.

And once your sex is satisfied with the woman, you are going to be very disappointed. You will find that this is not the same woman: you had fallen in love with somebody else. This is not the woman... But you know that this is the woman. So there is some deception, this woman deceived you. You are being deceived by biology, not by this woman.

This woman was also projecting on you. And once the honeymoon is over, the projection is over. Now she looks at you and finds just an ordinary man, nothing special about you. Everything was special before: the way you walked, talked, everything had something unique. Now you are just an Oregonian, nothing more. There is great frustration on both sides. Now you are standing face to face, seeing each other without any projection; hence the continuous fight. It is bound to be so.

In India, where even today ninety percent of marriages, or even more, are arranged marriages, this kind of frustration never happens. In an arranged marriage you are not given the chance of hallucinating. From the very beginning you are just standing on the earth, and there is no romance. You cannot even see the woman before you get married to her.

The very cultured families now allow the picture of the woman to be seen. Now a picture of the woman, and with all the photographic tricks – and that too only if you ask... You are going against the heritage, the culture, you are not supposed to ask. And particularly the girl cannot even see the picture of the man she is going to be married to. And even after marriage, they are not going to see each other in sunlight. They will meet each other in the darkness of the night. Of course, they remain to each other mysterious.

The mystery lingers longer in India than anywhere else. In the day they cannot talk to each other because in India there are joint families. They cannot talk in front of the children because that is a bad example, they cannot talk in front of the elders because that is disrespectful. And there are so many elders in the house, and there are so many dozens of children in the house, there is no possibility.

You will be surprised that the father of a child cannot take the child in his hands in front of others: that is disrespectful. I was told by my father, "I took you in my hands only when you were five years old." The grandfather can, that's why I became friendly with my grandfather. Naturally, he was acquainted with me, and me with him, from the very beginning. The father came after five years; he remained a stranger for five years. He never talked to me for five years.

I have asked my mother. There was no possibility of their talking or meeting or seeing. They did not see each other for years after their marriage. Children were born, but they had not seen each other because they would meet only in the darkness of the night. And in India, in a joint family, there are sometimes forty people, fifty people in the house. And those houses are just like Noah's ark.

For example, my grandfather used to have his horse tied to his cot in the night too. And I told him "The smell of the horse is so much that even if I want to meet you, your horse prevents me." Cows in the house, elders, children, everybody in the house – how Indians manage to make love is a mystery.

How they manage to produce dozens of children is simply mystifying. It all happens in darkness, without whispering a single word. What to say of loving chitchat and foreplay and afterplay. There is no possibility: only the play is enough! Fore and after does not exist; and the play has to be quick – so nobody comes to know.

I was staying with my grandfather in the house of one of his friends – and when a very close guest is there, in India, you don't allow him to sleep in a separate room, that is not hospitality. My grandfather and I were sleeping in the same room where my grandfather's friend, his son, and his son's wife were sleeping. And what I learned... My grandfather was old so once in a while he would cough; his friend was even older than him, and once in a while he would cough. And because of their coughing my sleep was difficult, so once in a while I would wake up. And once in a while I would see the son of my grandfather's friend making love to his wife – then I would cough.

That was enough! That was enough; he would jump into his own bed. And while I remained there I did not allow him to sleep with his wife. On the day we were leaving he pulled me aside and said, "You rascal!"

I said, "What? Why are you calling me a rascal?"

He said, "You coughed exactly at the time... Do you sleep or not? Those two old men, I know they cough – but not exactly at the time. I am so happy that you are going because for these two months I have not met my wife, because the moment I started moving towards her bed you would start coughing."

And coughing is such a thing that when I started then those two old men would hear it and start; it is infectious. One person starts, then the other starts feeling a temptation too.

Stop the sexual energy of people, then it will find some other outlet. Religions learned the trick: stop sexual energy – it moves, and gives the movement towards God. The military generals found it very soon: stop the sexual energy and the man is ready to fight, to quarrel; he is just hankering to fight.

In fact Sigmund Freud's explanation for all weapons is just sexual. He says that when you throw a knife into somebody's body, it is sexual penetration. A bullet is a sexual penetration from a faraway distance. He is a little bit obsessed with sex, but there is some truth in it, because sexually fulfilled people have not discovered weapons. There was no need.

So, all these explanations are about your dreams because your dreams are truer than your waking life. In waking life you don't beat your teacher, but in dreams you can. That's your real desire. If you were allowed, or if you were powerful enough you would have done it. But it is not possible, not practical. In dreams you are free to do it; it is a kind of substitute.

So below the conscious is the subconscious, which is the field of your dreaming. Below the subconscious is the unconscious, which is the field of your dreamless sleep, when you are in a kind of coma. You reach the same state as you were in your mother's womb; hence the relaxation, hence the feeling of rejuvenation. After a deep sleep, when you wake up you are fresh, young, full of energy.

If those two hours have been missed then you may have tossed and turned and dreamed a thousand and one things, but in the morning you will find yourself as tired as when you had gone to bed, perhaps more tired. That coma is needed, because in that coma your mind stops functioning and your body takes over.

When you are conscious, it is mind over body; when you are unconscious, it is body over mind. And the body has a wisdom because the body is far more ancient. Mind is a very late development, a very new comer, just amateurish. Hence, anything important, nature has not left to mind. Everything important has been left to the body, because body will take care more proficiently, more professionally, more wisely, without any mistakes, errors.

For example, breathing has not been left to the mind; otherwise sometimes you may forget, particularly in sleep. What will you do? – when deep sleep comes breathing will stop. No, breathing is not left to the mind. It is a body function because it is so essential for your life. And the mind is so amateurish and so stupid, because it is just trying to wake up, it is still not awake.

Nature has given every power to the body, all essential powers to the body. Your mind can be put aside and your body will go on functioning perfectly well. In fact, mind is always a hindrance in everything. He tries to overcome body, because mind is a power tripper, he wants to control everything.

What do these people go on doing in the name of Yoga? They are trying to control even their pulses, they are trying to control even their heartbeat. For what? – what do they gain out of it? I have seen people practicing for forty years how to stop the heartbeat; and certainly if they do that much practice they can stop the heartbeat for a time.

But what is the gain? You cannot see anything. I have seen these people: you don't see any aura, you don't see any fragrance. You don't see in their eyes that there has been any vision of reality. You don't see in their life any impact of the higher consciousness.

But they have immense power over the body. I have seen people lying down and a car passing over their body; they will simply stop their breath and the car passes over with no harm. I have seen one man stopping the body of a railway engine just with his hands. And all that he was doing was stopping his breath. By stopping his breath he was capable of stopping a railway engine or any car.

Strangely... It was as if he had become a rock, so heavy that it was impossible for the car, a four horsepower or six horsepower car, to push the man aside. With his breathing disappearing, it was as if all his hollowness had disappeared and he had become a solid rock. The earth and its gravitation is functioning perhaps ten times more on that person than it functions on you.

It is just like when you are in water: the gravitation functions less on you; that's why you can float on water. In water you can take a big rock in your hands without any trouble. You cannot pick up the same rock outside the water.

Water cuts somehow the power of gravitation. The water has the quality of levitation, of taking things up; levitation against gravitation. That's why you can take a bigger man's body in your hands in water, just like a child, as if he is a child. Outside the water you cannot do the same, he is so heavy.

Perhaps by stopping the breath – the quality of air must give a great levitation – the person becomes so heavy, and the power of gravitation is almost eight times more that he can manage normally. The wheels go on moving, but the car cannot move a single inch.

But what is the point of it? I have asked these people, "Yes, you have done a great job, but to me it seems idiotic. What is the point? How have you become more spiritual by this? You have simply proved that you are eight horsepower. The car is six horsepower, so you now have eight horses' power in you."

We still measure with horsepower because man takes a long time to forget the old language. Now horses are disappearing, horse-drawn buggies are disappearing. There are cars, there are airplanes, there are trains, but still we measure their power through the horse. An eight horsepower car means there are eight horses in your chariot.

"So of course you are more powerful than the car, but is that your goal – to become a powerful engine in a car? And you wasted forty years in learning the trick!" Yes, it influences people because everybody is a power tripper. It shows what great power this man has. It makes you feel inferior; he becomes suddenly superior.

Why do so many millions of people go on watching boxing matches? For what? Two fools beating each other for no reason at all. If there is any argument, sit down and settle it, negotiate. But there is no argument, no problem; the problem is only who is more powerful. That too can be decided in a more human way: just toss a coin and be finished. But why beat each other and break each other's bones? And the noses are bleeding, and the eyes are red, and millions of people are clapping, enjoying somehow a certain identity.

There are fans of Muhammad Ali, and there are fans of other Ali's. So these two fools are doing their stupidity, and a million fools are there to support and give them the idea that they are doing something important. I cannot see that in a little bit more enlightened humanity things like boxing can exist.

Boxing simply looks so primitive, so ugly, so inhuman; but millions of people... And these are not the only people: millions more will be sitting in front of their televisions. It seems the whole humanity is somehow after power. So whoever shows some power of any kind: power of money, power of body, power of politics, position, status, anything, people become impressed.

Sheela has just brought to me two days ago the news that since Indira Gandhi's assassination, her son Rajiv has been fighting the election to become the prime minister. He has chosen people very cleverly: he has chosen many of the film stars as his candidates. Poor Vinod, who is here, missed! If he had been in India he would have been in the prime minister's cabinet next month. His rival in the film world, Amitabh Bachchan... These two were the topmost actors of the Indian film world. And you will be surprised that India produces more films than Hollywood. Hollywood is number two; India is number one as far as film production is concerned.

These two persons, Amitabh and Vinod, were the top two. He has chosen Amitabh as one of his candidates, and Amitabh is going to be in his cabinet, absolutely certainly. And he will win, because film actors have a certain power, glamour, as if they are superhuman. He has chosen old descendants of royal families. One is a very strange fellow, but he will be elected.

Mysore was one of the richest states in India because Mysore jungles are jungles of sandalwood, and that is the costliest wood in the whole world. All the jungles were the private property of the maharajah of Mysore. And Mysore has the greatest population of elephants, so Mysore's maharajah has the biggest tusks of elephants in his palace. It is unique, because for thirty-six generations they have been kings.

Now there is a descendant of this family – the estate is no longer there, but he has his private property: a palace worth fifty million or more dollars, a vast palace all made of Italian marble. His throne must be priceless because it has so many diamonds, so many sapphires, so many rubies, emeralds – because Mysore has many mines, and the king had first rights to all the best stones found in those mines. Just the gold is worth nearabout fifty million dollars. The gold of the throne and all these diamonds and rubies and sapphires and emeralds – there is no way to count how much they will be worth. But that kind of throne is just one of its kind, there is no other.

This young man weighs three hundred and fifty pounds. He never goes out of the palace. He speaks in a nasal tone, almost inaudible. He has never spoken in public in his whole life because how can he speak? What he says is almost inaudible; perhaps only a few servants who are continuously with him understand him. He has an imported dog; his name is Kinky – and all that he does is go on playing with Kinky.

Now he has been chosen as a candidate for election in India by Rajiv Gandhi. He will win the election, because in Mysore, who can win against him? In Mysore the royal family is thought to be the descendants of God. And thirty-six uninterrupted generations of royal blood – and in no small quantity, three hundred and fifty pounds! There is no need for him to make a public speech. He cannot, he may not even go out of his palace, but he will win. And he has been chosen just because he has status and people worship him. So it is impossible for anybody to stand against him. And he has money, so he will give money to the election campaign, as much as they want.

People are not conscious of what they are doing. Now the people who are going to vote for this man, will you call them human beings? Perhaps Kinky the dog is far more intelligent than the man who goes on playing with him: he is an utter idiot. He has not done anything else in his life; but just to belong to a royal family is enough. And he has money, and money is power. Perhaps he may become a cabinet minister.

You are in your unconscious mind when you are fast asleep with no dreams. Freud had reached the unconscious just by analyzing dreams. If you are on the right track and you analyze a dream rightly, the miracle is, once the dream is analyzed completely – that means you become aware of its reason, why it happens, why it is, of what it is constituted – once you become aware of a dream, its total structure, root and all, it disappears.

To summarize: to be aware of a dream is the death of the dream.

And after a few years of psychoanalysis when all your dreams slowly disappear... Then Freud became aware that there is still another depth. He died before he could penetrate the other depth, but he had found it, discovered it: the unconscious.

Jung tried to go as deeply into the unconscious as possible. It is easier in hypnosis to reach the unconscious of any person, very easy. Hence in the future hypnosis is going to become part and parcel of every psychology. In India it always has been, because three years of psychoanalysis is a wastage of time. Within three minutes you can be hypnotized and all your dreaming process can be put aside; then there is direct entry into the unconscious.

Because Jung was interested in hypnosis, Freud condemned him as unscientific. It is not right. Hypnosis is a scientific method of digging deeply into you. And when Jung tried to go deep into the unconscious, he was surprised to find that underneath the unconscious there is still another layer: the collective unconscious, the unconscious of the whole humanity.

Everybody has it; and sometimes from that collective unconscious you get ideas, but because they come from so far away from your conscious, you think that they are coming from somewhere outside you. When Jesus hears the voice of God, it is not God speaking, it is the collective unconscious. But it is so far away that poor Jesus can be forgiven. He is simply mistaken, and he had no idea that there are depths within depths, depths behind depths.

This collective unconscious is to do with the mythological. Hence, Jung became interested in mythology to discover its existence, just as Freud became interested in dreams to discover the subconscious. Mythologies are dreams dreamed by the whole of humanity over thousands of years, but those mythologies carry some idea, some significance.

For example, the Indian mythology that life for the first time appeared as a fish. The first incarnation of God is Matsyavatar: incarnation as a fish. A strange mythology – how did they figure it out? Out of this vast world of animals, why did they fall upon the fish? – some indication from their collective unconscious. Now science says that perhaps life was born first in the ocean. It comes very close to the fish. And the child in the beginning, in the mother's womb, looks like a fish. He moves from there and passes through all the stages that man has passed through in millions of years – there is a point where he looks like a monkey.

Jung's discovery of mythology and its connection with the collective unconscious is of immense importance. But he stopped there because he was afraid, and obsessed with death, just as Sigmund Freud was himself obsessed with sex. Anything you brought to him – I say anything, and I mean anything – he would immediately manage to make it sexual. Whatever it was, it did not matter; he was capable of making it sexual.

Freud's whole mind was focused on one point; but perhaps that's the only way. In a small life, what can a man do? If he can work out only one idea in its totality, then he needs to be obsessed; otherwise it is difficult, life is so vast. If you go on jumping all around on everything, then it is difficult for you to move in one direction to the very end.

Hence all scientists, all philosophers, all thinkers, are obsessed with one particular idea. And then they try to fit everything into that idea. That's where they
go wrong. If they were a little more alert they would see that life is vast. Their idea
is meaningful, but meaningful only from a certain aspect.

Jung was very much afraid of death; he was death-obsessed. Just as
Sigmund Freud was sex-obsessed, Jung was death-obsessed. And the two obsessions are not very different. Sex is the beginning of life and death is the end of life.
Sex is the A and death is the Z; it is one alphabet, connected. It is not different but
distant, so distant that neither Freud nor Jung could see that they were both
concerned with one thing; but the poles were so far apart that they were unable to
join them.

Jung was very much afraid of death, and as he came closer to another layer
behind the collective unconscious he backed out. He tried many times to
approach the idea of death. He went to India because in India people have been
thinking about every possible aspect of life for thousands of years. Of course,
about death India has thought much more than anybody else – but he avoided
the man who could have been of some help.

He was asking people who were educated in the West – professors in the universities who had Western degrees, doctors who had Western degrees – because
he had a fixed idea that East and West can never meet. The idea was old; it was
given by an English poet, Rudyard Kipling, that East and West can never meet:
"East is East, West is West, and never the twain shall meet."

Somewhere in Jung's mind that idea remained his whole life, and he was
continually insisting to his disciples that the West had to discover its own methods; it should not use Eastern methods, because they could prove dangerous:
"They are not our heritage."

Now, this is a strange situation and a strange argument. A man who discov-
ers the collective unconscious still believes in East and West. Then there are two
collectives: Eastern collective unconscious and Western collective unconscious.
He never became aware of the simple fact that if you talk about collective unconscious then East is no longer East and West is no longer West. And if you think
they cannot meet then you can come and see here in Rajneeshpuram: they are
meeting. They have met!

Just a few days ago one man from South Africa declared a new conflict. He
said the real conflict is not between East and West, it is between North and South.
That was never thought of before, it is a real discovery. But it has a point in it.
There is a conflict, just like the one between East and West which has become
famous and well-known. But South and North are also in conflict, which has not
become so well-known. But then there will be four collective unconsciouses, and
it is going to be very difficult.

But Jung was not aware. One thing he was certain of: Eastern methods were
not to be used. So he avoided the only man alive in India, Raman Maharishi, who
could have taken him to the lowest level which Buddha called the cosmic unconscious. But that is almost a death. It is a death, because you are no longer there.
The cosmos is, but you are no longer there. The seeker disappears; he has

found what he was seeking, but he is no longer there. That's a quantum leap.

The subconscious, unconscious, collective and cosmic unconscious – these four layers are under your conscious. Above are also four layers. The question is how to reach the higher states of consciousness.

The method is a very strange one, but there is only one way. You have to go down first. You have to enter the cosmic unconscious. Unless you disappear into the cosmic unconscious, you cannot enter into the superconscious, the first level above conscious.

What actually happens: as you enter the cosmic unconscious, your subconscious, your unconscious, your collective unconscious all disappear, just like small rivers falling into the ocean – a vast ocean of cosmic darkness. It is a death. And unless you are born again you will not enter the Kingdom of God.

Jesus must have heard that statement somewhere in India from a Buddhist monk, because it has no source in Jewish religion. Its only source can be a Buddhist source, because that's what Buddha was teaching: that you dive deep into the cosmic unconscious, and as you enter into it, all is darkness, you are lost completely. But wait – don't be in a hurry and don't back out. Don't run back, because where will you go? You will go back again to the same routine world in which you had lived.

Don't run. Wait, wait a moment. And the darkness as you wait starts becoming less and less dark. It is almost as if you are coming from the outside in the hot sun, and enter in the house and you suddenly see darkness because your eyes are focused for the light outside. The sunlight is so bright that your pupils shrink. They cannot bear that much light going in, so they become small, very small. And then suddenly you enter your house; it takes a little time for your eyes to adjust to the new situation; the sun is no longer there. Your pupils start becoming bigger. When they become bigger, then the house has more light.

That's how thieves who come into your house in the night when everything is dark... You yourself in your own house cannot move around; you may stumble into this desk, that table, this chair. But a thief who has never been in your house, who knows nothing about the house enters in darkness, and without stumbling into anything finds exactly the place where you are keeping all your treasure. It needs training; it is an art. Of course it is a crime. That's another aspect; I am not concerned with that. But it is an art.

The famous Zen story is:

A very great master who was also a master thief was getting old. His son asked him, "Before you die, please teach me your art of stealing."

He said, "I was just waiting for you to ask because we never impose; art is something that you should have a feel for. If you are ready, I am ready. Today is the beginning of your teaching. Tonight you come with me."

The old man takes the young man. The young man is trembling, his heart is throbbing. He is looking from side to side, but the father is moving as if going for a morning walk, at ease. He cuts a hole in the wall – the son is perspiring and it is a cold winter night. And the father is doing his work so silently, and so artfully, the son is amazed.

The father goes in, calls the son in. They move inside the house. The father has the master key, he opens the doors. They reach the innermost chamber of the palace. The father opens a cupboard, a walk-in cupboard, and tells the son to get in. The son is trembling, just trembling. He gets in and asks, "What I am supposed to do?"

He said, "Simply get in. You are not supposed to do anything. Simply get in and then whatsoever happens, happens."

He got into it. The father locked the door and ran out leaving the son inside the cupboard, and while he was leaving the house, he shouted, "Thief! Thief!" so the whole house woke up. All the servants were running here and there, and were searching with torches everywhere. And they found the hole in the wall: certainly somebody has come in. A maidservant looking closely on the floor found some foot marks and went exactly to the wardrobe.

The son is aware; he cannot even breathe. He knows now that somebody is there, and is coming in with a torchlight: "Soon they will open it and I am caught. And this old man... In what unfortunate moment I asked him to teach me the art; and is this a way of teaching? He finished me in the first lesson!"

But suddenly – and that is God's voice – he heard somebody inside him saying, "Make the sound of scratching, as if a rat is inside scratching or eating." He could not believe it – who was speaking inside? He had never heard such a thing: making a scratching noise like a rat? But he made the scratching noise, and the woman opened the door, certain there was a rat inside... She opened the door, and he came out.

She was holding just a candle in her hand. He blew the candle out and ran away. When he was running out, people followed. He could not figure out who had said to him: "Blow the candle out." He had heard the voice say, "Blow the candle out and run away," but it was not his thinking because he had heard it; it was coming from somewhere.

And now in the dark night, he is running and people are following him, and they are coming closer and closer and they are shouting, "He is there! Catch him!" – they can see him.

He comes near a well, and the voice inside him says, "Take a rock and throw it in the well." So he takes a rock... There is no time to question why, and "Who are you?" and "What purpose will it serve?" These are questions which you ask when you are conveniently, comfortably seated in a classroom, when there is no hurry for the answer – neither do you mean that you really need the answer. But in such a situation when he is just about to be caught, the voice speaks and he follows.

He throws a rock into the well and runs away. Certainly, the rock falling in the well makes a big noise, and all the people who are following him stop near the well – they think that the man has jumped into the well. So now some arrangement has to be made: more light has to be brought, somebody has to go down and find out who this man is, whether he is alive or dead. Now their whole minds are diverted.

He reaches his home, really angry, almost ready to kill the father. And the father is sound asleep, covered with his blanket – it was a cold night. He pulls off his blanket, and he asks, "Is this the way to teach your own son?"

He said, "Are you back? That's enough; you have learned the art. Now go to sleep, we will discuss it in the morning."

But he said, "You should ask me how I managed to escape!"

He said, "That does not matter. You are back; about the how, we will discuss in the morning. And I know how, because the same voice that has been speaking in you has been speaking in me my whole life. That's why I was the master thief. It was not the working of the brain, it was not the working of the mind; it was from my very depths. I have followed only the deepest in me, and I have never gone wrong.

"You are back; that simply means you heard it, and that's the whole secret of the art. There is no other lesson. The first lesson is the last lesson. If you were not back it meant the student was not able to survive the first lesson: finished. He was not capable."

You have to take a jump. First it will be dark, very dark. Rest in that darkness: darkness has a beauty of its own.

You have known the beauty of light, and the beauty of flowers and trees, and men and women: that is all beauty in light, through light. It is all light reflected: different colors, different faces, different flowers, but it is all the world of light.

You have not known the silence, the depth, the unboundedness of darkness. It also has its own beauty, totally different.

It is the beauty of death.

And once you have allowed it to happen, once you relax in it, you say, "Okay. If it is death then let it be death, but I am not going back." Once you relax in this darkness of the cosmic unconscious, slowly it starts becoming lighter. And the first glimpse of light is the beginning of the superconscious.

When it becomes even lighter, so that you can see the tremendous emptiness, then it is the supersuperconscious. When it becomes so strong a light that it becomes unbearable – again you may feel like escaping – it is the collective conscious. It is not only your conscious, it is the consciousness of all human beings, of the whole history, in totality, condensed. Hence it is too bright.

Just as darkness makes you afraid, too much brightness also makes you blind and afraid. Don't be afraid, there is nothing to be afraid of. It is your nature; there is nothing to be afraid of, it is your being. If you allow this tremendous intensity of light of the collective conscious, you enter into the cosmic conscious.

Cosmic consciousness is neither dark nor light.

If you can find just the middle point between light and darkness – very soothing, warm from the side of light, cool from the side of darkness – it is the meeting, the ultimate meeting of the polar opposites.

And this cosmic consciousness is what I call enlightenment.

In darkness you were lost, but the fear, the trembling, the death surrounding you kept something of you still there: a very subtle ego which you cannot catch hold of. You feel you are lost but there you are still, because you are afraid. If you are not there, who is afraid? The darkness is so much that you are focused on darkness, and you are not in your focus at all.

In the cosmic consciousness you are really lost. There is no fear, there is no way of going back, or of going anywhere. Hence I call this the arrival – from where you had never departed in fact. It was always there above you, hanging above you, for millions of lives, just waiting, waiting. But to reach it first you will have to go deep down to the very roots.

Friedrich Nietzsche again – because this man I find tremendously insightful. On the whole he is a mess, but in fragments he has such penetrating insight, which is rarely available anywhere else. He says, "Before you can reach heaven, you have to reach to hell. Unless you have fathomed hell completely, there is no way to heaven."

It looks very absurd. And he used to write in maxims; he never wrote essays explaining anything, that was not his way. Insights never come in essays, in theses; they never come for PhD, DLitt degrees. No. For a PhD degree you have to sit in a library and do a clerical job, just collecting from here and there. You can simply take a pair of scissors and if you can cut from this book and that book, this journal and that journal, and just go on collecting them in a file, sooner or later you will be a PhD. There is not much more to it.

Men like Nietzsche only write maxims. One day suddenly he will write a maxim, and then for months he will not write. This is the meaning of what he says... Now, Jesus cannot understand it. Jesus says, "If you want to avoid hell, come follow me, I will take you to heaven. That's the only way to avoid hell." Nietzsche is saying, "If you avoid hell, heaven is already avoided, because heaven is a second step. You have missed the first step."

In another passage, a similar passage, Nietzsche says, "Before you can reach to the top of a tree and can understand the flowers blossoming there, you will have to go deep to the roots, because the secret lies there. And the deeper the roots go, the higher the tree goes." So the greater your longing for understanding, for cosmic consciousness – because that is the ultimate lotus, the lotus paradise – then the further you will have to go to the deepest roots in the darkest underground; and the way is only one.

Call it meditation, call it awareness, call it watchfulness – it all comes to the same: that you become more alert, first about your conscious mind, what goes on in your conscious mind. And it is a beautiful experience. It is really hilarious, a great panorama.

In my childhood in my town there were no movies, talkies. There was no cinema hall. Now there is, but in my childhood there was not. The only thing that was available was that once in a while a wandering man would come with a big box. I don't know what it is called. There is a small window in it. He opens the window, you just put your eyes to it and he goes on moving a handle and a film inside moves. And he goes on telling the story of what is happening.

Everything else I have forgotten, but one thing I cannot forget for a certain reason. The reason, I know, was because it was in all those boxes that came through my village. I had seen every one, because the fee was just one paise. Also the show was not long, just five minutes. In every box there were different films, but one picture was always there: the naked washerwoman of Mumbai. Why did it used to be in every one? – a very fat naked woman, the naked washerwoman of Mumbai. That used to be always there. Perhaps that was a great attraction, or people were fans of that naked washerwoman; and she was really ugly. And why from Mumbai?

If you start looking... Just whenever you have time, just sit silently and look at what is passing in your mind. There is no need to judge, because if you judge, the mind immediately changes its scenes according to you. The mind is very sensitive, touchy. If it feels that you are judging, then it starts showing things that are good. Then it won't show you the naked washerwoman of Mumbai, that picture will be missed out. So don't judge, then that picture is bound to come.

Don't judge, don't make any condemnation, don't make any appreciation. Be indifferent. Just sit silently looking at things, whatsoever is happening. And absurd things will be happening: a horse becomes a man... Now you need not ask why, there is no need to ask, simply see it.

For anything that is happening, you have only to be a seer.

That's the strategy that helps the whole scenery to slowly disappear from the conscious mind. And when the conscious mind disappears from the screen, the subconscious starts emerging. Subconscious is more colorful, technicolor. The conscious mind is just black and white, old style. But the subconscious is very colorful, much more meaningful, much more truthful.

But remember not to judge; otherwise the subconscious will slip down and you will be back into the conscious.

So two things: no judgment, just simple alertness.

Soon you will find these pictures also disappearing. Then the unconscious appears, which has very strange things to say to you, very mysterious. No need to be afraid; they are voices from the past, of your past lives and of other people's past lives. They carry pictures of your past life and other people's past life. Now you are moving into a denser forest, of a tremendous magnitude. Don't become afraid. The voices are very strong, and it is not only voices...

The unconscious remembers not only the voices, not only the pictures, it remembers all the experiences of all your senses. You will smell things that you have never smelled. But sometime in a past life somewhere, you must have smelled that smell; it is still there. You may hear music that is not known to you. You may hear languages which you are absolutely unaware of. You may taste the taste of strange foods. All the five senses will supply experiences of many, many lives. You have simply to remain a seer, no judgment. Then these start disappearing.

And when the collective unconscious opens, then animals and trees and birds – all are available to you. You are not separate from them. Stories like Saint Francis can be right. But there is no miracle in it. This man is perhaps the most important man in the whole of Christian history, because he talked to birds, animals, and they understood it. He would just sit on the bank of a river and start calling the fishes, and the fishes would start jumping all around him, listening to him. And he would talk to them. He would say, "Sisters, how are you?" His disciples would think he was mad, but they could not say that, because they could see that the fishes were listening, nodding their heads. Even the donkey on which he used to move he used to call "brother donkey." He just had to say, "Brother donkey, move right" – and the donkey would move right.

When he was dying, his last words were not said to any man, they were said to the donkey. He said, "Thank you, brother donkey; you have carried me your whole life and I am immensely grateful" – and there were tears in the donkey's eyes. As Francis died the donkey died. He could not bear the separation.

Now, there is nothing miraculous in it. This man has moved through the collective unconscious; perhaps just one more life and he will be able to enter the cosmic unconscious; and from there begins the upward flight.

It's very strange: if you want to go above consciousness, you have to go below consciousness. But there is only one method.

My name for it is meditation.

But meditation is equivalent to watchfulness, awareness, alertness.

awareness has its own rewards

Osho,
What do you want man to do? What is right and wrong according to you? Is there something like sin and its punishment too?

My concern with man is not about his doing, but about his being. And this is a very fundamental issue to be understood by you.

All the religions have been concerned about man's doings. They have been labeling a few acts as wrong, a few other acts as right, a few acts good, a few acts bad. They have not at all pondered over the real problem.

Man is asleep, and when a man is asleep the question is not what he should do or should not do. The question is: he should be awakened, he should be awake.

And remember, awakening is not a question of doing right, avoiding wrong; not committing sin, doing virtue.

Man's sleep is not an ordinary sleep. He walks, he talks, he does things, but it is all being done in sleep. So when I say man is asleep, I mean metaphysically, spiritually, man is asleep. He knows nothing about himself.

His innermost center is in darkness, and the society, the religions, the parents, the cultures, civilizations – nobody is bothered about his being awake. Their concern is that he should do things which are comfortable to them, convenient to them.

They reward you, they give you respectability, and they encourage your greed: so even in the other life, if you go on doing the right thing you will be immensely rewarded, and if you do the wrong thing you will be punished, heavily punished.

Centuries of conditioning have made you ask this question. I am not at all interested in what you do, because a man who is asleep, unaware of himself, whatever he does is wrong.

Let me repeat it: whatever an asleep man does is wrong. He may be doing virtuous acts: charity to the poor, opening hospitals, schools, colleges, universities; educating people, donating to every cause, helping in every calamity – but I still say whatever he does is wrong, because he is asleep. He cannot do right. In sleep it has never been possible to do right.

Just the other day, Sheela brought me the news: in India, in one of the biggest cities, Bhopal, a few days ago there has been a great accident. One big factory which produces some poisonous gas – must be for military reasons – exploded. It is just in the middle of the city. Two thousand people who were close to the factory died immediately, and one hundred thousand people have been seriously injured.

It is a big accident, and naturally – you can guess – Mother Teresa is running from Kolkata to Bhopal, because these people like Mother Teresa are praying every day to the Lord, "Give us an opportunity to serve." And the Lord, their Lord, is so compassionate, he goes on giving opportunities to serve. She went to Bhopal, moved around the injured, went to the families whose people have died, and what she said to them is very important. She said, "Don't take it as a tragedy."

This is what the religions have been doing for thousands of years: befooling people. This is a tragedy. She told people, "Don't think of it as a tragedy, it is a great opportunity. Look positively. It has brought the best out in man. So many people are serving others, helping in every way. Look at this side of it: the situation has brought the best out in thousands of people. They may never have done anything good in their life, but they are doing it now."

But do you understand the implications of it? It means it should happen in every factory! It should happen in every city, because it brings the best out in people. What can be more beautiful than this? A great opportunity to be good, to do good, to serve those who need your service, to help those who are in a helpless condition. This is a God-given opportunity for do-gooders. And nobody objected to her!

Perhaps I am the only person here, on this whole earth, who is objecting that this is befooling people. This is creating a camouflage, a bogus spiritual jargon. If God has any sense, any intelligence at all, he should find some better way to bring the best out in people. This does not seem to be very intelligent. If this is what God is doing then where is the Devil? And what will the Devil do? God has taken his job too; the Devil is unemployed.

And people applauded her; she is a great saint. And what present has she brought to them? – a small statue of Mother Mary. A great help: "Pray to Mother Mary, and don't take it as a tragedy and don't complain that it is the fault or carelessness of certain officers concerned; no, that is not good."

Of course if those people were not careless, and those officers had not allowed this tragedy, then Mother Teresa could not be a saint. Her sainthood depends on these stupid officers, this bureaucracy. Now she is consoling people, giving them the impression that it is a God-given opportunity.

Two thousand people have died, two thousand families are now on the streets; children, wives, old parents will become beggars. One hundred thousand people are seriously injured; many of them will die, and if they don't die they will live a crippled life: somebody blind, somebody without legs, somebody without hands, somebody deaf, somebody dumb. Mother Teresa is consoling these people, giving them a Madonna, Mother Mary's statue saying, "Pray to Mother Mary and everything will be okay – and don't complain against the officers."

Now, that's strange! Why? – because those officers, the government, go on showering money on her charitable trusts: "All help to Mother Teresa, all great titles of the country to Mother Teresa." Every university is competing with the others to give honorary degrees to Mother Teresa; naturally she has to protect those people also. These people should be punished if it is their carelessness – but she is protecting them: "Don't complain, because your complaining means you are taking things negatively. Take it positively."

So she is doing two things: consoling people – which is just rubbish, because this consolation is not going to help, the tragedy is not going to become comedy, they will have to suffer it. And secondly she is protecting those people whose fault it was. They should be really punished! But they are not to be punished, "Don't complain against them" – because she is gathering favor with the government, gathering favor with the officials, with the hierarchy, the bureaucracy.

And the last thing she did, which was her real purpose in going there, was to tell her secretary to write down all the names of the orphans. Many children have become orphans. That was her actual purpose in going there: she is in search of orphans. She has many orphanages, which are just factories to turn orphans into Catholics. You see the works, the miracles of saints!

All those orphans will be taken by her. The government will be happy, the people will be happy, the city will be happy that all those poor children... Who was going to take care of them? They would have been a nuisance. And in India if two thousand people die that means at least twenty-four thousand children must have been left as orphans. This great chance she could not miss.

Kolkata is far away from Bhopal – a thirty-hour journey by train – but she rushed immediately. Nobody takes note of where these orphans go on disappearing to. She goes on collecting these orphans, then where do they go on disappearing? She goes on giving them for adoption to Catholic families – but remember, only to Catholic families.

One American wanted a child; he simply went for that because the doctors had said that the situation was such that he and his wife couldn't have children; they would have to adopt. He simply went to India to get a child from Mother Teresa. But he forgot one thing, that he is a Protestant. He would have never thought about it. And when he wanted a child to adopt, the secretary asked him about his religion, because she had to fill in the form. When he said that he was a Protestant, she said, "There is a difficulty. Right now we don't have any orphans to give for adoption."

Now, in India you don't have any orphans...? Mother Teresa is collecting hundreds of orphans every day. And if there was no orphan, why did you want him to fill in a form in the first place? You should have told him before, "There is no orphan right now, we are helpless. We will inform you; you just leave your address."

But the secretary was willing to give him a child – just fill in the form, and you go in and choose a child – but as he was a Protestant... He is still a Christian, what to say about a Hindu, a Mohammedan or a Jaina. And those children belonged to Hindus, to Jainas, to Mohammedans.

For example, in Bhopal – Bhopal is a Mohammedan city – those children will be mostly Mohammedans. They will not be given to Mohammedans, to Hindus, to Jainas, no – even a Protestant Christian is denied. And what an excuse: "There is no orphan available." There were seven hundred orphans already inside that orphanage, and the secretary was denying that there was one orphan.

These children go on increasing the Catholic population. God is gracious, compassionate: let all the factories explode! Let everybody become an orphan so Catholics go on increasing by millions, and the pope again becomes the emperor of almost the whole world.

There is no wonder that the pope respects Mother Teresa and gives her all the great titles of the church. There is no wonder that she receives the Nobel Prize, because she is being recommended even by the pope. You can't get a Nobel Prize unless you are recommended by a certain category of people. Either they have to be Nobel Prize winners, or they have to be kings, queens, presidents, prime ministers.

The pope is the king of that small kingdom of the Vatican, eight square miles. He is the king of that kingdom – he has twenty soldiers, and six hundred million Catholics around the world. He has great power, and people like Mother Teresa are working everywhere to bring in more and more people.

You ask me what I want man to do. First thing: I want man to recognize that he is asleep, because unless he accepts and acknowledges that he is asleep there is no possibility of waking him up. Can you wake a man who thinks he is awake? He will slap you! "Stop all this nonsense, I am awake! What are you doing?" First you have to recognize it, create a recognition.

I have always loved this story:

A few friends, on a full moon night, got drunk. The night was so beautiful and they wanted to enjoy it, so they drank to the full and went to the beautiful river. The boatmen had gone, leaving their boats on the bank on the river. It was the middle of the night, the full moon was just above their heads, and it was a fairy-land all over.

Seeing the boats, one of the friends said, "It will be good if we go in the boat, on the river. Just look! The moon is reflected in the river, and when something, a waterfowl, runs over the water or takes a dip into the water, the whole water becomes silver. The moon spreads all over the river."

They were just a little bit awake the way man is: ninety-nine percent they were drunk. They went into a boat, they took the oars and started moving out into the river. The others who were just sitting went on telling the people who were rowing the boat, "Go faster, it is so beautiful. Don't move so slowly, make speed." And the oarsmen were trying hard and perspiring.

As the morning was coming closer, one of them said – because a cold wind started blowing and they came back to their senses a little bit – one of them said, "We must have come miles away from our place. Somebody should get out and have a look where we are, so that we can go back home. Soon the sun will be rising, and before that we have to get back; otherwise that boatman whose boat we have picked up without asking will create trouble."

One man got out and started laughing madly. They said, "Why are you laughing?"

He said, "Just come here and you also will laugh."

They all climbed out – and then they sat there laughing, because they had forgotten to unchain the boat! The whole night they had rowed and had tried to go faster and faster and they were exactly where they had started. Not a single inch... The boat was tied on the bank, it was locked.

This is the story of man as he is.

Now, Mother Teresa must be thinking that she is doing good. I have no doubt about her intentions, but I have tremendous doubt about her wakefulness. She is not awake, she is fast asleep. In sleep at the most you can go on dreaming good dreams or bad dreams; but what does it matter? If it is a dream, whether you dream of heaven or hell, what does it matter? In the morning you will find both were dreams.

In a dream you can be a thief, or you can be a monk. And of course in the dream you will enjoy being a monk and the ego that comes with it; it is part and parcel of a very polished, cultured ego. And if you are a thief, certainly, even in your dream you will feel bad that unfortunately you have to become a thief. You don't want to become one, but situations are forcing you to become a thief even though it is a sin.

You ask me: "Is there something like sin?" There is only one sin: that is not recognizing your sleep, not recognizing your state of deep hypnotic slumber. That's the only sin. There is no other sin.

Out of this one sin, millions of things can arise, but this is the root. And if this sin is there you cannot do anything right. Even if you try to do anything right you will do it for the wrong reasons, the wrong motives. The action may look right, but the motivation will be wrong. You are wrong; so from where can you get the right motivation?

Now, what is Mother Teresa running around for in her old age? There should be a time of retirement even for saints. These poor saints never retire; they become senile but still nobody retires them. Nobody tells them, "Now retire, you have done enough. Now let others do some good works; otherwise you will be the only monopolist in heaven. Share with other saints also. Now retire, and we will do the good things you were doing." But no, saints never retire.

Sinners retire but saints never retire. Strange... It's because the saint never gets tired, for the simple reason that his ego goes on becoming stronger and stronger. And he is collecting virtue; his treasure in the other world is increasing more and more. He is coming closer to God every day, so certainly he needs orphans, he needs accidents, he needs poor people.

On the one hand the pope says, "The idea of class struggle is a sin. The poor have to remain poor; they should not make any effort to change the structure of the society. This is the only society that has been given to them by God. Who are you to think that you can improve upon it?

"If the class structure is there it is a great opportunity, not a tragedy. If you are poor it is a great opportunity: Blessed are the poor for theirs is the Kingdom of God. If you want the Kingdom of God then don't make any effort to change the society, to create a revolution, to create some kind of structure where there is not so much distance between the rich and the poor."

I know it will be difficult for the asleep man to create a society where there is no class at all. A classless society can only be an enlightened society. Before that, a classless society is not possible. Marx is as much asleep as you are. Communists are as much asleep as the capitalists.

So in the Soviet Union, what happened? Sixty years, more than sixty years have passed. They changed the old structure; now there is nobody who is rich and nobody who is poor. That division they destroyed, but a new division has come in: between the bureaucracy – one who is in the government – and one who is just an ordinary citizen. Now all the power is in the hands of the bureaucracy: much more so than had ever been in the hands of rich people.

Rich people had power because they had money; through money they could purchase anything. But in the Soviet Union, the bureaucracy has every power over every individual: to let you live or to finish you off, to keep you in the country or send you to Siberia to die in that eternal world of ice. They have power over your life and death. Such power was never in the hands of the people who had money.

Yes, they had certain powers. They could have a better house than you, they could have more luxuries, more comforts than you, but they did not have the right over your life and death. If they killed you, then in the court they were treated in the same way as everyone else. Perhaps they may have managed a little bit by bribing the court, the judge, but that was very indirect, very difficult. In the Soviet Union it is blatantly naked: direct power is in the hands of the bureaucracy.

I have heard that when Stalin died… Stalin remained in power perhaps longer than anybody else in the whole world. Alexander the Great died very young; he was thirty-three, the same age as Jesus was when he died. Napoleon Bonaparte died on a small island, Saint Helena, as a prisoner. Adolf Hitler committed suicide.

Stalin seems to be the only man in the whole of history who ruled over the biggest of empires – because Russia is one sixth of the whole earth – for almost half a century. He had all the powers that you can imagine. He killed millions of people. Nobody could even raise a finger, because the moment you raised a finger against Stalin, the next day you disappeared.

When he died Khrushchev came to power, his second man, his very right hand. And at the first communist party meeting he spoke against Stalin. He said, "I have been watching all these years what this man has been doing. He has brought back the classes; only the name has changed. There are powerful people and there are powerless people, and the distance between them is the same as it was before. In fact the distance has increased, it has become bigger, tremendously big" – because in a capitalist country a poor man has every chance to move into a higher society: he can become rich.

Henry Ford was not born rich, and he became the richest man in the world, just through his own talent, his genius. When he was a child he used to polish boots for people. And when his children were born, he was already moving higher and higher, becoming richer and richer. When they came from college he said, "First, start polishing people's shoes in front of the factory" – where he created the Ford cars – "in front of the doors, start polishing shoes."

They were shocked. They said, "What are you saying? We are your sons and we should polish the shoes of your servants, your workers?"

Henry Ford said, "That's the way I made it, and I would not like you to just inherit capital; that is below your dignity. You are a Ford. You have to earn it, you have to show your mettle." And you will be surprised – his sons had to polish people's shoes in front of Ford's own factory. That man was absolutely right: those people, starting from scratch, became rich in their own right. And Ford said, "Now everything of mine belongs to you. You deserve it." But just being a son of Henry Ford was not enough.

In a capitalist society it is difficult for a poor man to rise, but not impossible. In fact rich people's children, because they are born in riches, don't know how to create wealth, and slowly, slowly their wealth disappears. By the third or fourth generation you will find them on the streets amongst the hippies. The poor man's son knows what poverty is; it hurts. He puts his total energy, all his talents to work. His only focus becomes how to get out of this imprisonment of poverty.

Yes, it is difficult, but not impossible. In fact, the richest people of the world come from poor families. But in a communist world it is almost impossible to enter into the elite few. It is almost impossible. First, to become a member of the communist party in the Soviet Union is very difficult.

The Soviet Union is not like other countries where you pay a little money and you become a member of the Republican Party or the Democratic Party, the Liberal Party or the Socialist Party. In the Soviet Union, to become a member of the Communist Party you have to prove that you are a communist every inch, that there is not even a lurking shadow of the bourgeoisie. And that you have to start proving it from your very childhood, because there are many layers of the communist party – even the kindergarten communist party!

Now what do you think of that – little kids, the kindergarten school? From there the conditioning begins. And the teachers recommend who is possibly the right candidate to become, one day, a member of the communist party. Then there are youth leagues. All those kindergarten children who have come with recommendations will not be chosen for the youth league, but only a few of them: a few fortunate ones who have proved their devotion.

And how do you prove your devotion? A very strange method of proving your devotion – to spy on your mother, to spy on your father, to spy on your family and to report to the communist party that your mother has been complaining against the government, that your father is deep down against communism... And it is not just a question of complaint; you are arranging murder, imprisonment – a life sentence, a death sentence for your mother and father – and you know it.

But this is the only way to prove your devotion. Wives spying on husbands and reporting against them, husbands are spying against wives and reporting them. And they know what that report means. It means that tomorrow the wife will be simply missing; you cannot even find where she has gone. There is no case in a court, there is no question of appeal – she simply disappears.

Either she is killed... Mostly they were killed, because Stalin never believed in unnecessarily burdening the economy of the country with people who were against communism, and if you keep them in prison you have to feed them, you have to give them clothes. And why should your country feed its enemies? What is the point? Get finished with them. Unburden the country. And he really unburdened in millions.

Khrushchev was very angry, and he said, "This man is the greatest murderer in history, and it is good that he is dead. We should remove his grave from Red Square" – because when Stalin was in power, at that time he had ordered his grave to be made near Lenin's grave in Red Square. While he was in power, the grave was already made according to his design, according to his idea. It had to be the grave of one of the greatest communists.

Khrushchev said, "We have to remove that grave. It is an ugly spot." And he removed it. Stalin's bones were taken out and sent back to the faraway Caucasus where he was born. There, near a monastery where he was educated, is now his poor grave, made with ordinary earthen bricks. That marvelous Italian-marble grave simply disappeared from Red Square.

While he was speaking to the communist party, a member at the back stood up and said, "You have been with Stalin all these years; why didn't you say these words then?" And the man sat down.

Khrushchev said, "I will answer your question; just please stand up again and say what your name is. Comrade, stand up again!" Nobody stood up again. He said, "This is my answer. Why aren't you standing up again and saying your name? And now you know why I was silent too; because tomorrow you would disappear. If I have lived to this day, it is because I kept absolutely silent." Even walls have ears in Russia; you cannot even whisper in your bathroom, because nobody knows... And particularly people who were in power, like Khrushchev, who was next to Stalin. His bathroom, his bedroom, everything must have been bugged. A slight suspicion and that was enough.

Stalin never wanted proofs for anything; just a suspicion was enough proof for him. The idea of justice that has prevailed in the world, the whole world, is that not a single innocent man should suffer. Even if ninety-nine criminals have to be left unpunished, not a single innocent man should suffer. That has been the criterion.

Stalin reversed it. He said, "Not a single criminal" – and criminal means one who is against communism – "not a single criminal should be left, even if ninety-nine innocent people have to be killed." Just the suspicion was enough; there was no need of finding proof.

And what harm was there? – because communism believes that man is only matter. Is there any harm if you dismantle your chair? Is there any harm if you take your clock apart and put the parts all over the place? Nobody can call you a criminal, although the clock was something alive, moving, and all these parts separated cannot show you the time and will not give the tick-tock of a clock.

Marx's idea about man is exactly like a clock; man is only a by-product of matter. In a certain arrangement, he speaks, talks, thinks, loves, feels – but all these are epiphenomena, not real phenomena. Put all the parts aside, take man apart: put the head on one side, leg on another side, hands there, heart here, and everything stops, nothing is left. And you can weigh all the parts, they will weigh exactly the same as the man. That is his scientific logic: that no soul has left the body. Nothing has gone, it is the same weight. You have just dismantled the organism – it was a machine.

According to Marx, in summary: man is a robot. So to kill a robot who is creating a nuisance can't be thought of as anything bad. Stalin did not think he was doing anything bad. He was serving the society, serving the great ideal of communism, bringing the classless society closer and closer. But all that he brought was a new class society, divided between the bureaucracy and the people. Now the bureaucracy is exploiting the people in every possible way, torturing them. Every property belongs to the government. There is no private property any more.

In the very beginning of the revolution, that is from 1917 to 1927, for ten years, the idea was discussed continually, "Should we do the same with women also as we have done with other property?" – because a woman is property. She should not belong to a single man; all women should belong to the nation.

But it seemed difficult, too difficult. The whole nation was against it. Nobody wanted his wife just to be public property like a public bench in the park or a public bus. Even the communists themselves were not ready for that, although Stalin was very much in favor of it. He treated his own wife almost like a thing; he used to beat her.

I have met Stalin's daughter, Svetlana. After Stalin's death she came to India. Just by chance I happened to be in Delhi, and the woman I was staying with... She is a rare woman. I will not tell you her name because what I am going to say refers to people who are still alive, and particularly to a person for whom I have tremendous respect. This woman is now nearabout seventy-five. I have never come across a woman that old and yet so beautiful.

She was in love with J. Krishnamurti. She wanted to marry J. Krishnamurti, but Theosophists did not allow Krishnamurti even to meet with any women. They wanted him to become a world teacher, and a married world teacher does not look right – I don't know why. Perhaps it creates the suspicion that whether you are a world teacher or not, if you have a wife she will be boss. And the world teacher should not have a boss. He is the boss. So they prevented it in every possible way. And finally J. Krishnamurti, even though he renounced the Theosophical movement – their world teacherhood that they were going to impose on him – he continued to have the idea that a man like him should not be married.

This is how millions of years of conditioning goes deep. If you don't want to marry that is perfectly okay; it is your decision to be married or not to be married. But to make it something unholy – that is strange. He still stays in this woman's house if she is in Delhi, because she is in a very high government post. Her principal house is in Mumbai. If he is in Mumbai then he stays in her house in Mumbai.

It is because of Krishnamurti that she became interested in me, because Krishnamurti was continually speaking against me to her. Naturally she became interested, because if Krishnamurti speaks against me... And he never speaks against anybody else by name, that is below him: this is a subtle kind of ego. For example, if I criticize Mahatma Gandhi, I criticize him openly. Krishnamurti criticizes him but he never mentions his name; that is below him.

But with me Krishnamurti is really cross, particularly because of my sann-yasins. Wherever he goes, anywhere in the world, they are sitting in the front row. And the moment he sees their red clothes and the *mala*, he freaks out. Then he forgets on what subject he was going to speak. Then he starts speaking against me, against sannyas, against the rosary, against disciplehood and against masters.

In Mumbai I have many sannyasins and they used to ask me what to do. I said, "Just go and sit in front. There is nothing you have to do, just smile and enjoy it." And the more they enjoyed it, the more he would beat his head; he would just go out of his senses. He would forget all awareness. He would act just like a bull does when you wave a red handkerchief or a red umbrella or a red flag: the bull becomes mad. I think Krishnamurti must have been a bull in his last life.

So he was continually speaking against me to this woman. And the woman's sisters, sisters-in-law – her whole family became very much interested in me; they were all my people. Krishnamurti was speaking against me and all the family was speaking for me. Finally the woman decided that she had to meet me. She invited me, saying, "If you pass through Delhi, stay with me this time."

I was staying with her and she told me, "Svetlana is here. Would you like to see her?"

I said, "That's very good. I wanted to meet Stalin, but no harm; some part of Stalin...at least royal blood!"

When I asked her, "How was he behaving with your mother?" she just started weeping.

She said, "He was a monster. He used to beat my mother. He used to beat me for any small thing and we could not say a single word against him, because he would do the same to us as he would have done to anybody else – he would kill us. We were treated just like servants."

Even Stalin's wife could not enter his room without knocking and asking per-mission. She had to make an appointment – and they lived just in the same house. Stalin was very much in favor of what he called women's liberation. And people thought it was not women's liberation; it was just making all women prostitutes. Everybody was against it. All of the communist party's high-ranking people were against it; not a single person was in favor. That's why the policy was dropped.

Otherwise everything that was private became public – and by public it simply meant it became state-owned. Your house, your horse, your hands, your land – everything became state-owned.

Hence, in the Soviet Union it is not communism. I call it state capitalism. The state became the only "monopolist." In America there are many capitalists; in the Soviet Union there is only one capitalist. And certainly to have many is better. Rather than giving all the power to one person... And it is like a pyramid: the communist party is the base and then slowly the pyramid becomes smaller and smaller with higher bureaucrats and finally and ultimately comes the central committee of the communist party with only twelve persons.

One of the central committee will be the president and one of them will be the prime minister. And the prime minister is the real power; the president is only a rubber stamp. He has to sign anything that the prime minister decides. Even if the prime minister decides that the president has to be sentenced to death, he has to sign it. He has no other power except to stamp it. Whatsoever comes from the prime minister, he stamps it. This is a new class structure.

Now, the pope seems not to be aware that to call the class struggle a sin means you are supporting not only America, you are also supporting the communist countries. Of that he is not aware. That's the situation of a man who is asleep. He does not know the implications of his own words, his own actions, because class exists everywhere on the earth. There is no country which is classless.

And yes, it is needed that one day the world becomes classless. And by a classless society I don't mean communism. I simply mean enlightened people who can see that there is no need for poverty to exist; we have enough technology to destroy it. There is no need to destroy the capitalist. All that is needed is to spread capitalism so that everybody becomes a capitalist.

Now, my approach is just the opposite of communism.

In Russia, in China, in other communist countries what have they done? They have destroyed all the capitalists and made the communist party the only monopolizing agency, the only capitalist alive. And what have they distributed? Poverty! – because after sixty-five years Russia is still poor, still starving, still without enough clothes, still without enough medicine. Seventy percent of their budget goes to the army. Only on thirty percent of the budget does the country live. Seventy percent is absorbed by arms and the army and the piling up of nuclear weapons.

It is such a small thing to see: if we stop the idea of war, which the pope does not call a sin... War is okay. He does not include war in his long list of sins. War is okay – because if he says war is a sin then all the popes up to now have been sinners because they have been continually warring, crusading against Mohammedans, against Jews, against everybody. And they have been saying that the crusade is a holy war!

No war is holy. No war can ever be holy. How can destruction be holy? How can killing be holy? How can butchering, slaughtering innocent people, children, women, old people, be holy? It must be holy in the same sense as the Holy Ghost: it is absolutely unholy.

But the classes are there. The capitalist wants the classes to remain because he feels that without the poor he will not be rich. That is wrong! That is absolutely wrong! Do you think that if poor people breathe then you cannot breathe? All that you need is enough air.

Certainly if air is in short supply then only rich people will breathe, because you will have to pay for it. Of course millions of poor people will die because they cannot pay – they don't have money to breathe. It is just like in a desert: you have to pay for water.

When Alexander came to India he met a fakir. The name of the fakir, he reports in his diary, does not seem to be Indian, but perhaps he misspelled it, mis-pronounced it, which is natural – just like me!

The Oregonians are very angry because I pronounce it Oreg-on; it should be Oreg-un. I cannot do that. I will go on pronouncing it Oregon. Ore*gun*? – sounds like son-of-a-gun. It doesn't feel right.

Alexander pronounces the name of the fakir, Dandamesh. *Dandamesh* is not an Indian name at all, it cannot be. It must have been Dandami. And there is in India a sect of monks who carry a staff in their hands called a *danda*: *danda* means "a big staff." These monks are called Dandadhari, staff holders; that is their symbol, their sect's symbol. Perhaps that man was carrying a *danda* and was known as Dandami: one who always keeps a *danda*. He was a naked man but the *danda* was absolutely necessary.

You may not understand why it is so. India is so full of dogs, and for certain reasons dogs are very much against monks, policemen, postmen: anybody who has a uniform. All the dogs are against uniforms. I don't know whether it is true in other countries or not, but in India... Indian dogs are absolutely against uniforms; anybody in uniform will be in trouble. And because of nonviolence dogs cannot be killed, so their population goes on increasing.

This staff was invented so that the poor monk, who has nothing, can at least protect himself against the dogs, because naked men also look like they are in a uniform, to the dog. In a way it is a uniform. All the naked monks, and there are many... And at the time when Alexander went to India, India was full of naked monks. The poor naked monk had to keep the *danda*, the staff.

He met Dandami, and a small dialogue between the two happened. Dandami was so blissful that Alexander felt jealous. He writes in his memoirs, "I felt jealous. That man had nothing except a staff and he looked so fulfilled, so contented, so immensely rich that I, Alexander the Great, the very great conqueror of the whole world, standing before him, looked like a beggar. The very flavor of the man was that of an emperor."

Alexander said to Dandami, "I would love it if you can accept my invitation. I would like to take you to Greece, particularly, because my teacher" – his teacher was Aristotle – "has asked me when I was leaving for India, 'If you come across a real sannyasin – because a sannyasin is something Eastern – if you find a real, authentic sannyasin, invite him as a royal guest and bring him here. I would love to see and meet a sannyasin. I have heard so much; so many rumors have been coming about sannyasins.'"

Dandami laughed and he said, "What can you give to me?"

Alexander said, "Whatever you ask."

He said, "If I ask for half of your kingdom?"

For a moment Alexander was stunned; what to say? But before he could say anything, Dandami said, "Okay, I ask for the whole kingdom. Don't be worried. I can see your worry – it is not up to your standards to give just half the kingdom. Okay, you give me the whole kingdom."

Alexander said, "You are asking too much. I had never thought..."

But Dandami said, "Do you think your kingdom is too much? In a desert you would give it for one glass of water; that's the value of your kingdom. Keep it, I was just joking. I am not going anywhere. If Aristotle wants to see a sannyasin he will have to come here. The thirsty go to the well, not the well to the thirsty. Tell Aristotle that you have met me. But your kingdom is not worth more than a glass of water. In the last stage in a desert, at the last moment when you are thirsty and dying, and somebody says, 'Here is a glass of water, but I want your whole kingdom' what will you say?"

Alexander had to accept it: "Yes, I would give the whole kingdom for one glass of water."

When water is scarce then of course rich people will be able to have control over water. If air becomes one day scarce, as is possible, because with more and more great happenings like Bhopal – that great opportunity, where the best comes out of man... The air is becoming polluted, so much so that soon you will see that only rich people will be capable of breathing – not everybody – because they will have stores of oxygen and oxygen masks. Just let there be a nuclear war anywhere and you will see that rich people will have facilities to protect themselves, and poor people will simply be dying.

There is no need for war; there is no need for poverty. We have enough money, enough resources, but seventy percent of the whole world's resources goes towards war. If that seventy percent is prevented from going towards bringing death to humanity, there is no need for anybody to become less rich. The living of all poor people can be raised higher. Marx's idea, Lenin, Stalin, Mao – their whole philosophy is to bring the richer people down to the level of the poor people. That they call communism; I call it stupidity.

My idea is to raise every poor person higher and higher and bring him to the level of the richest person. There is no need for poverty.

I will also have a classless society, but it will be of rich people. If Marx succeeds, he will also have a classless society – but phony. First, it will be of poor people. Secondly, because of those poor people, you will need a very strong and powerful bureaucracy to keep them down; otherwise they will revolt.

In America there is a possibility of a revolution, but in the Soviet Union you cannot conceive even the idea of revolution. You cannot talk with anybody about revolution. The very word will be enough for you to evaporate in some gas chamber.

Russia is not classless. America is not classless. Yes, there are different classes, but nobody is classless. And when the pope says that the idea of a class struggle is a sin, he certainly implies that the idea of creating a classless society is also a sin. No, the poor should remain poor, the rich should remain rich.

The very idea of class helps the so-called religions, because if everybody is rich and everybody has everything that is needed and everybody lives comfortably and luxuriously, who is going to bother about your heaven? Instead people will pray, "Please, send me back to the earth. I don't want to come to your heaven."

In the first place heaven will be a very ancient place – perhaps even bullock carts may not be available there, because I have never heard that God created bullock carts. And the spinning wheel... I sometimes feel sad for Mahatma Gandhi: if he has reached heaven, what will he be doing? – because the spinning wheel is not available there. There is no mention in any religious scripture that the spinning wheel is available to the angels.

Mahatma Gandhi will be simply dying to get back to the earth to find his spinning wheel again, because the whole day he was spinning. In the train, traveling, he was spinning; talking to people, he was spinning; dictating letters, he was spinning; dictating articles, he was spinning. He carried the spinning wheel everywhere.

There is no need for poverty, but the spinning wheel will keep people poor. Even if you spin for twelve hours a day you will not be able to create enough clothes for yourself. And there are other things to do, not just make clothes. You will need to eat something, drink something. And there are many other things you will need, not just clothes. Even if after twelve hours spinning you can make enough clothes to cover your body somehow, by that time the body will have disappeared because there will not be any food.

Gandhi wanted cultivation also to be done by ancient methods. That would mean that India had to fall back to Buddha's time, twenty-five centuries back. Then there were only twenty million people in India. Now there are seven hundred million people in India. You would have to cut out six hundred and eighty million people completely. And this will be nonviolent?

Yes, two million people, twenty million people are capable of living by ancient methods – a little food they can manage – but what to do with seven hundred million people? By the end of this century India will be the biggest country in the world, it will have gone ahead of China. Right now China has the biggest population: India will have passed beyond that by the end of this century.

But there will be more orphans, more poor people to be converted to Catholicism, to be made Christians, and more Saint Teresas.

No, a man asleep cannot do right. You ask me what is right, what is wrong?

I say to you to be awake is right. To be asleep is wrong. I don't determine acts wrong and right as such. My focus is your being. My effort is that you are there, in your being.

Then whatever you do is right.

A Zen monk used to steal – and he was a great master – but I say it was right because he was fully awake. Now, stealing in itself does not matter; whether it is right or wrong. It is a question of who is doing it. And why was this master stealing? He had never said why in his whole life.

All his disciples suffered for it because everybody was telling them, "What kind of master have you got? He talks about great things and then suddenly one day you find him stealing some small thing. And he always gets caught. Even ordinary thieves don't always get caught. And you say he is fully aware, careful, alert. And we understand, because even his disciples have a different quality surrounding them. And we know your master, we see him. We are surprised – why should he steal?"

And the disciples used to ask him and he would simply laugh.

At last, when he was dying, a disciple said, "Now at least tell us why you were doing this stupid thing. And you have not been stealing big treasures or anything, just somebody's cup and saucer, somebody's coat, somebody's shoes, even one shoe! – which is meaningless. What were you going to do with one shoe? And then too you would be caught. And the judges are tired of you, the jailers are tired of you."

At the last moment he said, "I was stealing because nobody takes care of those thieves and prisoners inside the jail. That's a great place to teach aware-ness; and those people are very innocent. And I love them because I have found them getting the idea more quickly than the so-called ordinary people. So I have been stealing and going inside the jail because that was the only way to get in. But those idiot judges would not send me for a long time, for two months, three months, because I am a great Zen master.

"I used to tell them, 'Give me as long a term as you can manage,' and they would say, 'What kind of man are you? We respect you. What do you want for just stealing one shoe – that we should send you for your whole life? Fifteen days will do.'"

He used to quarrel: "No, not fifteen days. At least three months, four months."

"But for what?" they said.

He simply said, "I love to be there. Outside I don't like it at all."

The jailers were tired, and they would see him and say, "Again!"

He said, "Where to go? Outside I don't like it at all. Inside the jail looks almost like my home."

And in fact it was his home because almost his whole life he had lived there. For just a few days he would be out, and then soon he would be in again. But he changed thousands of people inside the jail. He said, "Where can you get so many people? In the monastery people come, but not in such quantity; and not such qualitatively innocent people."

So to me it is not a question of what you do: the act is neither right nor wrong, the act is neutral. It depends on who does it, that person's integrity, awareness. If an awakened man is doing it, it is right. Otherwise whatever you do, it is going to be like Mother Teresa's work: on the surface looking really great; deep down just third-rate."

You also ask: "Is there something like sin and its punishment?" I have told you there is only one sin: that is unawareness. And you are being punished every moment for it. There is no other punishment.

Do you want more? Your suffering, your misery, your anxiety, your anguish

– and you are still hoping to be thrown in hell? You are not satisfied with all the misery that you are going through? Do you think hell is going to be better than Oregon? What more punishment is there?

Each moment of unawareness carries its own punishment, and each moment of awareness carries its own reward. They are intrinsic parts, you cannot divide them.

science plus religion:
the dynamic formula for the future

Osho,
It seems that all the pioneers in art and science have reached the unknown
spaces through some kind of obsession. What kind of obsessions has the
new religious man?

Science, art, and other dimensions open to the human mind are all one-dimensional – hence the obsession. The mind moves in one direction, dropping all others. It chooses a single point to be focused on, against the whole of life, hence the obsession. Concentration is obsession, but there is no other way – science and art can work only obsessively.

For example, a man like Albert Einstein... He is a man of tremendous intelligence, a superb genius, but he is obsessed. He is so much in his own dimension, the world of stars, the universe, that by and by he becomes completely blind to everything else. He forgets when he has to go to sleep, he forgets when he has to come out of his bathroom.

Sometimes for six hours Einstein used to remain in his bathtub – till his wife started making too much fuss, knocking on the door. And she was understanding, hence she tolerated as much as was possible – but six hours in the bathtub! And she would be sitting with his lunch getting cooler and cooler and colder and colder, and she knew it was not good to disturb him because even while he was in his bathtub playing with the soap bubbles, his mind was moving into depths of the universe.

He discovered his theory of relativity in his bathroom. He used to say, "Don't disturb me. Nothing is more important. When I am moving in a certain direction, and I am coming close to the clue, and you knock on the door... Let lunch be cold, throw it away, because just for your lunch you have distracted me. I was just getting close; now I am as far away as I was before. And nobody knows when again I will come so close to the point. It is not within my hands." Now, this man is certainly obsessed.

Edison was a great genius; perhaps nobody else has so many discoveries to his name, to his credit, as Edison: one thousand discoveries. But he was so obsessed that once he forgot his own name. That is a very rare possibility, most improbable – forgetting one's own name! Then you can forget anything.

It was before the First World War, when, for the first time in the world, ration cards were invented, and he had gone to take his ration. He was standing in a line and people went on moving forward. When his number came and he was at the front of the line, they called again and again, "Thomas Alva Edison, is there anybody by the name of Thomas Alva Edison?" And he looked here and there: who is this Thomas Alva Edison?

One neighbor standing behind, far back in the line, said, "What are you looking at? You are Thomas Alva Edison, I know you."

He said, "If you say so, then certainly I must be, because you are such a nice guy, you can't lie."

What happened to him? How did he forget his name? Even standing in the queue for the ration card, he was not there. He was in the world of electricity. He was figuring out things which had no concern with the place where he was standing or with the ration card or with the person named Thomas Alva Edison.

It is said... Perhaps it is just a joke, but it is possible that if a man can forget his own name it may be true and not a joke. He was going on a journey. He kissed his maidservant thinking she was his wife, and patted his wife thinking she was the maidservant. They both were shocked. But he said, "What is the matter? Why are you both looking shocked? Aren't you my wife and isn't she my maidservant?" And he was not joking; he was simply not there.

Obsession means you are possessed by some idea so totally that everything else becomes absolutely unimportant, everything else falls into darkness. Only one spot remains lighted, and it goes on growing narrower and narrower and narrower. That's the way of discovery. When it comes to be the narrowest, you have found the center for which you have been looking for years. But when your focus is narrowing, and when the circle of your focus is becoming smaller and smaller, what about you? You are also becoming narrower and narrower – one-pointed. The whole universe disappears for you.

The scientist is bound to be obsessed: the greater the scientist, the bigger the obsession. Hence, obsession is not a disease for a scientist, it is absolutely necessary. It is his way of working. If you relieve him of his obsession he will be an ordinary man, not a scientist.

It is defined, that science knows more and more about less and less. The object of knowledge becomes less and less, and your knowledge of it becomes more and more. If the definition is stretched to its logical conclusion, it means science ultimately will come to a point where it knows everything about nothing. That will be the logical conclusion.

And science is coming closer to that point where it knows all about nothing, because "less and less" is finally going to become nothing. And knowledge about "more and more" is finally going to become all.

The situation of religion is just the opposite. It knows less and less about more and more. Obviously a religious man becomes more and more non-obsessed. The more he becomes religious, the less obsessed he is. His method is to know less and less about more and more. His ultimate conclusion is to know nothing about all. That's why Bodhidharma says, "I know nothing." Socrates says, "I know nothing."

Nothing about what? – about all.

The focus is no longer there. The religious man is just a presence opening into all dimensions simultaneously.

Art is similar to science. Everything except religion is bound to be a kind of an obsession, for the simple reason that you have to go deeper and deeper to find the source of something; but your vision becomes narrower, and everything else starts falling out of your vision. You don't see, you become more and more blind about everything else except the one thing with which you are obsessed.

The painter, while painting, is not aware of anything; the poet also.

One of the greatest poets of India, Rabindranath Tagore, used to lock himself in his room or in his porch for days together. He was not to be disturbed for food or anything. Nobody knew what he was doing inside his room because he had locked it from the inside. Sometimes three days would pass and the whole family would be in a panic, wondering whether that man was still alive or dead. But there was no way to disturb him. They would all move around outside his room just to figure out if there was some noise inside or not, at least some indication that he was still alive.

When he was asked, "Why do you do it?" he said, "Unless I forget the whole world, and my family…" His family was a big family. His father was one of the richest men in Bengal, his grandfather was even richer. The British government had given them the title of rajah, the king, although they were not kings. But they had so much land and so much property and so much money that they were equivalent to any king; they had their own kingdom.

There were one hundred people in the family. Rabindranath writes in his auto-biography: "There were many people that I never came to know who they were. Guests used to come and then never go, and nobody would bother about it. Faraway relatives would appear – nobody had heard about them, they just used to declare that they were faraway cousins. That was perfectly okay, they were allowed in the family. They stayed in the family, they lived in the family, and they were so rich that nobody bothered whether these people should work or anything.

So, Rabindranath says, "In that family it was always a marketplace. It was impossible to be in that space where poetry becomes possible. It comes only when you are alone. It is very shy, it is very feminine; it won't come in a crowd.

It won't come if you are concerned with something else. It will come only when you are concerned only with it. It is very possessive, just like the feminine. Of course, as graceful as the feminine, and as shy as the feminine, but of course, as possessive too."

He said, "When I am possessed I don't want any disturbance. So many times I have missed, and a half poem has remained half. I could not manage that space again; the remaining lines never came. And I am not a poet who will compose poetry just intellectually. If it comes from the beyond, I am receptive."

And that beyond is really within your unconscious; it comes from there. But it looks like it is coming from the beyond.

Now, if you cure the poet of obsession, you kill him. Sigmund Freud is not needed by poets and scientists and artists. He will destroy them all. He will psycho-analyze them, disperse their obsession, and they will be reduced into ordinary human beings. But religiousness is not one-dimensional, hence there is no need for any obsession. In fact, if you are obsessed you cannot be religious.

Yes, these people – scientists, poets, painters, musicians, dancers – have sometimes reached into unknown spaces through their obsession. But those unknown spaces are not spiritual spaces; they are within the mind, and they belong to some part below the conscious mind, either to the unconscious or to the collective unconscious or to the cosmic unconscious.

The deeper the space is, the more unknown it is. But just because it is un-known does not mean that you have touched something spiritual. It is unknown but part of the unconscious world of your mind – it is not spiritual. It is tremen-dously exciting because it is so unknown. You have entered into an unknown corner of your being.

It is just a tremendous discovery, but still it is not religious. It won't bring you to the ecstasy and the blessing of a religious man. On the contrary, it may create a tremendous anguish in you, a tension which is unbearable, a nightmare which is pure suffering. Hence, you will find poets, musicians, scientists, in a kind of anguish. What they are doing is certainly a kind of fulfillment to them, but it does not bring solace to the soul.

Albert Einstein, before dying, said, "If I am born again I would prefer to be a plumber than to be a physicist." What anguish he must have suffered, that he is ready to become a plumber and does not want to be a physicist again! – because any obsession is a torture. You are being stretched. It is not a harmonious growth of your being because it is one-dimensional. It is as if a man's head starts growing and becoming bigger and bigger and bigger; the whole body shrinks and the head becomes so big that he can only stand on his head, there is no other way. The body cannot support the head.

In Japan they have dolls called *daruma* dolls. *Daruma* is the Japanese name for Bodhidharma. Those dolls are beautiful. They represent Bodhidharma: their bottom is heavy, very heavy, so you throw the doll in any way, and it will always sit in the lotus posture again. Because the base is heavy and the head is light, and the whole body is light, it cannot remain in any other position. If you put it in any other position it will immediately turn and sit in the lotus posture. The *daruma* doll was created because of a certain statement of Bodhidharma. He said, "When you become really centered in your being, nothing in the whole of existence can create even a slight trembling in you. No fear is possible. And when you are centered in your being, even if the whole of existence wants to throw you upside down, it is impossible; you will always come rightside up." That gave the idea of the *daruma* doll.

The religious man is multidimensional. All his windows and all his doors are open. His consciousness is available to everything.

He is not looking for a certain discovery, he is not looking even for God. That is why I am continually saying to you, "There is no God, don't look for him otherwise you will be obsessed. That's why I call all the religions that have existed up to now pseudo-religious: they are obsessed, just like anybody else – in fact, more obsessed.

What is a Tibetan monk doing his whole life? – just repeating the name of Buddha. If that is not an obsession, then what can be an obsession? – and a useless obsession too. If Albert Einstein is obsessed, at least he contributes to the world. He suffers, but he gives something to the world.

These Tibetan monks, what have they given to the world? The Hindu monks, what have they given to the world? What is their contribution? Of the Christian monks, the Catholic monks alone are one million in number. One million monks! And what is their contribution? They are just burdens on humanity – obsessed people, but obsessed with something that does not exist; hence there is no contribution.

The scientist is obsessed with something that really exists – he is obsessed with some objective reality. The poet is obsessed with something of subjective reality. But your pseudo-religious man is obsessed with a God which does not exist, and out of a non-existent God what are you going to get? Where are you going to reach? These monks are moving in circles their whole life. They are obsessed.

So let me make it clear to you. If you find a religious man obsessed, then that is enough proof that he is not religious. A really religious man is not obsessed at all. He is open to the whole. And he is not concerned in any way to discover something, to create something: a song, a painting, a dance, a sculpture. No, he is not concerned.

It is possible that a really religious man may create a song, but that is just play; he is not serious about it. It is just... You are sitting on the beach and you start playing and making a statue out of wet sand. You are not obsessed with it; there is no need to complete it. And when you leave you may give a hit to the statue that you have been creating for hours.

This was not an obsession, you were just being playful. Sitting alone... You were not doing something serious. A religious man sometimes composes poetry or music or dance or a statue or a painting, but they are all just games.

There are millions of statues in the East so beautiful that Michelangelo would feel jealous, but the sculptors have not even signed their name: that would become a serious affair. Millions of statues of the same caliber and quality as those of

Leonardo da Vinci or Michelangelo – but nobody knows who made them. The people who made them were just enjoying, playing. If something comes out of play, you cannot claim it is your creation and that you have to sign it.

Who made the Ajanta caves? – the Ellora caves? Who made the Khajuraho temples? Who made the Konarak temples? There is no way to find out. The people who made such tremendous beauty, incomparable, were not concerned at all to leave even a single trace behind. They enjoyed making it, of course, but that was all. It was not an obsession.

If you go to the Ajanta caves, which are Buddhist caves, where for thousands of years Buddhist monks must have been working... Many caves are incomplete. I used to go there, and I asked the guides – different guides – again and again... There were many guides, and I would always choose a different one so I could torture him. Incomplete caves, incomplete statues, Buddhas only half-made... And I would ask, "What was the matter?" And they would have no explanation.

Somebody said, "Perhaps the artist died."

I said, "There were so many other artists – there must have been thousands of artists for so many caves; each cave must have needed hundreds of artists to make it – couldn't they even complete a Buddha? Just the body is there, the head was just being started. This looks a little disrespectful to Buddha. You should complete it."

And they would say, "What can we do? Nobody knows who made them. Nobody knows why they stopped in the middle."

I said, "I know, that's why I am asking. This whole thing was just a big game. The person who was making it was not obsessed, otherwise he would have completed it. If he was dying, he would have taken a promise from a friend to complete it."

The obsessional man is a perfectionist. He will not leave anything incomplete, he will make it entire; he will not rest till it is complete. But to a religious man... They played as long as they enjoyed it. The moment they felt it was time to stop this game, they stopped the game. And because they stopped the game, no other artist – they were all religious people – would interfere with it.

Anybody could have completed it; just a little work was needed and it could have been completed. It was almost complete, but nobody interfered with it because that was trespassing. If that man wanted his Buddha to remain this way, it was his business. And that man may have started something else, because it was all play.

A religious man can create playfully but cannot be serious.

Seriousness is part of obsession. For example, Karl Marx is the ideal obsessional man. His whole life he spent in the British Museum library. He had no actual experience of poverty; he had never been part of the proletariat, the laborers for whom he was going to be the messiah. He had not a single friend who was a laborer.

He had only one friend, who was a capitalist, Friedrich Engels. And he had to be friendly towards Engels because who was going to feed him? His obsession was to create the whole philosophy of communism, in its entirety, so there would be no need for anybody else to add anything. He was a Jew – and somehow it is very difficult to get rid of your conditioning. Although he became an atheist, denied God, denied the soul, a Jew is a Jew – he wanted to make communism absolutely complete.

Before the museum library was open, he was standing there at the door. The librarian would come after him; before he came, Marx was waiting. And the whole day he was in the library. The library would be closed, and the librarian would be persuading him, "Now, please stop. Come tomorrow."

And Marx would say, "Just wait a few minutes longer; something is still incomplete. I have to complete this note."

In the beginning they used to be nice to him. Finally they found this was not going to help: they had to forcibly throw him out of the library. Four people would take him out, and he would be shouting, "Just a few minutes longer! Now, are you mad, or what? What are you doing? Tomorrow I will have to work hours to find those few sentences that I could write just now. Just wait!"

But the library has to be closed at a certain time, and those people have to go to their homes. They are just servants. They don't care about your communism and what philosophy you are writing. And you have been doing this for twenty years, thirty years, forty years! Forty years continuously! And sometimes it used to happen that he would not eat. The food would be with him, because he used to come with his food so that he did not have to go home or to a hotel and waste time.

So he would be just eating and referring to encyclopedias and books: with one hand he would be continually writing, and with the other hand he would be eating. And sometimes he forgot to eat; and as he became older, many times it happened that he was taken not to his home but to the hospital, because he was found unconscious: hungry, continuously reading, writing, reading, writing.

One feels sad that nobody reads this poor Karl Marx's book, *Das Kapital* – nobody! I have not come across a single communist who has read it from the first page to the last. Perhaps I am the only person who has read it from the first page to the last – just to see what kind of madman this Karl Marx was. And he was certainly a madman – so obsessed with economics, with exploitation, that he forgot the whole world.

He forgot small things. He was moving into the higher realms of mathematical theorizing, and he forgot simple mathematics, simple economics. He was a chain-smoker; he was reading, writing – and smoking. His wife, his physician, his friend Engels were all worried that this smoking would kill him.

One day he came home with big boxes of a certain cigarette that had just come on the market. His wife could not believe it: "Are you going to open a shop? Are you going to sell cigarettes? So many big boxes!"

And he was so happy. He said, "You don't understand. I have found this new cigarette, just introduced on the market. And the cigarette that I was smoking was costing double. Now with this cigarette you smoke one cigarette, and you save so much money; you smoke two cigarettes and you save so much money again. The more you smoke, the more money is saved! And I am going to smoke them because everybody has been torturing me, saying, 'You don't earn.' Now you will see how much money is saved."

The wife thought, "Your economics...!" She informed his friend Engels, and called him to come immediately. "Your friend seems to have gone completely mad, because this stupid thing even I can understand. How will money be saved? But he does not listen and he is just in his room smoking two cigarettes together, to save money!"

Engels came, took the cigarettes from his mouth and said, "Are you mad? What are you doing?"

He said, "I am just trying to do something so that I need not depend on you: I am saving money."

It was so difficult to explain to him, "Nothing will be saved, you will simply kill yourself. Yes, in figures it looks as if you smoke one cigarette and half the money is saved, but in actuality there is no money saved. And just to save that money you will be smoking double, treble, four times the number of cigarettes. So in fact you will be wasting more money than you were wasting before. And money is not the question," Engels said, "I take care of it. You need not be worried about it." He was a millionaire, owned factories, and he loved Karl Marx.

But Marx was so obsessed with making the system complete. And of course he has left a complete system; after Marx there has been no addition to it. To add anything to it, first you will have to read him, and that is going to drive you nuts.

Aristotle has created the whole system of logic; that was his obsession. Just a single man... His whole life, whole obsession was this: that the system of logic that he was creating should be complete; he should leave it as a closed chapter. So for future generations, for the whole future eternity, he would remain the logician, the only logician. And he completed a system. Of course he was obsessed. Day and night he was working: he wouldn't sleep until he fell asleep on his books. But these people are not religious people.

You ask me, what kind of an obsession will the new religious man have? The new religious man is simply the religious man. The old religious man was not religious, he only pretended to be religious. He made religion also an obsession. He was more obsessed than the scientist, than the painters and poets – because at least poets were going to the coffee house, meeting with the friends, doing things other than poetry. Painters were not only painting, they were doing a thousand and one other things too. But these pseudo-religious people were not doing anything else. They closed themselves in cells, in monasteries, and all that they were doing was nagging God.

Nietzsche said, "God is dead." Nobody asked him, "Who killed him?" I know: these so-called religious people! They nagged him for centuries. And all kinds of religious people, in all languages, nagging a single poor God – he must have committed suicide. His suicide is more probable than a natural death. He cannot die a natural death; he must have committed suicide.

But those people are still after him. Even in his grave he will be tossing and turning, because the Catholic is shouting in his ear, the Protestant is shouting in his ear, and then come the witnesses of Jehovah, who can drive anybody nuts.

All these people, all around the world, day and night, year in, year out, after just one single poor old God. These people must have provoked the desire for suicide in him.

It is a known fact that God never created anything after he created man. I have been wondering why. Why did he stop with man? Up to man's creation; everything was good. The horses were not becoming monks. The donkeys were not becoming priests. The monkeys were not declaring themselves popes. God was happy. It is said that he created each thing and said, "Good" – just the way I say, "Good." He must have learned it from me because I don't know anybody else who says good the way I say good. But when he created man he didn't say that.

He must have lost his nerve – "What have I done?" – because immediately man must have created the business of the so-called religions. He must have caught hold of his feet immediately: "God, my Lord…" Since then nobody has heard about him, where he is. Either he escaped to the farthest star – and physicists say those stars are running farther away; perhaps it is because of God.

Those stars are not static there. That was the idea up to this century, that the stars are static there, far away, but they are there. Now physicists say that they are not there. Where you see the stars in the night, there they may have been millions of light-years ago. The light has reached your eyes tonight, but light takes time to travel.

Where you see a certain star tonight. one thing is certain: it is not there. It may have been sometime far, far back – perhaps when the earth was not made, when even your solar system was not in existence, the star was there. That day the light started moving towards the non-existent earth and the non-existent sun, and it has arrived today. That much time it took to reach. Meanwhile the star is not sitting there. The light is coming towards you and the star is going farther away with the same speed as light – that is, at one hundred and eighty-six thousand miles per second, the light is coming towards you and the star is going away from the point where it was.

Perhaps God is riding on the farthest star and running as fast and as far away as possible from all these prying monks and religious people and churches, temples, mosques, synagogues. But it is good to say that there is no God, it saves God all the trouble. And one day it will save man also from this stupid obsession.

The religious man has no obsession. His life is simple, natural, spontaneous, moment-to-moment. He has no great ideas that he wants to bring to the world. He has no great ideologies that he wants to impose on humanity.

He is a simple man. That's why it is very difficult to find a religious man, because he will be so simple and so ordinary that you are going to miss him. He won't have any talent. He will not be a Picasso, he will not be an Einstein, he will not be a Stalin; he won't have any kind of talent. You will not be able to judge his genius because his genius is unobsessed, so he cannot produce science, he cannot produce new discoveries, new inventions.

It is not just a coincidence that in the East, where religion has existed for at least ten thousand years… And there have been a few authentically religious men. Of course there has not yet been an authentic religion; but here and there, once in a while, there have been authentic religious men.

But the East has not been able to create science. Do you think Buddha had not the genius equivalent to Albert Einstein? He had a far bigger, higher, deeper genius than any Albert Einstein could ever have. But he is not obsessed, hence his genius does not move in one direction. His genius becomes a fragrance around him, becomes a light around him. Those who have eyes can see the light. Those who have ears can hear the music around him, can hear the silence that surrounds him, can smell the fragrance of the man.

But Buddha is not going to invent a computer. He is not obsessed; he is absolutely unobsessed. So you can feel his genius, but you cannot see it reflected in some objective achievement. What is his achievement? Far smaller people have achieved much more. He has not achieved anything, but he has been just himself. If you can call it an achievement, then call it an achievement. But it is not achievement.

What he is, he has always been. An achievement means something that was not there and now is there. But to realize oneself; to know oneself, is not to bring any new thing into existence. It has been there; whether you know it or not does not make any difference to its existence. It has been there. It is there. Yes, there was a time when you were keeping your back to it, and now you have taken a one-hundred-and-eighty-degree turn and you are facing it – but nothing new has come into existence.

You can feel that experience – yes, it is an experience. All that you need is to be receptive, available, open, because a man like Buddha cannot even knock on your doors: even that will be interfering with somebody else's being.

Buddha can stand before your doors and wait till eternity: someday you may open the door, someday you will invite him in. Without your invitation he is not going to come in. There is not a question of ego. It is your house, you are the host, and unless you invite him it is not right to trespass on your privacy in any way.

Buddha became enlightened – but for seven days he remained silent. And he gave many arguments why he remained silent for seven days; in fact he wanted to remain silent forever. Later on when he was asked again and again why he had remained silent for seven days and then had spoken, he said, "Even to speak is to interfere; let the other understand the silence. And if he cannot understand the silence, do you think he will understand my words? – because my words will be far away from my silence, they won't be representative. There is every possibility he may be misguided by my words, and I may be helpless to prevent it. In silence if somebody comes to me, he cannot misinterpret it. He may understand, he may not understand; there are only two possibilities, and I will not be responsible for sending him on a track which was not my intention at all. But my words can take him in a direction which is not the direction I am pointing at."

So for seven days he remained silent and people asked, "Why did you speak?"

He said, "Now, this you will have to just take on faith, if you trust me. But there is no need to accept it, because it is meaningless. I was persuaded by other enlightened beings who are in the cosmos. But this you will have to take it on faith, unless you reach that state." He insisted, "This should not be part of my teachings; I am just fulfilling your curiosity. You can reject it because it is not an essential part of my teaching. But if you insist on asking why I spoke, then I have to answer you."

Buddha said, "People who have become enlightened before persuaded me, argued with me. They said, 'In thousands of years a man comes to the state of being where you are. Even if out of a hundred people, one person understands your words rightly, that is enough. Don't be worried about the ninety-nine because they will go astray even without hearing you. They are bound to go astray.

"'If they can go astray even hearing you, then what do you think – that without hearing you they will not go astray? Take it for granted: those ninety-nine are determined to go astray whether you speak or not. But what about that one percent? We appeal to you for that one percent who may not be able to find the path without your speaking.'"

And Buddha said, "I am speaking for that one percent."

Strangely, I am still speaking for that one percent.

The world has not moved a single inch. Twenty-five centuries and man is as blind, as asleep, and unconscious as he ever was.

Charles Darwin was absolutely wrong, because looking at man there seems to be no evolution: as far back as we can see, he is the same. If for ten thousand years there has not been any evolution in man, do you think one day suddenly a few monkeys jumped from their trees and, without any Patanjali to teach them Yoga exercises, stood – instead of on their four legs, on two legs? And their two front legs turned into two hands? And their monkey mind became man's mind?

It seems to be a far greater miracle than any prophet or messiah has been performing. It would have been far better for Jesus to turn a monkey into a man, because that would have proved poor Charles Darwin's theory of evolution. But he could not even turn man into man – what to say about turning a monkey into a man!

In English you have only one word for man; that is a poverty of language. In Hindi we have two words for man: one is *admi* – that is from Adam – and another is *insan*: both mean man. *Admi* is the lowest state of mankind; *insan* is the highest state of mankind.

One of the great poets, Mirza Ghalib, has a statement in which he says, "In this world the most difficult thing is the transformation of an *admi* into an *insan*. It is one of the most difficult things to make man really a man. He is subhuman."

So I say, still I am speaking for the one percent. And that one percent are not people having a special talent, a special quality, no – they just have an open heart, an open being, open from all directions, unobsessed with anything. They will be pure ordinariness – not in any way tense, pushed, pulled in any direction, as if there was a magnet. They will be relaxed, with no tensions.

Yes, if the whole of humanity one day turns into a religious commune, many things will disappear from the world which are not needed.

Ninety percent of scientific discoveries are used only in war; they are not needed. Ninety percent of paintings are just absurd; they are not needed. Ninety percent of problems that you continuously have to face are absolutely unwanted, unbased. They will disappear.

And whatever ten percent is left, the whole of humanity, radiant in its innocence and simplicity, will be able to cope with.

There will be no problems.

With that much innocence on the earth, and that much fragrance on the earth, and that much light on the earth, it is inconceivable that any problem could exist.

But many professions will disappear. What will the psychoanalyst do? What will the psychologist do? What will the therapist do? What will the priest do? Hence all these people are going to prevent the coming of the new man in every possible way, because his coming is their departure.

Who will bother about nuclear scientists? They will be simply cured from their obsession. Nuclear science? – you must be nuts! Man is starving, and you are piling up atom bombs and hydrogen bombs and neutron bombs – and man is starving. What kind of intelligence is at work? People are dying for small, little things: no shelter, no clothes, no food – and you are trying to reach the moon! For what? At what a cost!

Nobody asks, "Please at least let us know what the point is. Even if you reach there, then what you are going to do?" What did those people really do when they reached the moon? They must have looked absolutely foolish standing there – and they had risked their lives. They went through all kinds of strange training – in isolation tanks, in isolation rooms, in airless rooms, in gravitation-less rooms, for years. And then the whole journey, which was full of hazards – any moment anything could have gone wrong. And when you arrived what did you do there? What has been the attainment?

Now they are trying for Mars and other planets. Something seems to be crazy, buzzing in the politicians' mind, in the scientists' mind. Something seems to be basically wrong. And I say to you, it is the unobsessed religiousness that is missing. When a man is simple, innocent, ordinary, with no pretensions, no hypocrisy, his eyes are clear, he can see through and through: problems simply drop.

There is no need for problems to be. We create problems with one hand and we try to solve the problems with the other hand – and both are our hands! And where is this nonsense going to stop? Because with one hand we will go on creating problems, and with the other hand we will go on solving the problems. And it is our energy.

The religious man simply understands that these are both his hands; they have to learn to be together, they have to learn to function together in harmony.

If all the scientists of the world can have a little understanding of religiousness, they can at least refuse to create for war.

And if politicians are so interested, they can have wrestling matches. Everybody will enjoy it and there will be no harm. Why kill people? – people who have no interest in anything for which they will be killed. Why kill children? Why kill women? Why kill old people? They have no desire, no ideology; they simply want to live and be left alone to live. But the politicians won't let them.

Now, is it not a simpler thing that the president of America goes into a wrestling match with the president of Russia? Then whosoever wins, good. And drop all this nonsense – just a little sportsmanship will do; no politics is needed, no army is needed. If your generals are so interested in fighting, then let generals have boxing matches – or Indian-style wrestling, which is far better, far simpler, more human: you don't hit people's faces and their noses and their eyes and their lips and you don't disfigure them. And you don't break people's bones; there is no need. It is more articulate, more sophisticated. Just let the politicians – rather than have the Olympics for ordinary people, have Olympics for politicians, generals, and each year you can decide who is the winner. It is simple.

What I am saying is that to me it looks so simple that the world can be one. And *there* is the solution: the whole world, one. Poverty cannot exist. All the efforts going into war can move into production. All the sciences working to kill each other can work together – they are both our hands. And I don't see that there is any problem that cannot be solved; we only need a simple vision.

The religious man's vision is simple, uncomplicated, clear.

Unclouded is his being.

He is just a mirror. You can see your face in the mirror. You can see how you are creating your troubles, how you are creating your misery, your suffering, and then searching for solutions. Once you can see how you create the suffering, you stop creating it. There is no need for any solution, no question needs any answer, you just have to be simple to see that the question is meaningless, and the question drops. And in the dropping of the question, without finding any answer, you have found it.

Let me repeat: except for the religious man, every direction in life is in some way obsessional. The religious man is not moving in any direction, he is simply sitting in himself, just being himself, not going anywhere. He has no goal, no target.

He simply is, and in his is-ness there is no possibility of any obsession. He is the only really healthy and whole person. Everybody else is sick – in different ways, but sick all the same.

And I call the whole man the holy man.

Yes, once in a while these people have existed, but one person in centuries is not much help. It is just dropping a teaspoonful of sugar in the ocean to make it sweet. Obviously you simply lose the one teaspoonful of sugar which might have been used in a cup of tea. Make a cup of tea, that is understandable, but don't try to make the ocean sweet. The ocean is too big. For the ocean you will need oceanic methods.

My basic effort is to create communes – rather than the religious man, religious communes. Religious men have existed but they have not been of much help. Yes, to themselves – they arrived home – but the whole of humanity is still wandering in darkness. I want religious communes all over the world. Slowly, slowly in every city, create a religious commune. Many religious people together may perhaps be able to transform the face of the earth and to create a new world, which is urgently needed.

If we miss twenty years more then there is no hope, because the other side is coming to a climax. The mad side of man – the politician, the priest – is coming to a climax where the only conclusion is war.

And this war means total annihilation of all life from the earth, which will be the most idiotic thing to do.

positive thinking: philosophy for phonies

Osho,
I am a firm believer in the philosophy of positive thinking, and it was a
great shock to hear you speak against Mother Teresa and her philosophy of
positive thinking.

I am pleased that at least someone was listening, someone was awake, someone
was not asleep. This is what positive philosophy is: you are shocked and I
am happy!

But I am not a believer in anything at all. Belief as such is against my way of
looking at things. Belief is a blind man's groping in the dark. I do not believe in
anything, I do not disbelieve in anything – because both are belief systems. Either
I know or I don't know. I am absolutely clear about it.

You are saying that you are a "firm believer." What does it mean? A firm
believer – why have you used the word *firm*? There must be some infirmity hiding
behind it. Is not just being a believer enough? You know it is not; hence you have
to add something more, make it more solid, more strong. But whatever you do,
a belief is a belief, and can never become knowing. Your firm believing simply
proves that your doubting is very firm. A firm doubter needs a firm believing. An
ordinary doubter simply believes.

Belief is to cover something. If the doubt is too big then you have to stretch
the belief into a firm belief. You have to repress your doubt very strongly, because
you know that if it is not repressed strongly it will throw off the cover of belief
and you will be naked before your own eyes – hence the shock. The shock is not
irrelevant.

If I criticize Mother Teresa, why should you be shocked? Either you see that what I am saying is right and there is no question of shock, or you see that what I am saying is wrong; then too there is no question of shock. From where comes the shock?

Shock needs two things: one part of you – the deeper part of you, the repressed part of you – sees the truth of what I am saying, and the repressor part of you does not want to see it. This conflict creates the shock.

You may be a firm believer in the philosophy of positive thinking, but I don't think you understand what the philosophy of positive thinking means.

First, the philosophy of positive thinking means being untruthful, it means being dishonest. It means seeing a certain thing and yet denying what you have seen; it means deceiving yourself and others. Positive thinking is the only bullshit philosophy that America has contributed to human thought – nothing else. Dale Carnegie, Napoleon Hill, and the Christian priest, Vincent Peale – all these people have filled the whole American mind with this absolutely absurd idea of a positive philosophy. And it appeals particularly to mediocre minds.

Dale Carnegie's book, *How to Win Friends and Influence People,* has been sold in numbers just next to the Christian Bible. No other book has been able to reach that popularity. The Christian Bible should not be a competitor in fact, because it is more or less given free, forced on people. But Dale Carnegie's book people have been purchasing; it has not been given to you free. And it has created a certain kind of ideology which has given birth to many books of a similar kind. But to me it is nauseating.

The very idea that you want to influence people is the idea of a salesman, and that's what Dale Carnegie was – salesman turned philosopher. It has happened many times. Just recently Werner Erhard, the founder of EST... He was a salesman of encyclopedias, dictionaries, but in trying to sell encyclopedias and dictionaries he became aware of salesmanship. Then why bother about encyclopedias? Why not sell ideas directly? – which are a more invisible commodity.

People can't see it and yet they go on purchasing it. And once you have paid two hundred and fifty dollars for a certain idea which you can't see, you have to pretend that you have got it; otherwise people will think you are a fool. Two hundred and fifty dollars, and you have not "got it"...? It is very simple.

In the East there is an old story...

A king caught his prime minister fooling around with his wife. Naturally he was mad. In those days, this was a common punishment: he cut off the nose of the prime minister. And the nose was cut off only when somebody was caught fooling around with somebody else's wife, so that became a signboard. Wherever you went, your missing nose went ahead of you as a declaration.

But the man was a politician, he was a prime minister. He simply escaped from his kingdom to another kingdom and entered the other kingdom as a saint. Now, nobody can doubt a saint. The nose was certainly missing, but to doubt a saint is to commit a sin. But some curious people asked him, "What happened to your nose?"

And the saint smiled; he said, "That's a secret. It is a certain technique to attain to the ultimate truth. But you have to lose your nose: the nose represents the ego." He is on the right lines: he is creating a philosophy – people's egos are written on their noses. The crowd thought that what he was saying was significant. The nose represents the ego, and the ego is the only barrier between God and man. There must be some technique that if you remove the nose, the ego is removed and you meet the ultimate truth, you realize it.

One idiot immediately was ready. The politician-turned-saint called him in the night, alone, because it was an absolutely private matter. Before he cut off the nose of the man he said, "When I cut off your nose, keep your eyes closed. When the nose is removed I will say, 'Open your eyes,' and you will see God standing before you."

The nose was cut off, and the saint said, "Now you can open your eyes: God is standing before you." The man opened his eyes – there was nobody.

He said, "But I don't see anybody."

The saint said, "Now it is your problem. If you don't see God, people will think you are an idiot. Do you think I see him? I don't see him either, but now try positive thinking. What is the gain in being proved an idiot? Say that you have got it."

Werner Erhard may think that he has created the philosophy of EST. That is not so. It was created thousands of years before by this politician who cut off the nose of that idiot. That was the first EST graduate.

The idiot thought it over and he said, "That seems to be the right thing; yes, I see it."

The saint said, "You have also become a saint. From tomorrow start spreading the philosophy by word of mouth."

It was just as Werner Erhard has been doing: no need to advertise in the newspapers and the magazines; no need – just by word of mouth. It is more impressive, more alive: there is an eyewitness. An advertisement in a newspaper may be just not true, but the man with the nose missing, smiling, radiant with the realization of the ultimate truth…

The next day people saw there were now two saints. And the number started increasing by the same strategy. First your nose is cut off, then the alternative: either you prove yourself an idiot, or you become a saint. Now who is going to choose to be an idiot? Even an idiot cannot be that idiotic – when he can become a saint so easily. And now there is nothing left, he has to become a saint. It seems to be perfectly right – people are respectful, and the crowd around the saints is increasing, and the saints are increasing…

Even the king of that kingdom became interested; he asked his prime minister. The prime minister said, "Wait a little, because I know this man – he was the prime minister of the neighboring kingdom. I don't think that he has attained ultimate truth, he has simply lost his nose."

Politicians easily understand the language of politicians. He said, "Wait. Let me inquire of the other king, and investigate the whole thing before you lose your nose and realize God. Give me just a little time."

He inquired of the other king. He said, "That man is really a nasty man. It is my fault because I cut off his nose. I should have cut off his head. I never thought that he would do such a thing as cutting the noses off thousands of people. Every night hundreds of people are turned into awakened souls, enlightened people, God-realized."

He got the whole information and then he said to his king, "This is the information I have got. Now I will invite the great saint to the palace and give him a good beating."

The saint was invited and of course he was very happy; and all the other saints also were very happy that now even the king was becoming interested in the positive philosophy. That's what he was saying: "This is simply positive philosophy. Now, bothering about the missing nose is a negative approach. It is gone; what is the point of all this crying over spilled milk? Why not make something positive out of it? And I am giving you the ultimate truth, just for the price of a nose."

They were all happy. They all went and waited outside the palace. The great sage entered – by now he had become a great sage. The prime minister closed the doors. He had two wrestlers, strong men, there, and they started beating the man. The sage said, "What are you doing?"

The prime minister said, "Now tell the truth, otherwise the beating will continue. We will not kill you, but we will not allow you to live either. We will keep you hanging between death and life. It is better that you say it quickly."

Seeing the situation he said, "Okay, the truth is that my king has cut off my nose because I was fooling around with his wife. Now, what do you suggest? What should I have done? In this situation, with a nose missing, wherever I went I would have been condemned, boycotted. So I found this positive philosophy. In the same position, wouldn't you have done the same?"

The prime minister said, "Of course I would have done the same – but now it is time that you move from this kingdom, because even my king is becoming interested, and I don't want his nose to be removed by you, and him to become a sage. Move from this country to another. The world is large; there are fools everywhere, and you will find them everywhere. Right now you already have a great following."

When Werner Erhard or people like him found that they could sell encyclopedias, worthless encyclopedias which nobody is going to read, and nobody is going to look into... People keep encyclopedias simply for show, in their study or in their sitting room. They look beautiful. They are not to be read, they are to be looked at. If you can sell encyclopedias – and people are so foolish that they will purchase useless books, highly-praised but meaningless books, at a high cost – why not sell ideas? Once you know the simple technique of salesmanship you can sell anything.

Positive thinking is just deceiving people. If influencing people and winning friends becomes your ideology, you will have to do two things. One is you will have to act, behave the way people like you to act and behave. That's the simple way to influence them, there is no other way.

The whole philosophy can be condensed into a simple sentence: if you want people to be influenced by you, just behave the way they think is the right way to behave. You prove to be their ideal, which they also want to be but have not been able to be yet. Of course, you cannot become anybody else's ideal, but you can pretend. You will become a hypocrite.

And if you are going to influence many people, then of course you will have to have many personalities, many masks, because each person is influenced by a different mask.

If you want to influence a Hindu, you have to have a different kind of personality than when you are trying to influence a Christian. To Christians, Jesus crucified on the cross is the symbol of the greatest sacrifice anybody can make to redeem humanity.

To the Hindus, crucifixion simply means this man must have committed a great sin in the past. Their philosophy is of karma and its consequence. You cannot be just crucified without any karma on your part. You must have acted in evil ways, and this is the outcome of that. The crucifixion of Jesus does not prove to the Hindu or the Jaina or the Buddhist that he is a messiah.

But to the Christian, Mahavira, Buddha, Krishna, Lao Tzu – nobody seems to be comparable to Jesus. In fact to a Christian mind they all look very selfish: they are just working for their own redemption while Jesus is working for the redemption of the whole of humanity. A man who is interested in his own ultimate realization is obviously the most selfish man in the world. What selfishness is possible which can go beyond this selfishness?

If he renounces the world, that is selfish because he simply wants his soul to be freed from the wheel of life and death. He wants to meet the universal spirit of God, or he wants to enter nirvana and disappear into the cosmos where there is no suffering, where there is only bliss, eternal bliss. And this man does not bother about anybody else. You call him a saint? – an incarnation of God? – a *tirthankara*? No, not to the Christian; that is not appealing.

If you want to influence many people you will have to have many personalities, many masks. You will have to continuously pretend that which you are not, and you will have to hide that which you are. Now this is what makes a man phony. Dale Carnegie's whole philosophy is for phonies.

In fact, the word *phony* is also a contribution of America. Strangely, it means exactly what *personality* means. In Greek drama the actors used masks and they spoke through the mask. *Sona* means sound, and sound coming from a mask is called *persona* in Greek – it is not the real man, but the mask. You don't know who is behind it; all that you hear is the sound, and you see a mask. The mask is a mask, it cannot speak. And the one who can speak you don't see; he is hiding. From *persona* comes the English word *personality*. And *phony* is exactly the same.

Since telephones came into existence, you can hear people's voices through the telephone, and you don't see the person. And of course the voice also is not exactly the same; coming through wires or by wireless much is changed. It is phony; *phony* comes from *phone*. Strangely, *persona* and *phony* mean exactly the same. You don't see who is speaking, you only hear the voice. That too has gone through a change, through the mechanism; it is not exactly the same voice.

Dale Carnegie's philosophy creates phonies, but the real purpose is to influence people. Why? To win friends, but why? What is the need? Two things have to be understood. First, influencing people is only a means to win friends. The word *win* has to be underlined. It has the whole of politics in it. The more people are under your influence, the more powerful you are. Your power depends on how many people are supportive of you, how many people you have influenced so much that they will be ready to do anything for you.

Hence, the politician speaks in a language which is always vague, you can interpret it the way you like, so that many people can be influenced. If he is very clear and what he says is absolutely scientific – without any vagueness, certain – if it has only one meaning, then perhaps he will succeed in annoying people.

That's what I have been doing my whole life – how to lose friends, how to create enemies... If somebody wants to learn it, they can learn it from me. And the reason is that I don't want to influence anybody. The very idea is ugly, and against humanity. To influence means to interfere, to trespass, to drag you onto a path which is not yours, to make you do things which you have never thought of before.

To influence a person is the most violent act in the world. I have never tried to influence anybody. It is another thing if somebody saw some truth in what I was saying or I was being, but it was not my effort to influence him. If, in spite of me, he was able to see something, then the whole responsibility is his.

Jesus says to his people, "On the judgment day I will sort out my sheep and tell God that these are my people – they have to be saved. For others I am not concerned." If there is something like a judgment day – there is none, but just for the argument's sake – if there is something like a judgment day, and if I am to do the sorting out, I will not be able to find a single sheep, because I have never influenced anybody. And when you influence somebody, certainly you become the shepherd and that person becomes just a sheep. You are reducing human beings to sheep; you are taking their humanity away. In the name of saving them you are destroying them.

Don't be influenced by anybody. Don't be impressed by anybody. Look, see, be aware – and choose. But remember, the responsibility is yours. You cannot say, "Lord, I followed you – now save me." Never follow anybody, because that's how you go astray from yourself.

Dale Carnegie started this whole school of positive philosophy, positive thinking: don't see the negative part, don't see the darker side. But by your not seeing it, do you think it disappears? You are just befooling yourself. You cannot change reality. The night will still be there; you can think that it is daytime for twenty-four hours, but by your thinking it, it is not going to be light twenty-four hours a day.

The negative is as much part of life as the positive. They balance each other.

After Dale Carnegie, the great name in the tradition of this positive thinking is Napoleon Hill. *Think and Grow Rich* is his greatest contribution to the world – a beautifully written book, but all crap. Think and grow rich: you don't have to do anything, you only have to think in absolutely positive terms and riches will start flowing towards you. If they don't come, that simply means that you have not been thinking absolutely positively.

So these are beautiful games in which you cannot defeat the man who is proposing the game. He has the key in his hands. If you succeed by chance, then he succeeds because his philosophy – think and grow rich – has succeeded. You have been thinking and thinking and thinking and positively thinking that dollars are showering on you – these are not snowflakes but dollars showering on you – and suddenly your uncle dies and leaves you a big inheritance. Naturally, positive thinking works!

But if you don't succeed... And ninety-nine percent of the time you are not going to succeed – you know perfectly well that your positive thinking is not absolutely positive; you know that there is doubt. Once in a while you open your eyes to see whether they are dollars or just snowflakes. You see they are just snowflakes, and you again close your eyes and start thinking that dollars are showering. But the doubt is there, that these really are snowflakes. Whom are you trying to befool? All these thoughts *are* going on: "This is just nonsense, I shouldn't waste my time, I could be earning some dollars; this way I am losing rather than gaining."

But Napoleon Hill writes beautifully and gives examples of how people have succeeded by positive thinking. And you can find people – this world is big enough. For everything you can find an example. Why one? – you can find hundreds of examples if you just look around and try to find them. And all these people have been doing just that: they find examples, and they place the examples in beautiful poetic prose. And of course you want to be rich, so they exploit your ambition, your desire. They give you such a simple method – and they don't ask anything of you in return.

About Napoleon Hill I remember... He himself was a poor man. That would have been enough proof to disprove his whole philosophy. He became rich by selling the book, *Think and Grow Rich*. But it was not positive thinking that was making him rich – it was fools around the world who were purchasing the book, it was his work, his labor, his effort. But in the very beginning days, when his book came out, he used to stand in bookstores to persuade people to purchase the book.

And it happened that Henry Ford came in his latest model car and went into the bookshop to find something light to read. And Napoleon Hill did not want to miss this chance. He went forward with his book and he said, "A great book has just been published – you will be happy with it. And it is not only a book, it is a sure method of success."

Henry Ford looked at the man and said, "Are you the writer of the book?"

Napoleon Hill said proudly, "Yes, I am the writer of the book." And he can be proud: that book he has written is a piece of art. And to create a piece of art out of crap is real mastery.

Henry Ford, without touching the book, just asked one question, "Have you come in your own car or on the bus?"

Napoleon Hill could not understand what he meant. He said, "Of course, I came on the bus."

Henry Ford said, "Look outside. That is my private car, and I am Henry Ford. You are befooling others; you don't have even a private car and you write a book called *Think and Grow Rich*! And I have grown rich without thinking, so I don't want to bother with it. You think and grow rich! – and when you grow rich then come to me. That will be the proof. The book is not the proof."

And it is said that Napoleon Hill never could gather up the courage to meet this old man, Henry Ford, again, even though he became a little richer. But compared to Henry Ford he was always a poor man and was bound to remain a poor man, always. But Henry Ford's logic was clear.

Out of these people, one Christian priest, Norman Vincent Peale, has created a positive philosophy. And he has tried to convert the whole Christian attitude, as if it is a philosophy of positive thinking. And of course he could have quoted all the religions of the world, but he wants to spread Christianity, so he doesn't take account of any other religions.

And in Jesus you can find... All the religions have been doing the same harm that Jesus did: "Blessed are the poor for theirs is the Kingdom of God" – now Mother Teresa is not saying anything different. Norman Vincent Peale has become a world-famous preacher. His whole standpoint is: don't look at anything from the negative, critical attitude. Look from the positive, accepting, receptive attitude. And he says that if you do it, you transform the nature of the object – which is absolutely wrong.

Just by saying, "Blessed are the poor because theirs is the Kingdom of God," you don't change poverty. Otherwise in two thousand years Christian priests would have made poverty disappear. Poverty goes on growing, the blessed people go on growing.

In fact, there will be so many blessed people that in the Kingdom of God, shared by all these blessed people, they will again be poor; they are not going to get much share in it. All these shareholders in the Kingdom of God will make God also poor. It will be a company of poor shareholders and directors – the directors of course must be the beggars who are poorer than the poor.

Two thousand years of continuously teaching... Has it changed the nature of poverty? No. It has done only one thing – it has killed the revolutionary spirit in the poor. Poverty remains in its own place and goes on growing in leaps and bounds.

But it has done one thing certainly: it has taken away the guts of the poor man. His rebellious spirit has been poisoned. And on one thing only I agree with Karl Marx – that religion is nothing but opium for the poor people. I have to agree with him because that's what all the religions in the world have done. They have given opium, a drug, so you can have beautiful dreams.

In India it is a common routine... In Indian villages poverty is such that if only the man goes to work, it is not enough; the wife also has to go. It is against the Indian idea which is that women should not go to work; their place is the home, and they have enough work there. But even if it goes against the Indian culture, the Indian civilization, poverty is so great that just the man earning cannot feed the whole family – the woman has to go.

And the woman may be carrying a small child, because Indian women are constantly either pregnant or getting ready to be pregnant again; meanwhile they raise the other child. They have to carry the child to the place where they are working, maybe on the road, making the road, or in the field or in the garden, or in construction, anywhere. But what to do with the child? They will be continuously at work and the child will be lying down by the side of the road.

So the routine method is that they give a little opium to the child. All over India that is done, even though opium is now illegal; but nothing can be done about it. And everybody understands that that is the only way. The child remains hungry but happy. Just a little opium and for six to eight hours he is floating in the lotus paradise. He will not cry, he will not weep; he will not disturb the mother.

Religions have done the same to the whole of humanity: be hungry, be uneducated, be sick, suffer every kind of misery possible – but take it positively. No. I do not believe in any philosophy of positive thinking; nor do I believe in the opposite, in the philosophy of negative thinking – because both are there. The positive and the negative make one whole.

My philosophy is holistic – neither positivist, nor negativist, but holistic, realistic. See the whole in its totality, whatever it is. Good and bad, day and night, life and death, they are both there.

My approach is to see exactly what is the case. There is no need to project any philosophy on it.

Mother Teresa says to these people in Bhopal, – "Take it positively." Two thousand people dead! Certainly through some mistake of some lazy Indian. And it has been happening in many places all over India; it is not a singular case. Bridges fall down after millions of rupees have been put into years of construction. The first day the train passes by... And with the bridge, the train and the passengers all go down into the river – but take it positively.

Dams continually go on flooding thousands of miles because they break. India goes on borrowing money from all over the world, from the World Bank and from other sources, to make new dams. And with all the engineers and all that expertise, what happens? It does not happen anywhere else in the world, it happens only in India! India is a very positive country because the people who are responsible are not punished; otherwise it would stop.

The contractor should be punished when a bridge kills thousands of people and destroys the labor of thousands of people and makes the country borrow more and more – which India will never be able to repay. That is absolutely clear, because how are you going to pay it back? Slowly, slowly you are becoming slaves again – economic slaves.

Political slavery is gone; now economic slavery is coming from the back door. If you cannot pay money, then you will have to substitute it with something. If you owe to America, or if you owe to Russia, then you will have to give them bases for their military forces. You have to, because there is no other way to pay them back. And why do these countries go on giving to these poor countries, knowing perfectly well that they cannot get it back? In fact they don't want to get it back! This is a new form of slavery.

People don't understand that forms go on changing but things remain the same. Political slavery became costly, very costly. To those who were the masters, it became more costly to have a slave country than not to be bothered with slave countries. That was more economically profitable. Leave these poor countries politically free – but what are they going to do with their economy? They will beg from you, and then you can exploit them economically. And in fact that is the real exploitation. Political slavery was useful because you were powerful enough to exploit them economically.

All such exploitation is economic – if you were politically powerful then of course you could exploit them economically. By the end of the Second World War it became clear that it was no longer feasible, no longer economically useful to have political slavery in the world. But the real thing was economic exploitation. Drop the political slavery, influence people, make friends – and go on exploiting them economically the way you were doing before. Now you will do even better because you are friends, you are helping in every possible way – but for what reason are you helping?

Soviet Russia goes on pouring money into India. In Russia itself there is poverty; they are not too worried about that poverty, they are more concerned to create factories in India, steel plants in India. Go on giving as much money and expertise as India asks, because soon they will be so much in debt that while politically they can remain free, it will make no difference – your armies, your military bases will be inside their country; they will have to give in to you. Their political freedom will be just paper freedom: underneath they will be slaves again.

And in India nobody is punished for all these things which go on happening. In India there are really miracles that happen. They have five-year plans just like Russia used to have five-year plans. In those five-year plans so many dams have to be made, so many roads, so many bridges, and the country is given a great hope that within five years everything will be changed: poverty will be gone, every village will have a school, a hospital, and everything.

And on paper these things do happen. You can see the road has been made, on the map. The contract has been given, the contractor has taken the money, the engineers have been working, the laborers have been paid, the machines have been purchased. Five years of work and the road is ready. The road is even inaugurated by a great leader – and there is no road!

You see the picture of the leader in the newspaper, inaugurating the road. They have made just a small piece for the inauguration, so that a small piece of road is shown in the picture. And the leader is inaugurating it, cutting a ribbon with the scissors, and people are all around, clapping. And it is a miracle! If you go just one furlong ahead, there is no road – and the road was going to be one hundred miles in length. It is non-existent.

Great miracles! But take it positively, and don't complain against anybody, otherwise everybody will be caught: the leader who inaugurated the road will be caught and asked, "What road have you inaugurated? Where is it?"

The minister who gave the contract must have been bribed. The contractor must have taken the major portion of the money that was going to make the bridge, and everything else is fictitious. Engineers have been paid, workers have been paid; for years the work goes on, and reports go on coming into the files that the work is going well, and the road is coming along, and it will be ready even before the time set for it.

It can be ready any day; the way it is going it can be ready any day. And then the great leader comes to inaugurate it, and people are clapping because they believe in positive philosophy. They know the road goes only one furlong, but still they are clapping because a great leader has come, and they have all been given money to clap, praise the leader, wave flags to welcome him. And these pictures will be the proof. All these people have to be punished.

And Mother Teresa says to those poor people, "Don't complain." Whom is she going to save? The criminals? Yes, I use the word *criminals*, because I don't know anything worse than that. I cannot call them sinners because I don't believe in sin. But they are criminals. If it is the carelessness of one person who did not lock the plant correctly, and it kills two thousand people...

And this is a government report of two thousand people killed. Whenever there is a government report, particularly from India, multiply it by five and you will be almost right. If they say two thousand people have died, that means at least ten thousand people have died. If they say one hundred thousand people have been seriously injured, don't believe their numbers – at least five hundred thousand people must have been injured. Who is going to count? The government officials reduce it as much as possible so that there is no negativity in people, and positive philosophy goes on living. And then they call in these people like Mother Teresa who say, "Don't complain." Why?

Then what about Adolf Hitler's gas chambers? Take it positively – and yes, if you want to take it positively, it can be argued in a very positive way: those millions of Jews that evaporated in the gas chambers of Adolf Hitler... Now think positively. If they had lived they may have been poor. They may have suffered any kind of disease, tuberculosis. cancer. And they were all Jews, so you can understand they could have suffered from AIDS, because Jews are the oldest homosexuals in the world. And it is not that I am saying it, I am simply quoting the Old Testament.

Even God could not take it positively! He had to destroy two cities, Gomorrah and Sodom, in the Old Testament. It is not written by me. God had to destroy both the cities completely! Why? Sodom became so famous that now we have the word *sodomy* because of Sodom. People were making love to animals – that's what sodomy is. Now sodomy means making love to animals, but it comes from the name of the city, Sodom. People were making love to all kinds of animals.

And Gomorrah – just the sound of the name is enough to give you an idea what else must have been happening there – homosexuality, sodomy, other kinds of perversions. I have always wondered why people have missed on this name Gomorrah; it is so phonetically connected with some sexual perversion. God had to destroy both cities completely.

God could not take it positively. God has never taken anything positively, otherwise why is there hell? If God takes things positively then he will just hug and kiss criminals and say, "Come on, boys! I was just waiting for you. This paradise is yours because I take things positively. I have read the books of Norman Vincent Peale." But he goes on throwing people into hell. Mother Teresa seems to be very anti-God. But all these religions are in a contradiction.

Here they go on saying one thing, and there they go on saying, "You will be punished. Each sin will be counted, calculated. And you cannot hide anything from God; he will read you just like an open book – there is no way to hide – and accordingly you will be judged." So Christians have judgment day: if God believes in the philosophy of positive thinking, then what is the need of a judgment day? All are to be forgiven, and whatsoever they have done has to be looked at positively. Then what is the need of a day of judgment? Saints and sinners will be the same, they will receive the same welcome – but that creates trouble.

That is why nobody has raised this question: what about God and his philosophy? If you say that God is going to forgive everybody, then sainthood loses all charm. Then who is going to suffer all the austerities and fasts and prayers, and renounce all the pleasures of life – knowing perfectly well that those who are having all the pleasures here on earth will again have the same pleasures that you will have in heaven? So you are a loser!

And perhaps because your whole life you denied yourself pleasures, you may not be able to enjoy them, because you will be so inhibited that when beautiful girls in the Hindu paradise appear dancing before you... The saints are certainly bound to close their eyes, just out of habit of millions of lives – for Hindus it is a question of millions of lives.

Gandhi used to have three monkeys just by his side on the table. They were presented to him by a Japanese saint; in fact, four were presented, but the fourth has been missing from all the pictures. When I went to Gandhi's ashram I asked his son Ramdas, "Where is the fourth monkey?"

He said, "How did you come to know about the fourth monkey? – because when they came, all four were joined together, they were not separate, and immediately the fourth was separated and destroyed. How did you come to know? – because this thing happened long ago."

I said, "I am really an explorer of strange things. Tell me about the fourth."

"But," he said, "it has been completely destroyed. How did you...? Who told you?" – because except Gandhi, Ramdas, his son, and Ba, his mother, nobody knew about it. "We opened the parcel, and we destroyed the fourth."

I said, "That's okay. I was also present."

He said, "You must be joking."

And nowhere is it mentioned that there were four monkeys.

But I know because originally those four monkeys were Chinese. They are very traditional, Taoist monkeys, at least three thousand years old, so I knew the fourth was bound to be there. From Taoism they traveled to Japan, and they had never been three. But his whole life he kept those three monkeys by his side; they are still preserved in the Gandhi memorial museum in Delhi. But it is a lie, because the fourth is missing.

One monkey has his hands over his eyes, closing them. "Don't see anything evil" is the message. The second one has his hands over his ears: "Don't hear anything evil." The third monkey had his hands over his mouth – not to throw a kiss at you, but: "Don't say anything evil." What was the fourth doing so that they destroyed him? The fourth was keeping both his hands over his sexual organ: "Remain celibate, don't do anything evil." Now, Gandhi was worried that this monkey would create trouble. "Anybody coming will ask what he is doing. And just sitting by my side... Destroy this one; these three are okay."

All the religions have been teaching these saints to practice it but when they are in paradise and have freedom, it is going to be difficult for them, really difficult. The sinners will enjoy paradise; the saints will hide just at the sight of an approaching *apsara* – that is a young woman that is made available to all in paradise – and there are thousands of beautiful *apsaras*. You can call them divine call girls. I don't know how to translate that word because in the Christian heaven *apsaras* don't exist.

What the saints will do is start shaking and feeling nervous and perspiring, and they will immediately close their eyes because that is what they have been doing their whole life.

To make the distinction clear, they had got to be realistic, the way I am telling you to be realistic – to see the wholeness of a thing.

Now this woman, Mother Teresa, is a bigger criminal than those people who created the calamity of Bhopal, because she is not only trying to cover their laziness, their mistake, their error; she is giving the idea that wherever such a thing happens you just cover it up.

So I say that when millions of Jews are evaporated, Hitler must be doing great, positive work: perhaps with a smaller population there will be less poverty. And these Jews were the richest people in Germany, so let their money and their riches be distributed. And anyway they are going to die sooner or later, so why not sooner? What could they have done by living? So why make so much fuss? They may have died from a very terrible disease – AIDS, cancer, or something – and Hitler has given them the simplest and the quickest death, a painless death. Look at it positively!

But Mother Teresa will not have the guts to say, "Look at it positively," because the Jews in America who go on giving respect to her will be immediately enemies. She cannot say that.

Why not take the Russian revolution positively? Stalin killing millions of people – has she ever said to take that positively? It is good: those millions of people are freed from life's miseries, sufferings, troubles. But she will not say that. Communism cannot be taken positively – her master, pope the Polack, has just declared that the very idea of class war is a sin. Now, is that taking things positively? Then class war is not a sin but a virtue, if you take it positively.

But why do such an ugly thing to the poor Indians? And your purposes are clear. Your purpose is political: to keep the government happy. Because in India it is a problem... Many missionaries have been deported from India, and there is constant pressure from the Hindu population that missionaries should be deported from India because they are exploiting poverty and converting people to Christianity – not by argument, because as far as argument is concerned Christianity has nothing compared to Eastern religions. They cannot win in any argument; Christianity has no argument at all.

India has had ten thousand years of continual argumentation and nothing else! As far as argument is concerned, nobody can come close to the Indians because they have done only that one thing for ten thousand years – nothing else. They have tried to split hairs, and they have succeeded. There are books which cannot be translated even today because scholars find that it is impossible to find any Western words equivalent to them. For example, Indian logic is impossible to translate – Aristotle is just a pygmy. Indian logic has gone so deep in continually splitting hairs and has created such words because it needed them.

Words are created only when you need them. For example, here you have *snow*, *ice*, and perhaps one more word I don't know. But ask the Eskimo; he has a dozen words for snow. No other language has a dozen words, but the Eskimo has. And the reason is he knows those twelve different qualities. He has lived for thousands of years with snow. He is acquainted with it. He can make differentiations which nobody else can.

Now, after ten thousand years of continually arguing, India has come to words that no other language in the world can translate. Even to understand them is as difficult as to understand Albert Einstein's theory of relativity, perhaps more difficult.

So India is continually deporting missionaries; the pressure goes on becoming bigger and bigger. The reason... Hindus are not worried about argument. If you want to argue they are ready, the Jainas are ready, the Buddhists are ready. About argument there is no problem; your Christian missionaries will not have any chance of winning. But they can convert people by giving bread, by giving medicine, by opening a hospital, by making a school, a college, by creating institutions for the orphans, for the widows.

All these things Indians cannot do; they have never done them, they have never bothered about them. In fact, they have reasons, explanations, arguments why: if somebody is an orphan, it means in his past life he has done something wrong. Now let him suffer, don't interfere; otherwise he will have to be an orphan again in the next life, and you will be simply prolonging his suffering. Let him be finished with it and the accounts be closed, so that in the next life he comes fresh and is not an orphan. Widows – it is their fate; if their husbands have died, it is nobody else's business. According to Hindus these women must have done immense wrong in their past lives, so they are suffering.

So nobody is going to do anything about any real problem. Christian missionaries tackle the real problems. And naturally, when they feed, give medicines, serve the poor with their doctors, their nurses, their hospitals, their schools, their teachers – those people become impressed: "No Hindu ever cared, nobody bothered about us. If we were dying they just left us dying. You care for us – certainly you are really religious." And if they start getting more and more involved with Christianity, it is simple. But they are not converted the way conversion should happen. It is smuggling them through the back door.

They don't know about their own religions, because nobody has taught them. But Christians are teaching them about Christianity; that is their only knowledge.

And they see these people and their service, their compassion, their sympathy, and naturally they think this is the religion you should belong to. And if these missionaries are doing so much, what about Jesus, the messiah? If he says that he will redeem the world, he means it. These people are his representatives.

But Hindus are pressuring the government that these people should be thrown out because they are misguiding people, taking advantage of their poverty, of their sickness, of their old age. But nobody can dare to say, "Deport Mother Teresa," because she is continually protecting the government. This is a political strategy: protecting the officers, protecting the rich, and underground doing the real work of converting people to Christianity.

I am not against anybody being converted to Christianity. If with understanding, with feeling a person moves towards Christianity, it is perfectly good; nobody has the right to prevent him. But if he is in some way bribed, seduced, then this should be prevented. Whether he was going to become a Mohammedan or a Hindu or a Christian or a Buddhist, it does not matter: nobody should be allowed to cunningly change a person's life, his vision, his thinking. He should be left alone. All missionaries – it makes no difference to which religion they are connected – all missionaries are against humanity. But people like Mother Teresa do their work in a very sophisticated way, a very polished way.

You ask me if I am against positive philosophy. Yes, because I am also against negative philosophy. I have to be against both because both choose only half the fact, and both try to ignore the other half.

And remember: a half-truth is far more dangerous than a whole lie, because the whole lie will be discovered by you sooner or later. How long can it remain undiscovered by you? A lie, of course, is a lie; it is just a palace made of playing cards – a little breeze and the whole palace disappears. But the half-truth is dangerous. You may never discover it, you may continue to think it is the whole truth. So the real problem is not the whole lie, the real problem is the half-truth pretending to be the whole truth; and that is what these people are doing.

The philosophy of positive thinking says: "Take everything positively. The negative should not have any space in your approach, there should be no negative part." This is making a part, the positive part, almost the whole.

The same is true about negative people, although there are none who preach the philosophy of negative thinking, because who is going to listen to them? They will say, "If somebody is smiling, find out – there must be something he is hiding behind the smile. In fact, he must want to cry or weep. Find out – don't be deceived by his smiling; find the negative. If he is looking very happy, that means certainly there is something that he is trying to hide behind his happiness."

People are so miserable, who is going to listen to such a philosopher? They will say, "We are already so miserable, and you are teaching us to search for more misery! Even if a false smile is there, at least it is there. Please forgive us, we can't go on digging and finding the tears. We have enough tears. And just a smile – although it may be just a mannerism, a formality, just a civilized way of meeting somebody..."

When you meet somebody and ask, "How are you?" he says, "I am perfectly well." Now, if you are a negative philosopher you have to find out what this man is hiding: "How can he be perfectly well? Have you ever heard of anybody in the world being perfectly well? He is lying!" But nobody will listen to a negative philosopher. You also say, "I am perfectly well. You are perfectly well? – good." And you depart in good spirits. What is the point of showing one's wounds to each other and making each other more miserable than before?

So there is no school of negative philosophers. But there are more people who believe in negative philosophy without knowing it than there are people who believe in positive philosophy.

In fact, all these believers in positive philosophy are basically negative. To hide that negativity they believe firmly in the positive philosophy.

I am not in support of either side. I am in favor of taking the whole truth, and that's what I would like you to do too: take the whole truth, because the negative is as essential as the positive.

You cannot create electricity with only the positive pole; you will need the negative pole too. Only with both the negative and the positive pole can you create electricity. Is the negative absolutely negative? It is complementary, so it is not against the positive.

If I had been in Bhopal I would have told them, "Find the people who are responsible for this calamity; it is manmade." Of course we cannot find God when there are natural calamities. If we could then I would be in favor of catching hold of God and punishing him, because this is not even a human way – what to say about a divine way! But we cannot catch hold of God because he is nonexistent – so we are helpless.

But when manmade calamities are there, please don't say such stupid things to people as, "Take it positively. Don't complain." No, find out who the criminals are and let them be punished as heavily as possible. You punish a single man if he kills somebody, and perhaps a single man was behind the whole explosion which has killed thousands of people, crippled thousands of people. But he will be left completely free to do it again, and people like him will also not feel any necessity to be more alert, to be more careful.

If India has become a country of lazy and lousy people, the reason is simple and clear: nobody has bothered to deal with the sources from where this laziness and lousiness arise. And everybody *is* lazy and lousy.

When I joined the university I was puzzled because the whole years' course was not enough for more than two months; in two months it could be finished. I used to finish it in two months. My professors, senior professors, the head of the department, the dean all told me, "This is not the way. You simply finish in two months a course which has to be finished in ten months. That makes us all feel guilty."

I said, "That is your business. If you don't want to feel guilty, finish your course also in two months, or change the syllabus – make the syllabus in such a way that the course is really for ten months. This is lousy, absolute laziness, and I cannot be part of it."

It is because of this that I used to travel so much. My students were not at a loss at all. I would finish their course quickly and then would say, "Now unnecessarily you will be bothering and I will be bothering... What is the point? Once in a while, whenever I am here, I will come. If you have any questions you can ask them, otherwise I will see you when the examinations come round."

And my professors, my department, my head were not courageous enough to report me because they knew that if they reported me, then I was going to expose the whole thing: that these people were lousy. And my students would have been my witnesses that I had finished my course – now for what did they want me here too?

I was moving around the country. Everybody knew because the newspapers were publishing that I was in Kolkata addressing the university, I was in Benares... And they knew that I was supposed to be there in Jabalpur. My principal once asked me for dinner, and at his home he said, "Do at least one thing: Go wherever you want, but don't let it be published in the newspapers because then it becomes a problem. People start asking us, 'If he is in Chennai... But we don't have any application for leave. He never informs us when he goes or when comes back.'"

I said, "I cannot do anything about that. How can I prevent the journalists reporting? What can I do? I don't know who is reporting; I simply speak and move on, and whatsoever they want to do, they do. But if you have any problems, if anybody reports to you, you can call me. I can put that man right, there and then."

For nine years I managed this way. The whole university was just in a state of shock. They could not believe that nobody raised any question against me. I got the whole salary, and I was rarely seen. But the reason was that my department was afraid to report me, for the simple reason that I had said that I would expose the whole thing.

The country has become lazy. I told the vice-chancellor, "All your courses are not enough for the whole year. What you teach in six years can be taught very easily in two years; you are wasting four years. In those four years you could teach so much that the degrees of no other country could be compared to your degrees. Right now no country even accepts your degrees."

He said, "Perhaps you are right, but no professor will agree because they are happy with the way things are going; they have always done it this way. So I don't want to take the responsibility on myself."

Doctor Radhakrishnan, who became president of India, was basically a professor of philosophy. First he was professor of philosophy, then he became vice-chancellor of the Hindu university in Varanasi, and then he managed and manipulated to become the president of India. When he became the president of India, he declared his birthday as "teachers' day."

That is a very cunning strategy that is being done in India. Jawaharlal Nehru's birthday is "children's day," because once Jawaharlal was dead people would soon forget about him. But children's day will continue because children are not going to disappear from the world, and on children's day Jawaharlal will be remembered.

So Doctor Radhakrishnan created a teachers' day. On the first teachers' day in my university, I asked the vice-chancellor, who was presiding over the meeting,

"I want to inquire about a simple thing: why do you call it teachers' day?"

He said, "You don't know? It is so simple. A teacher has become president of the country."

I said, "Who is being respected, a teacher or the president of the country? I will call it a teachers' day if a president drops his presidency and becomes a teacher. Then it will be a teachers' day, putting teaching higher than the presidency of the country. Let him resign from the presidency and become a teacher.

"This is my challenge to Doctor Radhakrishnan: resign from your post, become a teacher, and we will celebrate the teachers' day. Right now this is absolutely absurd. Tomorrow a shoemaker becomes a president and so then a 'shoemakers' day'; someday, somebody else is a cloth merchant, then 'cloth merchants' day'. But in all these days you are respecting the post of the president. So simply call all these days 'president's day'. Why drag the poor teacher into it?"

My vice-chancellor said, "Will you please keep it to yourself! Soon the media will be here, and if they hear your challenge or anything, then I at least am in difficulty because it is because of Radhakrishnan that I have been appointed vice-chancellor here in this university. I am his student, and what you are saying is perfectly right, but – forgive me – don't say it in front of people."

I said, "Everybody goes on: 'Be truthful, be honest, be authentic,' and whenever I try to be truthful, honest and authentic, immediately I am stopped."

I am certainly against people like Mother Teresa, because I count them as criminals, not as saints. And I will not take them positively because they are doing certain harm – and so subtle a harm to humanity that it cannot be forgiven.

It may have shocked you. Think about your shock and look at both the sides of the shock, the negative and the positive, so that you can understand why the whole phenomenon happened to you.

And this is going to be my approach to everything.

Look holistically. Be a realist and you will be surprised, amazed. When you look at both sides they fit together, they complement each other. They are just like the Chinese symbol of yin and yang.

Have you seen the Chinese symbol of yin and yang? – two fish in a circle, one fish in one half-circle, the other fish in the other half-circle; but both fish fitting together, making it a whole. Yin means the feminine; yang means the masculine.

This is applicable to all polarities, positive and negative; they are just like two fish moving in such a way, so closely, that they make a circle.

Then you look at existence with the eyes of a religious man. Then there is no saint, no sinner; they are all complementary to each other. They both are needed in some way.

Yes, better ways can be found so that they can complement each other more lucidly, more gracefully, more beautifully.

the magic of self-respect

Osho,
What is the place of surrender in your vision of a new religious consciousness?

I do not teach the ego, hence I cannot teach surrender, because surrender is nothing but the subtlest form of the ego.

Surrender is not against the ego, it is in fact an act of the ego. Who surrenders? And by surrendering, who becomes humble? Who becomes meek? It is the ego standing upside down. It makes no difference whether the ego is standing on its legs or on its head. In fact it is more dangerous when it is on its head because then you will not be able to recognize it.

Jesus says, "Blessed are the meek," but what is meekness? "Blessed are the humble," but what is humbleness? Can a man who has no ego be humble? How can he be humble? Who will be humble? A man who has no ego has no way to be meek or to be humble. He cannot be an egoist on the one hand; he cannot be a humble person on the other hand.

To teach surrender is to give you a strategy to hide your ego, to sublimate your ego. Yes, that's the right word, *sublimation*. A Freudian word, very significant. You can sublimate anything, so much so that recognition becomes impossible. You may even start thinking that this is the very opposite of the original thing. Meeting a humble man you will feel how egoless he is – he also feels how egoless he is. The ego has come from the back door and now it is no longer condemned, but appreciated.

And why is a meek person, a humble person appreciated? That too is a strange story. He is appreciated because he fulfills everybody else's ego. Just see the whole game of it. Why do you appreciate a humble person? – because being humble to you, he buttresses your ego. And because your ego is buttressed, you in response buttress his humbleness.

Now a vicious circle is created. He will become more and more humble because everybody loves his humbleness. He gains respectability, and everybody enjoys his humbleness because everybody is being satisfied by his humbleness – it is a deep satisfaction for the ego.

Yes, blessed are the humble and the meek because without them how are the egoists going to be contented? And when you say, "They shall inherit the kingdom of God," then naturally one is ready to do anything.

I want you to understand it clearly: ego and surrender are two sides of the same coin. I don't teach the ego, so how can there be any place for surrender in my vision? I don't teach you to be meek, I don't teach you to be humble.

I teach you to be authentic, integrated individuals with immense self-respect. The word *self-respect* may create doubts in your mind because self-respect seems to again mean the ego. It is not so. You have to understand both words, *self* and *respect*; both are significant.

Self is that which you are born with. Ego is that which you accumulate; ego is your achievement. Self is a gift of existence to you. You have not done anything to earn it, you have not achieved it; hence nobody can take it away from you. That is impossible because it is your nature, your very being.

Ego is all that you go on accumulating through education, manners, civilization, culture, schools, colleges, universities... You go on accumulating it. It is your effort, you have made it, and you have made it so big that you have completely forgotten your real self.

To know the real self is enough: the ego falls flat on the ground without any effort to surrender it. Unless the ego falls on its own, without your effort, it is not going to leave you. If you make effort to drop it, and that is what surrender is... All the religions teach surrender, hence I say they don't understand even the very basics of psychology. Ego has not to be surrendered, it has to be seen. It has to be understood through and through.

That is the meaning of *respect*. It is one of the most beautiful words in the English language. It does not mean what it has come to mean: honor. No – respect simply means *re-spect*, to look again. That's the literal meaning of the word; there is no place for honor. Just look again, look back, look deep. *Spect* means to see, look; *re* means again. Once, you had known it.

Before you entered and became part of a society, a culture, a civilization, you knew it. It is not a coincidence that people go on thinking that their childhood was the most beautiful part of their life. It is a long-forgotten memory, because there have been days in your life, the earliest days, which you cannot remember exactly; only a vague feeling, a kind of fragrance, a kind of shadow is there.

If you *re-spect*, if you look again and go deep into your existence, you are going to find the place from where you started losing yourself and gaining the ego.

That moment is a moment of illumination because once you have seen what the ego is, the game is finished.

So I cannot say to you, drop the ego, because that means I accept the reality of your ego. And how are you going to drop it – you are it. Right now, you *are* it. The self you have lost far away back in the past. There is a great distance between you and your self. Right now you are existing at the periphery of your self. That periphery is pretending to be your self. That pretender is the ego. Now telling the ego, "Drop! Surrender! Be humble!" is simply idiotic.

I used to go at least three or four times a year to Mount Abu in India. Mount Abu has one of the most artistic temples in the whole world. They are Jaina temples, Delwara temples. The carving in the marble is incomparable. When for the first time I went to Mount Abu, the priest of the Delwara temple came to invite me. I went with him to his office. The Delwara temple is a very precious temple, very ancient, and yet as fresh as if it had just been finished, just created.

Marble has that quality of freshness: for thousands of years it remains young, fresh, innocent. And Delwara temples are just marble and marble. The Taj Mahal is nothing compared to Delwara temples. The Taj Mahal is a simple structure, but Delwara temples are the artwork of thousands of artists, perhaps over hundreds of years. Each inch is carved.

In his office – and he had a beautiful office, because governors, governor-generals, and even George V, the king, had come to visit the Delwara temples. If you miss the Delwara temples you miss much of India, the India that was. Delwara has something of the past beauty and glory. So he had a beautiful office because he was continually receiving guests from foreign countries, prime ministers, presidents, kings, queens.

I went into his office. And in his office there was carved on the marble wall, a beautiful sentence, a statement from Mahavira. The statement is such that nobody could object to it, and nobody had ever objected. The priest was almost seventy years old and the priest's forefathers, and their forefathers from generation to generation, had served the temple. The statement was simple. The statement was: "The humble man is respected universally. Be humble."

But the reason you are given for being humble is that you will be honored universally. The whole statement of Mahavira is: "The king is honored in his own country, but the humble man is honored universally" – there are no boundaries to his honor. A king's honor has boundaries – within his own kingdom. Beyond those boundaries he is nobody. But the humble person has no boundaries to his kingdom, the whole universe is his kingdom; he is universally honored.

But to whom is this idea going to appeal? The ego will immediately catch hold of it. That's what the ego wants: to be honored universally! And if humbleness is the way, then okay, the ego is ready to be humble. If surrender is the way, the ego is ready to surrender.

People used to come to me and they would say, "We want to surrender to you."

I would say, "But what will you surrender to me?" And they would say, "It is such a simple thing – we want to surrender our ego."

I would say, "That is okay, but what will I do with all these egos? You are tortured by one, I will be tortured by the thousands of egos you surrender to me.

It is as if somebody comes and says, "I surrender my cancer to you." Great surrender! You are obliging me? And how can you surrender your ego? Have you ever met it? Have you even seen it? Have you seen its subtle ways of movement, its workings? Do you know it? You don't know it."

I asked the priest, "Remove this sentence from this temple. Mahavira has no understanding about ego because what he is saying is an appeal to the ego. Yes, he will get people ready to surrender, ready to be humble, ready to be meek; but behind their meekness will be a sophisticated ego, far more dangerous than the ordinary raw quality of the uncultured ego, which can be easily traced to where it is."

The sophisticated ego becomes more and more difficult to find. It becomes so subtle that it goes on slipping from your hands. And it becomes so clever at changing its faces. If it can change its face to meekness, humbleness, surrender, then what else do you want it to do? It is doing almost the impossible: it is pretending to be its opposite.

And the religions have been exploiting the idea; they say, "Blessed are the meek for they shall inherit the earth." Now, to inherit the earth... What more can your ego demand? And what more can your ego find? And this man is giving you a simple proposal: "Be meek, and the earth is yours." It is a bargain! And you are not going to be the loser. What you are losing? – you are simply gaining. Karl Marx, in his most famous book, *The Communist Manifesto*, has a beautiful sentence at the end. With that sentence he concludes the communist manifesto. The sentence has some great insight in it. It says, "Workers of the world, unite. You have nothing to lose but your chains."

He is calling on the workers, the proletariat, the poor people of the world, the laborers, to unite, to fight for their rights, to rebel against the whole system of exploitation, because what have you got to lose except your chains? You don't have anything else except your chains, so there is no need to be afraid of fighting. The other party has to lose. If you win, you gain. If you are defeated, you lose nothing, because you don't have anything in the first place.

He was giving a great incentive. He thought that the revolution would happen first in America. He had never even dreamed that it would happen first in Russia. He must have been puzzled in his grave, almost shocked.

He had never thought that the revolution would happen in Russia, in China, in Poland, in Yugoslavia, in Czechoslovakia – those names had never occurred to him, could not have occurred to him. He thought the revolution would happen where capitalism had come to its peak, where the class division was perfect, where you could see the rich and the poor.

Marx forgot just one thing, and that changed the whole course of communism. He forgot that the American poor have something to lose. He forgot his own declaration. When he predicted that the revolution would happen first in America, he forgot completely that the American poor have something to lose. The Russian poor have nothing to lose, the Chinese poor have nothing to lose. The wonder of wonders is India! It has the poorest people in the world; you cannot conceive what they can lose, but no revolution has happened there.

In India it could not happen because the religious tradition is so deep that it has told the poor people, "You are the blessed people. Your poverty is just a test of your faith. All these small troubles are nothing before the blessings of paradise. This life is just a life consisting only of four days."

That's a proverb in India, that life is nothing but four days. Two days pass in desiring, the remaining two days pass in waiting. It is so small that half of it – while you are young, you have ambitions and desires to be someone, to be somewhere, to get your name carved for the coming generations – those two days pass in desiring. And the other half, when you start getting older, those two days pass in waiting for some miracle to happen and your desires to be fulfilled. This is all your life is: a soap bubble.

For this small life are you going to lose the blessings, eternal blessings of heaven? Be patient. Have faith. Your poverty is a God-given opportunity. If you can pass this fire test – which is not a long journey, just four steps – the doors of paradise open, and you will be received with bands and singing and dancing.

In India revolution seems to be impossible. It should have happened first in India, because what Karl Marx says has a truth in it. When you don't have anything to lose, what is the fear of fighting, of rebelling, of risking?

I have told this ancient story many times, but each time that I have told it I have loved it more...

A master is going from one place to another with his chief disciple. They have to cross a jungle. The disciple is puzzled because the master says, "Move a little quicker, we have to pass through the jungle fast. The sun is coming down and soon it will be night."

The disciple has been with the master for many years and the master has never been afraid of the night. He has never been in such a hurry. Moreover, he is keeping a bag hanging from his shoulder. He is clutching that bag, and once in a while he puts his hand inside and feels something there, and then looks at ease.

The disciple was very puzzled: what is the matter? What is he carrying in the bag that he is so afraid? But the path was long, and although they were almost running, in the middle of the jungle the night came. The disciple saw for the first time the master trembling, almost in a nervous breakdown.

He said, "What is the matter? We have been in jungles many times, and we have stayed in jungles. We are sannyasins – we have renounced the world. Even if a wild animal comes and eats us, there is nothing much to be worried about. One day one has to die. There will always be some excuse – about some disease, wild animals, some enemy. And it does not matter when one dies; what matters is how one dies. And you know and I know how to die. So why be afraid?"

But the master is no longer in a state to listen to him. They stop at a well, and the master says, "I am tired and thirsty so let's pull up some water so we can wash our faces and drink some water and do our prayer: the prayer that is done at sunset." In his nervousness he even forgot that the sun had already set.

He gave the bag to the disciple and told him, "Be careful with the bag."

The master went to pull water from the well. This was the chance the disciple had been waiting for, to look into the bag to find out what was the matter. He opened the bag and found what the matter was – the master was carrying a brick of solid gold. Now he knew what the fear was. It was not death, it was not wild animals, it was not the night – it was robbers, thieves. This gold brick was the cause.

So he took out the brick, threw it away in the jungle, found a stone of the same size, weighing almost the same, and put it in the bag. And when the master was back, the first thing he did was take away the bag. It was as heavy as before – the brick was inside.

They started walking again, faster than before. The disciple said, "Now there is no need to go so fast."

The master said, "What do you mean?"

He said, "I have thrown away the cause of fear, long ago."

The master said, "The cause of fear? How can you throw away the cause of fear?"

He said, "You can look in your bag."

The master took out the stone. He said, "My God! You have thrown away my gold brick. Now there is no need to rush, we can stay here the whole night." And they stayed in the jungle.

In the morning the master thanked the disciple: "You did right. Because I had something to lose, there was fear. When there was nothing to lose, there was no point in the fear. I slept such a beautiful sleep. With that brick I could not have slept the whole night. At least a dozen times I would have touched the brick and felt whether it was still there or gone. But you did the right thing."

When you have something to lose, there is fear. That's why in America the revolution has not happened, and is not going to happen – because America has really rich people and poor people, but the poor are almost in the same position as the middle classes in poor countries. The middle class never revolts because it has something and it can hope for more; it can invest for more, it can desire, be ambitious, wait. So of course the middle class can never go into revolution. Who knows? – you may lose even that which you have got.

America has two classes, the middle class and the rich class, hence there is never going to be a revolution. In Russia it happened, in China it happened, because they were class-divided societies with clear-cut divisions. Now, in India ninety-five percent of the people have nothing to lose. Four percent of the people, the middle class, have a little bit to lose. One percent of the people, the super-rich, have much to lose.

But in India the revolution has not happened in five thousand years. Religion is the cause: it goes on giving you the whole of paradise, for nothing. Why bother about the revolution? What are you going to gain? Rather, be patient, prayerful, faithful; surrender to God and you will have everything.

Jesus says to the poor people that it is possible for a camel to pass through the eye of a needle, but it is not possible for a rich man to pass through the gates of heaven. I don't believe it. This is simply a consolation. This is poison, pure poison. There is every possibility that the rich man will get through the gates of heaven. He may bribe the gatekeeper – and if the gatekeeper is Indian, there is no problem.

And the rich man, whom Jesus says cannot pass through the gates of heaven, has done everything to be qualified to get through the gates of heaven. He has made synagogues, temples; he has been donating to the poor, giving charity, making hospitals, schools. What are the poor doing? Do you think just being poor is a qualification?

At the gates of heaven will you be just saying, "Because I was poor, I claim... And where is that guy Jesus who said, 'Blessed are the poor, for they shall inherit the Kingdom of God'?" You won't find Jesus there either. He himself was poor – who will allow him to enter heaven? There is no possibility.

Poverty is not a qualification for anything.

The rich man will find a thousand and one ways. All the priests will be there to support the rich man. All the scriptures will be there to support the rich man – because they were all created by the money of the rich man. The priests have lived off the money of the rich man. Even God is the creation of the rich man to befool the poor. And you think the poor will enter heaven?

In fact, there is no heaven. It has been created to give hope to the poor, to give consolation, to titillate their greed – using simple methods which the poor can afford, like being humble. In fact, what else can he do? His poverty has humiliated him enough and now you are saying, "Be humble." No, I cannot say that. I cannot humiliate anybody. And this teaching is nothing but a strategy to make peace with his humiliated state.

You have been humiliated by everybody, you have been trodden on by everybody, you are crushed by everybody – and then comes the priest to give you the opium: "Don't be worried, my son, this is just a passing phase. If you remain humble and surrendered, everything is going to be okay for you. And these rich people who are treading all over you – they will be thrown into hell."

And this priest lives on the money of the rich. He knows there is no hell. The rich know there is no hell, there is no heaven, that this is a strategy for the humiliated to be consoled. No, I am not at all in favor of surrender.

My religion has no place for surrender. It teaches you integrity. It teaches you individuality. It teaches you selfhood. It teaches you self-respect. And the magic of self-respect is that the moment you start searching for yourself, you will come across many shadowy selves, all phony. And it is not difficult to see what is phony because anything that you come across is phony. A simple criterion: anything that you find within you and think, "This is my self," know well that it is phony.

It is the finder who is the true one, not the found. The found is just the object that you have achieved and accumulated. Discard all those selves that you go on finding within you: "This is the self... No, this is the self..." Go on discarding them. A simple criterion, there cannot be a simpler criterion: anything that you find as your self is not your self.

Go on discarding, and a moment comes when you cannot find any self anywhere. You cannot find anything – all is empty. And that is the moment of awakening. Suddenly the seer is seen.

You are awakened to your own awareness.

You don't find an objective self, you find a subjectivity, and finding it is such a blessing, such an ecstasy that you will not care a bit about paradise. And you will not be bothered any more about surrendering because there is nothing to surrender. You have discarded all that was phony, that was only pretension.

You have been told you are this, you are that, and you have accepted it. You have started playing the game of being this and being that, and nobody has told you – nobody *can* tell you – who you are. It is only you who can discover it. In discovering it, the ego evaporates. It is not surrendered, because it is a non-existential, a shadowy thing, it has no substance in it.

A famous incident...

One of the kings, Bimbisara, came to Buddha. That day a rare thing had happened. A poor man, a shoemaker, Sudas was his name... S*udas* means a good slave, a nice slave, a slave who has no ideas of rebellion, of revolt or anything, who is absolutely contented with his slavery. He had a small hut and a small pond behind the hut.

That day, in his pond a lotus flower blossomed out of season. Once in a while things like that happen in nature. It's nothing to brag about, nothing to make a miracle out of. Sudas asked his wife, "I should take this to the richest man in the town because he goes every day to Gautam the Buddha, and he will be delighted. And at least he is going to give me one rupee as a reward."

The wife said, "Go, be quick – he may be leaving."

He went out on the road and found that the chariot of the richest man was coming, going towards the mango grove where Buddha was staying. He stopped the rich man and said, "Out of season a rare lotus flower has blossomed in my pond, and I thought it would be good if you could present it to your master, Gautam the Buddha."

The rich man was really happy. He said, "Of course, because even my master will be surprised to see it. This is not the season for lotuses. I will give you one thousand rupees as a reward."

The poor Sudas could not believe it – one thousand rupees! In those days rupees were solid gold. In fact the word *rupee* comes from the Sanskrit word *rup*, which means gold, pure gold. The coins were pure gold – one thousand gold coins! The poor man said, "Please say it again, I cannot believe my ears."

The rich man thought that perhaps he was not willing to sell for one thousand rupees. He said, "Don't be worried: I will give you ten thousand, or you can ask and whatever you ask I will give you, because I would love to put this rare flower at Buddha's feet; perhaps nobody has ever presented such a thing to him."

Sudas was so shocked, he lost his voice. He could not say, "Yes, ten thousand is enough."

And the rich man said, "Why are you silent? Are you not willing?"

While this negotiation was going on another chariot, the chariot of King Bimbisara, came by. Seeing the lotus flower, the king stopped and said to Sudas, "Sudas, whatsoever the rich man is going to give to you, I will give you five times more. Whatever he is giving, just come to the palace and collect five times more."

Sudas was almost on the verge of falling dead. The rich man was giving ten thousand, and he was willing to give even more. And now comes the king who says, "Five times more, whatever!" – he is not even inquiring. Kings are kings, they should not inquire the prices of things. And of course in front of the king the rich man could not say anything. He knew well that whatsoever he says, the king will give five times more. He had lost it.

The king asked Sudas... Sudas opened his mouth and said, "Forgive me, but if this flower gives you so much pleasure, just presenting it to Buddha – then I am going to present it myself. You can keep your money.

The king could not believe it. The rich man could not believe it. They both said, "What are you saying?"

He said, "I am a poor man, but I manage to live. What am I going to do with all your money? But I am not going to miss this chance that you think is so precious. I am going to put this flower at Buddha's feet myself."

But kings cannot be denied. The king said, "Then you should be aware that you will never reach Buddha; your head will be cut off. I will give you ten times."

Seeing the situation, the poor man had to give the lotus to the king. The king was already going with a very precious diamond to present to Buddha. That diamond that Bimbisara had was the biggest diamond known in those days. Now he had two presents. When he went to Buddha, both hands were full; in one a very precious diamond, in the other a very rare flower. Which to present first? – of course he thought of the diamond.

As he was going to place the diamond, Buddha said, "Drop it!" He did not give him the chance to put it at his feet, he said, "Drop it." And when Buddha says drop it, he has to drop it – unwillingly, reluctantly, because such a precious diamond... In the whole country, all the kings were jealous of the diamond – he was the owner of a rare piece – and Buddha says, "Drop it!" He is not even giving him the chance to put it at his feet.

Then he raised the other hand with the flower, and Buddha said, "Drop it!" So he dropped both and stood there empty-handed.

Buddha said, "Drop it!"

Bimbisara said, "Either you are mad or I am mad. Both my hands are empty – now what can I drop?"

Sariputta, one of Buddha's disciples, said, "You have not understood Buddha. He is not interested in your diamond or in your lotus; you can take them away. Drop the real thing."

"What real thing?" he said. "I have only brought two things."

Buddha said, "Drop yourself!"

"But," Bimbisara said, "myself? I don't know who I am."

Buddha said, "That was the point. Go home, find out, and when you find out who you are, then come back."

It was very insulting in a way. In front of ten thousand sannyasins – and Bimbisara is told to go back and look into himself and find out who he is. But he was a man of tremendous courage, intelligence, integrity. He told the palace,

"Nobody should disturb me. Whatsoever time it takes, I am going to find what this man says."

For three days he remained in isolation. The fourth day he came out, radiant, and went to Buddha. And when Buddha saw him, Buddha said, "Now there is no need to drop anything because what you have found cannot be dropped. I can see it on your face, in your eyes. I was telling you to drop that which you were not."

But you cannot drop it unless you find who you are. And the moment you find who you are there is no need to drop it, it simply drops of its own accord.

Let me repeat your question. You asked me: "What is the place of surrender in your religion?" From my side, there is no place.

I do not ask you to surrender. I ask you to seek and search your being. Surrender will happen, but it will be a happening, not a doing. Neither I will ask you for surrender nor have you to do it. But what I am asking you to do, if you do it, surrender is going to happen. And when it happens of its own accord then it is a totally different phenomenon, qualitatively different. Then it is not ego pretending to be humble and meek and surrendered. Then it is a state of no-ego.

The ego disappears in a very simple way. It is just like you are doing some arithmetic and for two plus two, you put five. Somebody draws your attention to the fact that two plus two are four, not five, and you see the point. Do you have to drop five? Will it take effort to drop five? – struggle, austerities, fasting? You simply erase it. It was just a mistake, and you will write four.

The ego is just a mistake – just like two plus two is equal to five. Just like that, when you look inwards and search for the real self, you come to know that two plus two is four, not five. Nothing has to be dropped, but something has disappeared from you. Something that was continuously pretending to be your self, something that was destroying your whole life, something that was messing up everything is found no more.

When the ego is not found, I call that surrender from your side; it is not part of my religion. I will not ask you to surrender, but I will ask you something else which brings the surrender of its own accord. But then you are not humble, you are not meek, you are very grounded, very centered, very self-respectful. And only a man who is self-respectful is capable of respecting others.

The man who respects himself cannot humiliate anybody else, because he knows that the same self is hidden in every being, even in the trees and the rocks. Perhaps it is fast asleep in the rock, but that doesn't matter; it is the same existence in different forms.

A man who respects himself suddenly finds himself respecting the whole universe. He cannot humiliate anybody, he cannot be disrespectful to anybody.

But remember – he is not humble, he is not meek; you cannot exploit him in the name of meekness and humbleness. He will not allow you to put him in a position of humility, and he will not care about your kingdom of God.

He will say, "You can go to your kingdom of God. I have found my Kingdom of God; it is within me. I don't need any messiah to take me to the Kingdom of God, all I need is an inner search. Except me, nobody else can do it. I am responsible for losing my self; I have to be responsible for finding it."

The truly religious man is difficult to understand because he will not fall into any category of yours. Your categories are opposites: arrogant-humble... Now where can you put a religious man? Arrogant? – he is not arrogant. Humble? – he is not humble. He is simply himself.

A religious man cannot be categorized. All your categories fall short. He is beyond all your categories, hence he is bound to be misunderstood.

I am not an arrogant man; I am not humble either. But then the question arises, where do I stand? I don't even stand in the middle of both because that will be just half and half, something of arrogance and something of humbleness. No, I don't even stand in the exact middle. That's where I disagree with Gautam Buddha. He teaches to be always in the middle: don't be arrogant, don't be humble, just be in the middle. But I say: exactly in the middle you will be something of both.

No, the really religious man is beyond the categories of opposites. You cannot categorize him. He is neither on this pole nor on that pole. He is not in the middle either; he is just above.

He is a watcher on the hills, and everything else is deep in the valley. Nothing touches him.

So sometimes you can interpret him as arrogant, sometimes you can interpret him as humble, but those are your interpretations. As far as his own experiences are concerned... And I can say it with my authority, I do not need any scriptures to support me. I am not arrogant, I have never been arrogant; I have never been humble either. I have been just myself. So whatever the situation demanded, I acted, responded, neither with humbleness nor with arrogance, but just whatso-ever the moment needed – with awareness.

Hence my teaching is in a way very simple if you can see the point.

If you miss the point it is very difficult.

I will not say to you to turn your other cheek if somebody hits you, no. Jesus can say it because he teaches humbleness. I cannot say that. I can only say one thing: let that moment decide. Sometimes perhaps you have to turn the other cheek. Sometimes perhaps you have to hit the man harder than he has hit you. Sometimes perhaps you have to hit him on both cheeks – but nothing can be given to you as a ready-made formula. It will depend on you, the person, the situation.

But act with awareness, then whatever you do is right.

So I don't label acts as right and wrong. To me, the quality of your awareness is decisive. If you can respond with awareness, then whatever your response is, I declare it right. If you lose your awareness and react, then whatever you do – you may be turning the other cheek – is wrong. Do you see I have used two different words? With awareness I used the word *response*; with unawareness I used the word *reaction*.

Response comes from yourself.

Reaction is created by the other man: he has hit you. He is the master of the situation, and you are simply a puppet. You are reacting. His action is decisive, and because he has done something, now you are doing something in reaction. This is the unconscious man's behavior. That's why the unconscious man's behavior can be manipulated very easily. You smile, he will smile. You be angry, he will be angry.

It is because of this that people like Dale Carnegie can write books like *How to Win Friends and Influence People*. All that you have to know is simple reactions. He himself describes a situation...

He was functioning as an agent of an insurance company. And there was a rich woman, the richest in the town, a widow, who was very much against insurance and insurance agents; so much so that insurance agents could not even see her – just from the gate they were thrown out. Her orders were, "Throw them out!" No question of an appointment...

And when he came to the city, all the other agents said, "You have written this book, *How to Win Friends and Influence People*, now, if you can insure this old lady we will think that you have something to say, otherwise it is all hocus-pocus." Dale Carnegie managed to insure the woman. How did he do it? A simple method.

Early in the morning he went around the woman's house. She was in the garden. Standing outside the fence, he said, "I have never seen such beautiful flowers."

The old woman said, "Are you interested in roses?"

He said, "How did you know? I am mad about roses; the only flower that attracts me is the rose."

The woman said, "Why are you standing outside? Come in. I will show you my roses. I am also mad about roses, and you will not come across such big rose flowers as I have got." And he was invited in. They went around her big garden, full of beautiful roses. And he was all praise, and all the poetry that he knew... The woman was so immensely impressed that she said, "You seem to be such a wise man that I want to ask you one question. What do you think about insurance?" – because she was tortured by these insurance agents continually, and they were being thrown out.

He said, "For that I will have to come again because I will have to think it over and do a little research on it. I never advise anybody unless I am certain."

The woman said, "That is right. You are the first man who is not too eager to advise. That is the sure sign of a fool: too eager to advise."

He said, "No, I will have to look at the whole matter. Perhaps it will take a few days." And during those few days he used to come every morning and stand outside the fence.

And the woman said, "Now there is no need to be standing out there – I have told all the servants that for you the doors are open twenty-four hours a day. Whenever you want to come into the garden, you can come. If you want to come into the house, you can. It is your house, don't be shy."

And within a few days he came with all the forms, the files and everything. He said, "I have worked out the whole thing. In fact I had to become an agent of an insurance company to find out absolutely all the details, the inside story, because from the outside you cannot know much. Now I am absolutely certain that this is the thing for you."

Now, this is the way the whole of humanity functions: reaction. You just do something that you know how the other unconscious being is going to react to. And it is very rare that an insurance agent will meet an awakened man, a rare possibility. In the first place the awakened man will not have anything to be insured. Only with the awakened man will Dale Carnegie fail, because he will not react, he will respond. And about response you cannot be predictable.

The man of awareness is unpredictable because he never reacts. You cannot figure out beforehand what he is going to do. And each moment he is anew. He may have acted in a certain way in a certain moment. The next moment he may not act in the same way because in the next moment everything has changed.

Every moment life is continuously changing. It is a moving river; nothing is static except your unconsciousness and its reactions, which are static.

I was expelled from one college – I was expelled many times. I loved it, I enjoyed it; I am not complaining. I have no complaint against anything in my life. Everything has been tremendously beautiful. That expulsion was also beautiful. I had to search for a new college, but before I could be admitted I somehow had to persuade the principal, because the whole city knew – there were twenty colleges – the whole city was aware that I was continually being expelled from one college to another.

I have been educated in many colleges. People ordinarily for one degree go to one college; for one degree I have gone to a dozen colleges. For two or three months at the most they were able to withstand me. So I went to the principal's house, not to the college. I inquired about him from the neighbors, what kind of man he was. They said, "Very religious; every morning... He is a follower of the goddess Kali." He himself was a very strong man, black – *kali* means black – very tall and very fat. He never needed any microphone, there was no need; he could address ten thousand students without any loudspeaker system.

So the whole neighborhood told me, "Early in the morning for two hours, three hours, he is such a nuisance because he just continues, '*Jai* Kali! *Jai* Kali! *Jai* Kali!' – and you know the man and his voice!" "*Jai* Kali" means victory to the mother goddess Kali. "And he gets so agitated that he gets louder and louder. First he starts by sitting, and then he stands up. And he almost looks like Kali himself."

Kali is a very ugly goddess, a very ugly woman with four hands, with a necklace of human skulls. With one hand she is holding a head, freshly cut off, blood dropping from it; in another hand, a sword. And she is standing on her husband's chest! – a real woman. The world needs such women.

So I inquired about everything, and then I went early in the morning at six o'clock and he was doing his thing, and really he was hot! He had a small temple in his house. I simply went in and sat there by the side. When he was just coming to the end of it I started, "*Jai* Kali!"

He looked around and he said, "Who are you?"

I said, "Don't disturb me," and I started again: "*Jai* Kali!"

He said, "But this is strange. For the first time – and you are so young. Are you a devotee of Kali?"

I said, "What do you think? Do you think you are the only devotee of Kali in this city?"

He said, "I used to think that nobody was such a devotee as I am, but you certainly seem to be!"

I said, "No, not compared to you. You are far ahead. You are almost a saint; I am just a beginner, an amateur."

He said, "No, you are not an amateur! What do you do?" He wanted to talk and he pulled me along: "Come with me, have breakfast." So I had breakfast with him. He said, "You are the only man who has understood me – when you said, 'You are almost a saint...' Nobody thinks me a saint, they think that I am a monster. And these neighbors would kill me if they could manage, but knowing me they are afraid, they are cowards. You are the only man in my whole life who has understood me. What do you do?"

I said, "I study in a college."

He said, "Drop that college. Join my college."

I said, "If you say so, I can drop anything. Dropped! Done!" And I joined his college.

After a few days he came to know. Then he called me and said, "You are a rascal."

I said, "You should have understood, even on that day. You are not a saint either, but I wanted admission. What else to do?"

Unconscious people are predictable. You can manage them easily. You can make them do things, say things, even things that they never wanted to do or never wanted to say, because they react.

But a man of awareness, an authentically religious man only responds. He is not in your hands; you cannot pull him down, you cannot make him do anything. You cannot manage to draw out even a single sentence from him. He will do only that which in that moment he finds – through his awareness – is appropriate.

Yes, surrender happens. But remember, in my religion there is no place for "doing" surrender. Surrender is not expected of you, it is not asked from you, but it happens. I am simply making you aware of it. And when it happens nothing can be done about it. But the happening is so graceful and beautiful it does not leave any trace behind it.

The ego simply evaporates and you are left without ego – neither humble nor arrogant, just without ego.

You cannot even say, "I am egoless," because there is no longer an "I" to declare it; there is only a kind of am-ness, there is no "I" in it. The "I" goes with the ego.

Am-ness remains with your existence and becomes really a tremendous force, changing everything that you have been before.

It cuts you from your past.

It gives you a new birth.

about the author

Osho defies categorization. His thousands of talks cover everything from the individual quest for meaning to the most urgent social and political issues facing society today. Osho's books are not written but are transcribed from audio and video recordings of his extemporaneous talks to international audiences. As he puts it, "So remember: whatever I am saying is not just for you... I am talking also for the future generations."

Osho has been described by *The Sunday Times* in London as one of the "1000 Makers of the 20th Century" and by American author Tom Robbins as "the most dangerous man since Jesus Christ." *Sunday Mid-Day* (India) has selected Osho as one of ten people – along with Gandhi, Nehru and Buddha – who have changed the destiny of India.

About his own work Osho has said that he is helping to create the conditions for the birth of a new kind of human being. He often characterizes this new human being as "Zorba the Buddha" – capable both of enjoying the earthy pleasures of a Zorba the Greek and the silent serenity of a Gautama the Buddha.

Running like a thread through all aspects of Osho's talks and meditations is a vision that encompasses both the timeless wisdom of all ages past and the highest potential of today's (and tomorrow's) science and technology.

Osho is known for his revolutionary contribution to the science of inner transformation, with an approach to meditation that acknowledges the accelerated pace of contemporary life. His unique OSHO Active Meditations are designed to first release the accumulated stresses of body and mind, so that it is then easier to take an experience of stillness and thought-free relaxation into daily life.

Two autobiographical works by the author are available:
Autobiography of a Spiritually Incorrect Mystic, **St Martins Press, USA**
Glimpses of a Golden Childhood, OSHO Media International, Pune, India

OSHO international meditation resort

Location
Located 100 miles southeast of Mumbai in the thriving modern city of Pune, India, the OSHO International Meditation Resort is a holiday destination with a difference. The Meditation Resort is spread over 28 acres of spectacular gardens in a beautiful tree-lined residential area.

Uniqueness
Each year the Meditation Resort welcomes thousands of people from more than 100 countries. The unique campus provides an opportunity for a direct personal experience of a new way of living – with more awareness, relaxation, celebration and creativity. A great variety of around-the-clock and around-the-year program options are available. Doing nothing and just relaxing is one of them!

All programs are based on the OSHO vision of "Zorba the Buddha" – a qualitatively new kind of human being who is able both to participate creatively in everyday life and to relax into silence and meditation.

THE DETAILS

Meditations
A full daily schedule of meditations for every type of person includes methods that are active and passive, traditional and revolutionary, and in particular the OSHO Active Meditations™. The meditations take place in what must be the world's largest meditation hall, the Osho Auditorium.

Multiversity
Individual sessions, courses and workshops cover everything from creative arts to holistic health, personal transformation, relationship and life transition, work-as-meditation, esoteric sciences, and the "Zen" approach to sports and recreation. The secret of the Multiversity's success lies in the fact that all its programs are combined with meditation, supporting the understanding that as human beings we are far more than the sum of our parts.

Basho Spa
The luxurious Basho Spa provides for leisurely open-air swimming surrounded by trees and tropical green. The uniquely styled, spacious Jacuzzi, the saunas, gym, tennis courts...all these are enhanced by their stunningly beautiful setting.

Cuisine
A variety of different eating areas serve delicious Western, Asian and Indian vegetarian food – most of it organically grown especially for the Meditation Resort. Breads and cakes are baked in the resort's own bakery.

Night life
There are many evening events to choose from – dancing being at the top of the list! Other activities include full-moon meditations beneath the stars, variety shows, music performances and meditations for daily life.
Or you can just enjoy meeting people at the Plaza Café, or walking in the nighttime serenity of the gardens of this fairytale environment.

Facilities
You can buy all your basic necessities and toiletries in the Galleria. The Multimedia Gallery sells a large range of OSHO media products. There is also a bank, a travel agency and a Cyber Café on-campus. For those who enjoy shopping, Pune provides all the options, ranging from traditional and ethnic Indian products to all of the global brand-name stores.

Accommodation
You can choose to stay in the elegant rooms of the Osho Guesthouse, or for longer stays opt for one of the Living-In program packages. Additionally there is a plentiful variety of nearby hotels and serviced apartments.

www.osho.com/meditationresort
www.osho.com/guesthouse
www.osho.com/livingin

for more information

Thanks for buying this OSHO book.

You can find more OSHO unique content in multiple languages and formats at the following websites online:

The official website of OSHO International is www.OSHO.com and a comprehensive inventory of OSHO-related links can be found at www.OSHO.com/AllAboutOsho

You can search the open access OSHO library for your favorite topic at www.OSHO.com/Library

A complete presentation of all the OSHO meditations and related music can be found at www.OSHO.com/Meditation

To plan a visit to OSHO International Meditation Resort you can visit www.OSHO.com/MeditationResort

Latest updates about events, festivals, media releases and quotes are updated daily on www.facebook.com/OSHO.International

All latest happenings, including information about the OSHO Multiversity courses, are updated daily on www.facebook.com/OSHO.International.Meditation.Resort

You can wake up to a daily OSHO quote at www.twitter.com/OSHOtimes

Your instant access to OSHO video channel can be found on www.youtube.com/OSHOInternational

To make OSHO available in your local language you can register and transcribe or translate OSHO Talks at www.OSHOtalks.info

Please take a moment to **register and browse** these sites as they provide much more information about OSHO. You may also discover many fun and exciting ways to **get involved** in making OSHO available around the world.

Happy reading.

www.osho.com/meditationresort

www.osho.com/guesthouse

www.osho.com/livingin